WALES
Says YES

I Ann, am byth, cariad

WALES
Says YES

The Inside Story of the Yes for Wales

Referendum Campaign

LEIGHTON ANDREWS

Foreword by Peter Hain MP

seren

We now stand ready to build a new participatory democracy in Wales. As an outsider who has become a Welsh insider – a Pretoria boy turned Neath man – I have felt a real privilege in playing a part in giving birth to it. I salute all those, including the author, who against steep odds achieved a change of the greatest possible significance for Wales – arguably the most significant for centuries.

Peter Hain
Under Secretary of State for Wales and Labour MP for Neath

8

Contents

One: A Referendum is Announced

On the kitchen wall of Peter Hain's house in Resolven, Neath, there is a frame containing photographs of a party held for his constituency on 20 July 1996, a scorching summer Saturday. One of the pictures shows Peter Hain and myself in animated conversation. We were discussing the likely consequences of the Labour Opposition's decision, announced just three weeks earlier, to hold a referendum on its plans for Welsh devolution. Unknown to those partying around us, who included many local Labour activists, and media and sporting celebrities such as BBC Wales' Roy Noble and the former England cricketer Tom Cartwright, this was no ordinary exchange of pleasantries. Hain, then a junior Opposition whip, said that he planned to be active in getting an all-party campaign off the ground. He had already cleared this with Ron Davies, the Shadow Secretary of State for Wales, who was very enthusiastic about the idea. Peter felt a broad all-party campaign was crucial to winning the referendum. I had recently moved back to Wales following my marriage two weeks before. I told Peter I intended to leave the BBC, where I was the Head of Public Affairs, in October, and would be delighted to help.

I had known Peter through politics for nearly twenty years. I told him I would sketch out an initial campaign plan, and would send it to him over the summer. I remembered the previous Welsh referendum in 1979, held when I was a student union official at the University College of North Wales, Bangor, and the disappointment and gloom as the results came in. Peter and I both agreed to meet a few weeks later to see where things were going.

The referendum announcement on 27 June had come as something of a shock to many of us, but not least to Tony Blair's own Front Bench colleagues. They had woken on the previous morning to find articles in the *Independent* written by that paper's political editor, Anthony Bevins, and their new editor, Andrew Marr, which declared that Labour would be announcing new plans to deflect the Conservative government's attack on Labour's constitutional plans by holding referendums in both Scotland and Wales. For both George Robertson, Shadow Secretary of State for Scotland, and

9

Ron Davies, this posed something of a problem. Only three days before Davies had explicitly ruled out a referendum once again. He had told the *Western Mail*, "The problem with a pre-legislation referendum is that there are so many questions which you cannot answer." Just three weeks before that, he had taken part in a joint *Western Mail*/Radio Four debate and pledged the same thing. That had become the newspaper's front-page lead on Thursday 6 June under the heading 'No re-run of '79 poll'. It was going to be very difficult to explain his way out of that, particularly to the other pro-devolution parties, the Welsh Liberal Democrats and the nationalist party Plaid Cymru.

"No re-run of '79 poll" was what the pro-devolutionists in Wales had wanted to hear. They had taken half a generation to restore a commitment to devolution for Wales in Labour's policy. They held bitter memories of the 1979 referendum. Then Labour was badly divided as Neil Kinnock had led a Back Bench and public campaign for a No-vote.

At the *Western Mail*/Radio Four debate, held at Cardiff's Coal Exchange, and attended by more than 400 people, Shadow Welsh Secretary Ron Davies had insisted that a Labour election victory would be enough for the commitment to a Welsh Assembly to be honoured. Davies had come under some pressure at the debate, notably on the issue of proportional representation for the Assembly, which his party had so far ruled out. Some devolution campaigners were planning a campaign to get Labour to change its mind on PR, believing that Labour should be as inclusive in its policies for Wales as it was in its policies for Scotland where PR was part of the proposition. A large advert was planned for the *Western Mail* a few weeks later. But Davies' comments on the question of a referendum seemed unequivocal, and campaigners were reassured by this.

Only a month before that, in May, Labour's plans for Welsh devolution had been outlined by Ron Davies in a press conference. A new document, *Preparing for a New Wales*, published in advance of Labour's Welsh conference, set out the plans to reform the quangos, create an economic powerhouse, establish committees on key areas, create a Welsh Comptroller and Auditor-General, ensure fair representation for women, form a business advisory forum, as well as an executive committee comprising the leaders of the different committees and many other matters. While the document did not get much applause from either Plaid Cymru or the Liberal Democrats, these were clear commitments.

But it was Scotland that was causing the most concern to Tony Blair. He had inherited the devolution policy from his predecessor John Smith, and was widely felt to have misgivings about aspects of it. Blair and Gordon Brown were particularly concerned about the tax policy, which they felt could undermine their attempts to be seen as a party of low taxation. Blair was anxious for clarity on the issue by the launch of Labour's draft manifesto. In Scotland, however, Labour's devolution policy was coming under considerable pressure. An effective campaign against Labour's plans for a tax-raising Parliament – tagged the 'Tartan Tax' – was being conducted by the Conservative Scottish Secretary Michael Forsyth. The influential and independent Constitution Unit published a report arguing that the number of Scottish MPs would have to be reduced and the Scottish Secretary lose his place in Cabinet, and that the Barnett formula, under which Scotland (and Wales) received its financial allocation, would have to be reviewed.

The Constitution Unit also made similar comments on the Welsh Assembly which were less than favourable to Labour's plans. The Unit itself had suggested that "if it wanted to test opinion in Wales, the Government could hold a referendum in advance of introducing legislation for a Welsh Assembly. A referendum could help decide the question of principle." It said that ultimately the Welsh Secretary would have to go; there would have to be fewer Welsh MPs; and the Assembly should have revenue-raising and law-making powers otherwise it would be ineffectual.

The Constitution Unit's report on Scotland was seized upon by Michael Forsyth, who said "it is a supreme irony that those who claim to want a voice for the Scottish people refuse to give them a say on the issue." The *Scotsman* on the morning of Monday 24 June headlined its main story 'Labour to hit back on devolution'. Its Political Editor Ewan MacAskill wrote, "The Labour Party is planning a huge counter-offensive over the next fortnight to blunt a Conservative campaign against its plans to create a Scottish Parliament." He said that Labour was keeping its plans under wraps, but intended to embarrass members of the Cabinet and other Conservatives who supported devolution in the 1970s. There was to be a Commons debate on the Constitution that week, one that Conservative Prime Minister John Major was said to be looking forward to.

One day later the London *Independent's* political columnist Don Macintyre hinted at the change, apparently based on a call he had had over the weekend from Peter Mandelson. This hint was completely missed by everyone. A heavier briefing by Labour Press Officers the next day signalled the change in Labour's position, and the *Independent* responded with the two articles which shocked the Labour Party and other pro-devolution supporters. The *Independent's* editor Andrew Marr, a Scot himself, said that by campaigning against Scottish Home Rule, the Conservatives had changed Labour's policy. Marr said that Major's potent 'Save the Union' message in 1992 had been a lesson to both the main parties. "The Tories think it helped them win. Labour is worried that they're right." Marr forecast that Labour would go for a multi-option referendum: and that they would do so publicly within days.

Mari James remembers the day of the *Independent* story well. As Acting Chair of the Parliament for Wales Campaign, at that point the leading pressure group for reform, she received a call from John Adams, Research Assistant to Ron Davies, alerting her to the story. "He asked me if I was likely to go on the record opposing it," she recalls. "I had BBC Wales on the other line at the time requesting an interview on just this point." Mari was convinced that a referendum could not be won, since support within the Wales Labour Party was, she felt, precarious. "Persuade me we're not going to lose," she told Adams. She went on air and told BBC Wales that the referendum was yet another hurdle in the way of a Welsh Assembly but she was confident that it would not stop campaigners continuing to work for the democratisation of Wales. Mari was the only person John Adams called, but he was on the receiving end of a lot of calls, and warned people that there would be a press conference the next day and, off the record, that there would be a referendum. Journalists were also briefed that Davies would announce the introduction of an element of proportional representation.

The proposal created a storm in both Wales and Scotland. "Tony Blair is facing a civil war in the Wales Labour Party" said the *Western Mail*. "Labour faces split over referendum" said the Glasgow paper *The Herald*. The suggestion was made that the decision had been taken by a special Shadow Ministers' Committee on devolution, membership of which seemed to vary depending on which newspaper you read. The Scottish newspapers claimed that it consisted of Tony Blair, Chief Whip Donald Dewar, Shadow Scottish Secretary George Robertson, Shadow Chancellor Gordon Brown, Shadow Leader of the House Ann Taylor, and Shadow Home Secretary Jack Straw. Derry Irvine, likely to be Labour's Lord Chancellor, was also consulted. It was suggested that the deal had been finalised when Tony Blair stayed with Shadow Scottish secretary George Robertson during the aftermath of the Dunblane massacre in March. The question of whether Ron Davies had been in the know was immediately raised. The briefing given out by Blair's office seemed to say that Davies had been informed as soon as matters concerning Wales had been discussed. It seems likely now that while there had been discussions behind the scenes over a period of months as to whether a referendum was appropriate, neither Davies nor Robertson really knew what was coming and were rocked by the announcement, as were their colleagues. To some extent, it is possible to see the proposal for a referendum as originating in Wales. Pontypridd MP Dr Kim Howells, a Shadow Constitutional Affairs spokesman in Jack Straw's Home Affairs team, had argued the case privately. Howells, who had caused a major row when he had warned that devolution should not be about "the balkanisation of Britain", believed that the referendum principle was critical to getting the devolution proposals through. The issue was debated in the Labour Party Policy Commission, which had been considering devolution for three years, but rejected. It had also been discussed by Welsh Labour MPs, and in the relevant informal working groups of shadow ministers that Blair established to review in detail the range of Labour policies, after he was elected Leader of the Labour Party in 1994. Davies had resisted the referendum throughout these discussions.

Labour sold the plan as wrong-footing the Conservatives. Labour rebels on the devolution policy in Wales welcomed it as giving people the opportunity to vote for Labour at the election and against devolution in the referendum.

Behind the scenes, Davies had achieved something significant as a result of the referendum announcement. He managed to move the debate significantly on the question of proportional representation for elections. Previously Davies had found it difficult to sway the Wales Labour Party in favour of PR. Blair called Davies in to see him to discuss the referendum on Tuesday 25 June, the day before the referendum stories appeared in the *Independent*. Some believe that Blair had been working that weekend on Labour's draft manifesto document and had finally concluded that Scotland would have to have a referendum. Others believe that the decision had been reached earlier but now action had to be taken to stop the plan leaking. It seemed that Blair had not yet concluded that Wales should have a referendum, but Davies said that if Scotland were to face a referendum, then Wales would have to do so as well. Blair would have backed Davies if he had said there was no case for a referendum in Wales. Instead, Davies told Blair that he wanted to use the opportunity to re-introduce the issue of electoral reform. Blair himself was already persuaded of the case for this. In June, Davies had arranged for some of the Wales Labour Party's leading officers to come to Westminster and discuss the issue with Blair, who made it clear to them what his own views were. Davies calculated that if there were to be a referendum, he had to have the support of the Welsh Liberal Democrats and Plaid Cymru for the campaign. The only way of achieving that was to ensure that they could see that Labour now supported an element of electoral reform. Blair asked the Wales Labour Party executive to look at PR, and meanwhile Davies also suggested that they look at reducing the number of Assembly seats from 80 – Labour's existing proposal – to 60, with 20 of these elected by PR. Hain and others believe that Davies used the referendum issue adroitly to ensure that PR was brought into the frame.

Announcing the plans in Cardiff, Davies said, "We have set out our plans for a Welsh Assembly and Tony Blair has made clear his intention to legislate on these plans in the first year of a Labour government. Our plans will be good for Wales and good for Britain. We believe they are supported by the people of Wales who want to have more control over what happens here in Wales. The Tories say the people of Wales do not want an Assembly. They are wrong and we will prove that. We will publish a White Paper as soon as possible after the election and hold a referendum here in Wales before legislation passes through the House of Commons."

Davies pledged that the Labour government led by Tony Blair would "campaign all-out for the full-hearted support of the Welsh people for our proposals." The test would be a straightforward majority of the votes cast. A positive vote in the referendum would be the best security a Welsh Assembly could have. Davies had also agreed with Blair that there should be another look at the choice of electoral system. The UK Parliament would remain as the sovereign Parliament. Devolution was neither nationalism nor a half-way house to nationalism.

The Wales TUC welcomed the move. Alex Carlile, for the Welsh Liberal Democrats, cautiously welcomed the referendum, but said that there would have to be significant changes to Labour's policy on PR. Plaid Cymru MPs were shocked by the referendum announcement and criticised Labour's commitment to the project.

A similar statement was made in Scotland by George Robertson, flanked by other leading Scots in Blair's Shadow Cabinet. But one of his Front Bench spokespersons, John McAllion, resigned, saying Labour had "lost control" of its policy. Lord Ewing, a former Labour Front Bencher, resigned as Joint Chairman of the Scottish Constitutional Convention. Scottish Liberal Democrats were even more critical. Their leader, Jim Wallace, said "The history of a devolution referendum is of rigged rules designed to wreck the scheme. We want no part of that." He picked out the statement that sovereignty rested with the UK Parliament and contrasted this with the document *A Claim of Right for Scotland*, signed by George Robertson, which said that sovereignty rested with the people. Privately, he said that if Labour had taken them into their confidence, then the Liberal Democrats could have been more supportive.

Blair went to Scotland that Saturday, June 29, to sell the plan to Labour's Scottish Executive. The executive welcomed the commitment to introduce the Parliament in the first year of a new Labour Government and to lead the campaign for the Scottish referendum. Shortly after, Blair addressed an almost universally hostile meeting of the Welsh Parliamentary Labour Party. It was a very tense meeting, and feelings were not disguised, as MPs wrangled over the reasons for the referendum. Pro and anti MPs said sharp things, with most MPs contributing. Blair's move was welcomed by one of the anti-devolution MPs, Alan Williams, who saw the referendum as likely to be lost. Hain waited until near the end to speak, saying that what had to happen now was a campaign to mobilise opinion inside and outside the party. Even before this, one pro-devolution MP, Paul Flynn, Labour member for Newport West, wrote to Tony Blair to tell him that any loyalty he owed New Labour was now dead. "Surely Welsh Labour MPs have a right to decide the most important Welsh policy we have had?"

The other pro-devolution parties in Wales began distancing themselves from Labour. Plaid warned that there was no guarantee its members would join in a Yes campaign. Dafydd Elis-Thomas called for a referendum for England as well, claiming that it was wrong that the English were excluded, and that it was necessary to avoid a backlash. "Devolution is not an expression of Scottish and Welsh self-determination," he told the *Western Mail*. "It is a profound adjustment of the political and legislative partnership with England in a continuing unitary state."

The Liberal Democrats in Wales wanted a new forum made up of all the political parties plus the voluntary sector and the unions to discuss the form and make-up of the Assembly. Without that forum, the Liberal Democrats would not give their active support to a referendum campaign.

Whatever the public reactions of the politicians, few in Welsh public life were convinced that the referendum could be won. One of Wales' top broadcasters told me "Well, that's it then. That's the end of the Assembly". One of those who did believe it could be won was the *Western Mail's* veteran columnist Clive Betts. A week after the referendum announcement he said that Wales had changed dramatically since 1979 and urged that preparations for the campaign should start straightaway. Most devolution campaigners in Wales were stunned by the news. Eluned Morgan, MEP for Mid and West Wales, felt "absolute frustration, because I didn't think we needed it". She felt it could be won but that it would be a struggle. Val Feld, a Labour activist then seeking nomination for the Gower Parliamentary seat, later to be Treasurer of Yes for Wales, said "I remember being in deep despondency". John Osmond, who had resigned as Chair of the Parliament for Wales Campaign only a month before to take up the post of Director of the Institute of Welsh Affairs, was very depressed. "It was very hard to believe that we could turn around '79."

Some, however, were more positive. Professor Kevin Morgan, later to become Chair of Yes for Wales, was delighted. "I was a referendumist from the outset." He recalls becoming more apprehensive when he realised how much work would have to be done to achieve the level of mobilisation necessary.

It was in this climate that Peter and I had our first conversation. At the time it was announced, Hain had welcomed the referendum, saying that Blair's proposals would have "unchallengeable authority and popular legitimacy. No-one will be able to defy the will of the people and retain any credibility."

Over the summer, we began to work in earnest on the campaign. We were both clear that the existing organisation, the Parliament for Wales Campaign, was too narrowly focused to be able to collect the wide degree of support necessary. Interestingly, though we did not know it at the time, this was also the view of some of the Plaid Cymru MPs who were concerned that the Parliament for Wales Campaign now appeared to be following a more sectarian approach. They and others, including Mari James, had had a number of conversations at the National Eisteddfod in Llandeilo about the need for an all-party campaign. Labour was particularly hostile to the Parliament for Wales Campaign and had refused to allow it a stand at their conference.

I felt we needed something broadly-based. The Welsh historian, Gwyn Alf Williams, had called in 1989 for a popular front in Wales, "focusing in the first instance on a set of minimal objectives around which a majority can unite." That was what we needed. Ours was not the only initiative at that point, however. The Institute for Welsh Affairs put together a working group to establish the practicalities of the approach to the referendum. Business, in the shape of the Wales CBI, had also begun to express its concerns about the Assembly, claiming CBI members were opposed to an Assembly by more than 2:1. (This debate would reverberate throughout the months up to the referendum vote.)

The Labour Party was also trying to pull together its own campaign. Peter Hain had privately spoken to Andrew Davies, a former regional organiser for the party, and a lecturer at Swansea College. Both Peter and Ron Davies wanted Andrew to begin work in the autumn. Davies said he had agreed the appointment with Blair, but internal tensions within the Labour Party were to delay Andrew's appointment as referendum organiser until April 1997.

A crucial role in the Labour campaign organisation was played by Don Touhig, MP for Islwyn and campaign officer of the Wales Parliamentary Labour Party. Appointed Referendum Campaign Coordinator for the Wales Parliamentary Labour Party, Touhig began talking to Labour activists and councillors around Wales. The strategy to which he had been working was agreed by the Labour Welsh Front Bench team in July. Its paper had argued that the campaign could be won by targeting Labour voters in the old county areas of Gwent, Mid, South and West Glamorgan and Clwyd. It assumed that Labour voters would need to be persuaded to vote Yes, and that most Tories would clearly vote no. The assumption was that both Plaid and Liberal Democrat voters would vote Yes. In order to get the message across the focus would need to be on the bread-and-butter issues of health, education, training and the economy. It was necessary to make the Assembly relevant, and keep the message simple, concentrating on the direct benefits to everyday life in Wales. The paper noted that in 1979 the No campaign had three key arguments: cost, bureaucracy, and separatism. The Front Bench team recognised that some in Labour would be hostile to PR and might not therefore join in. There was a feeling that after a year-long election campaign, people might lack the motivation and energy for a referendum campaign. It was also seen as essential to win over Labour councillors and try to keep the council leaders on board. Money would also be needed.

The paper noted that a short referendum bill was possible, with subordinate legislation dealing with issues such as funding of pro- and anti-campaigns. It recognised that a White Paper should be published so that people knew what they were voting for. The paper looked to an autumn referendum if there was a May general election. It recognised that a small majority might require concessions being made to the Liberal Democrats and Nationalists.

Unaware of this, I drafted an outline campaign document as a basis for discussion with Peter. Ultimately, after some revisions, it became the founding statement of the Yes Campaign and set out the aims of the campaign. My main concern was that the devolution movement appeared divided within itself, focusing on points of detail rather than on the strategic goal of winning people to the principle of devolution. The new campaign's objective was to secure a Yes-vote in the referendum on Welsh devolution. "It is not a forum for debate on the merits of different forms of devolution to or within Wales, or on the nature of the Assembly's tax-raising or law-making powers. Its sole purpose is to secure a Yes-vote in the referendum on the terms offered." Peter added a qualification to this, to clarify that people were not being asked to downplay their own views outside the campaign, but that within the campaign they should focus on points of unity. The paper went on to state that the campaign would be non-party and all-party. It would be organised around a National Forum "representative of the civic life of Wales, North and South, East and West, rural and industrial, denominational and non-denominational, voluntary, private and public organisations, ethnic minority organisations, language organisations, cultural, sporting, business, trades unions, youth and student: everyone who wishes to see Wales take a step forward in terms of controlling and democratising its own affairs via a Yes-vote in the referendum." It would be directed by a Steering Committee "based on a core group of some twelve or so individuals prepared to work hard for devolution." The National Forum would have an advisory role and would have the job of drawing in new groups (Doctors Say Yes, Teachers Say Yes, Farmers Say Yes).

Organisationally, the paper recognised that the referendum could be as early as the autumn of 1997 – about a year away. The campaign would need full-time support: certainly a campaign organiser, possibly more. There would need to be local Yes campaigns, drawing people into local activity in their communities.

Both Peter and I believed that the campaign had above all to be popular. My draft said "the campaign will take the argument for devolution out to ordinary people. It will be a popular campaign, drawing people in, giving them a reason to vote and hopefully work for the devolution cause. It will be confident about the prospects for Wales after devolution.... We aim to identify popular celebrities at an early stage, and they must be celebrities of today, not yesterday." Peter added the words "the campaign will only succeed if it engages with popular contemporary culture." An ambitious list of celebrities was attached.

We met in Westminster in September to run through the paper. High on our list were the need for funds, the need for an office, the question of who should front the campaign, and its launch. We decided to approach Rowntree for money, and I undertook to speak to Professor Sir Trevor Jones, Chairman of the Joseph Rowntree Reform Trust (who had been Peter's tutor at Queen Mary College in the 1970s). Peter suggested that the Wales TUC could find office space in Transport House, Cardiff. He had spoken to David Jenkins, General Secretary of the Wales TUC at the Royal Welsh Show in July, receiving a friendly but cautious response. Jenkins had favoured delaying the launch until after the General Election. Peter and I felt that would be too late. I thought that Transport House wasn't right for the campaign, and said I would look for an alternative. A number of names were discussed for Chairman, including Peter himself, David Waterstone, former Chief Executive of the WDA, and Geraint Stanley Jones, former Controller of BBC Wales and former Chief Executive of S4C. We agreed on a January launch for the campaign. We also agreed on the need to talk to other pro-devolution parties. The name of the campaign was becoming fixed in our minds: either Yes for Wales or Wales Says Yes.

The other pro-devolution parties were developing their own positions, in part in reaction to Labour's changing views. At the Liberal Democrats' UK Conference in Brighton in September, Mike German, the party's Welsh campaigns and elections director, attacked Labour's emerging plans for 40 Assembly members elected by first past the post and 20 topped up by AMS. He said that the Liberal Democrats would not be able to support this. Alex Carlile startled some of his party members by saying he thought the Liberal Democrats should move closer to Labour and he could envisage Ashdown sitting in a Blair Cabinet. Ashdown said he did not agree with this. He also pledged the party to vote against a Labour plan for a Scottish Parliament that did not have tax-varying powers. By late October, it was clear that the Liberal Democrats and Labour were involved in wide-ranging constitutional discussions at UK level. They were embarked on formal talks through a Joint Consultative Committee co-chaired by two Scottish MPs, Robin Cook for the Labour Party and Robert MacLennan for the Liberal Democrats.

Plaid Cymru outlined their policy for a multi-choice referendum at their own conference in the autumn, but also suggested that they could stomach campaigning for a Yes-vote in a simple yes-no choice if there was an additional question on law-making powers. The party decided to hold a special conference immediately a Labour government published details of its referendum plans. That conference would decide the party's stance in a referendum. Plaid MPs and activists were concerned about a repeat of 1979, with Labour MPs campaigning against their own party's proposals. Their party leader Dafydd Wigley said in an article in the *Western Mail* in October: "all the signs point to a re-run of the 1979 charade in Wales. Labour dissidents like Llew Smith are already raising their voices against their own party's proposals." He called for "a fair referendum" with four choices: the status quo; a limited assembly as proposed by Labour; a law-making Parliament, as supported by the Liberal Democrats, Wales Labour Action and the Parliament for Wales Campaign; and full self-government in Europe, Plaid's own position.

At Labour's conference, Ron Davies said that the referendum would "offer a measure of protection against the unwelcome attentions of any future centralising government". He spoke of the "coalition of ideas for progress" in Wales, acknowledging that there were many in Wales who shared Labour's aspirations: "There are many in business and industry, the trades unions, the universities, the media, churches, right throughout our social and cultural life." It sounded like the coalition we were seeking to put together.

Peter and I held a further meeting in October. Both of us had spoken to Rowntree, and they could take an application for a small grant immediately. Peter's letter, calling the campaign Wales Says Yes, went off on the 27 September. In it he said "Our strong belief is that – especially given the much less secure majority for devolution in Wales than in Scotland – it is essential to get the campaign planned well in advance of the General Election, so that it can be up and sprinting immediately afterwards towards a referendum expected in the early autumn of 1997. At present the focus of everyone else is understandably on the General Election. Unless the

Welsh campaign is well prepared it could encounter similar difficulties to those in 1978/9, though support for devolution is much stronger now." He confirmed that a fuller application would be put to the Trust meeting in December. I had identified a possible office in a building owned by the PR Company, Harrison Cowley, in St Andrew's Place, just around the corner from Cardiff City Hall and the Welsh Office. The office was modern and had the benefit of access to a conference room. I thought I could get it for a nominal rent.

Rowntree came through with an initial donation of £3,000 on 14 October. I spoke to Alex Carlile MP, Leader of the Liberal Democrats in Wales. Carlile felt that he could not, at this stage, come out in favour of an all-party campaign. For the Liberal Democrats, there would have to be some movement on PR from Labour. However, he felt that Lord Geraint (the former MP for Ceredigion) might be prepared to help publicly from the start. Peter talked to Dafydd Wigley MP and Dafydd Elis-Thomas. He concluded that though Plaid could not at this point come out in favour, it was likely that many of their activists would be supportive. He was made firmly aware of Plaid's worries about Labour's ability to deliver, and Elis-Thomas sharply warned Peter that he himself would not repeat the mistakes of 1979, with Plaid having to support Labour's campaign while Labour MPs campaigned actively against it. Peter understood that Plaid and the Liberal Democrats saw Labour's proposals as weak but argued that they could maintain their own integrity and their distinctive positions while acting alongside the all-party Yes Campaign.

During November 1996, the pace quickened. Meetings were held with David Waterstone and with Lord Geraint. Peter talked to Lord Cledwyn who suggested several Welsh grandees who might be supportive. At Ron Davies' request, Peter also informed Don Touhig about his attempt to marshal a broad base of support. Touhig was unenthusiastic but accepted that matters were proceeding apace anyway. Several conversations were had with Geraint Stanley Jones, who eventually declined the suggestion that he should be Chairman, believing that he was not the right person. Names of potential supporters were pulled together, as were names of potential donors. Waterstone wrote to a few potential sympathisers in business.

Peter had identified a potential National Organiser. I met Daran Hill in Cardiff's Post House Hotel on November 1st. He was bilingual, a former Vice-President of NUS Wales, experienced in student politics, working as Research Officer for University College Swansea Students' Union, and a member of Onllwyn ward in Peter's Neath constituency. I thought he had a clear grasp of what was needed, and an appreciation of the urgency of the campaign. Now we just needed to get a proper grant from Rowntree. All this preparation was being done in secrecy. Where people were sounded out, it was on a confidential basis. Remarkably, in Wales' small and incestuous political community, the news did not leak.

By late November, both Peter Hain and I were concerned that we had not been able to identify the right person to be Chairman. Peter suggested Eluned Morgan, the young MEP for Mid and West Wales. I also knew Eluned well from working with her in Brussels, as she sat on the European Parliament's Media Committee, which I had addressed on several occasions on behalf of the BBC. I felt that it would not be right to have an elected party politician as Chairman, and that both the Liberal Democrats and Plaid would be likely to see the new campaign as a Labour front if this happened. Another name that was considered was that of the former Chairman of Welsh Water, John Elfed Jones.

During the month, the nucleus of the key names for the Steering Committee had come together. Peter had spoken to a number of people, including Waterstone, Eluned Morgan, Professor Kevin Morgan of the University College of Wales, Cardiff, television executive Ron Jones, Geraint Stanley Jones, Professor Hywel Francis of University College Swansea, Labour activist Val Feld who was Director of the Equal Opportunities Commission in Wales, Peter Polish of Democratic Left, Eleri Carrog of Siarter Cymru and a former agent for Dafydd Wigley, Derek Gregory of Unison, Alun Jones of the teachers' union NAS-UWT, David Jenkins of the Wales TUC, and Alun Wyn Bevan, a former BBC sports commentator. Peter had also hoped that Plaid activist Adam Price would be able to be part of the campaign, but his work commitments would not allow this. I had also approached Mari James, whose experience as former National Co-ordinator and now acting Chairman of the Parliament for Wales Campaign I thought would be invaluable, and Huw Roberts, formerly Director of Public Affairs at SWALEC and now running his own political consultancy. A date was set for the first meeting of the putative Steering Committee: it was to be held on 20 December in Cardiff, in the Harrison Cowley Board Room.

Rowntree had a full Trust meeting in early December, and I

drafted a submission to go to them. The submission went in the name of Yes for Wales.Ie Dros Gymru. After weeks when we had been calling the campaign Wales Says Yes I told Peter that I had tried the name out on a number of Welsh-speakers who felt that this did not work so well in the language. The correct Welsh would be very long-winded. So it was as Yes for Wales that the campaign went forward.

The submission to Rowntree stated that "The Yes for Wales campaign has been established in shadow form in advance of the General Election to ensure that the groundwork for the Welsh devolution campaign is done well before the referendum is called. Our overriding objective is to avoid the mistakes of the 1979 campaign by ensuring that we have a cross-party pan-Wales campaign which draws in the maximum possible popular support and endorsement. Our campaign has one aim, and one aim only: to deliver a Yes-vote in the referendum. There are other organisations in Wales seeking to influence the scope and detail of the devolution legislation – without a Yes-vote in the referendum, the finest and most elegant arguments concerning powers of the Assembly and nature of the electoral system will be irrelevant. First, we have to get the popular support of the Welsh people."

The document said that the campaign planned to launch in the New Year of 1997. Pre-election tasks included building databases of supporters for fundraising and campaigning purposes, preparing key arguments, and recruiting prominent supporters. £25,000 was sought from Rowntree in year one, with a further £25,000 in year two if matching funds were raised. (I was not yet convinced that an incoming government could deliver a referendum in 1997). An initial budget was set out. The submission concluded with a statement reflecting a view that would feature heavily at the launch of Yes for Wales: "Over recent months there has been less attention focused on the merits of devolution and disputes between devolution-supporting parties have tended to hog the headlines. This has boosted the morale of those opposed to devolution and the merits of devolution itself have gone by the board. We believe that the case for the Yes-vote has to be made again and that creating a cross-party campaign for a Yes-vote, focused on a very practical objective, not concerned about the merits of one form of devolution or another, will be critical to re-positioning the campaign for devolution."

Rowntree's approval of the grant in December meant that the campaign could properly take off. Daran Hill was hired, and an office rented at Harrison Cowley. Mari James made contact with Charter 88 who agreed to administer the salary payments. I commissioned a logo from the multimedia company Splash!

Meanwhile, in the wider world, debate on devolution continued. The Labour Party Policy Commission was examining how to take forward the need for an element of proportional representation agreed at the time the referendum was announced. A number of Labour members were pressing for the adoption of a form of electoral reform, namely the additional member system. A paper calling for that option was produced by Cardiff Cllr Kevin Brennan, a researcher for Cardiff West MP Rhodri Morgan, one of Labour's Front Bench spokespersons. It was written with the support of Huw Edwards, former Labour MP for Monmouth and now the Party's candidate for the seat, and Mary Southcott of the Labour Campaign for Electoral Reform. The paper recognised that the STV system was preferred by many but was unlikely to command sufficient support within the Wales Labour Party. The pressure group Wales Labour Action was pressing for stronger commitments on PR and on tax-raising and law-making powers for the Assembly. Its leading light, Gareth Hughes, had already been voted off the Policy Commission, which did not bode well for its conclusions. Meanwhile the Chairman of the Commission, Ken Hopkins, former Director of Education in Mid Glamorgan County Council, had come out in favour of first past the post in the *New Welsh Review*. But Ron Davies held out for electoral reform, writing in the *Western Mail* at the end of November, "We have to be consensual, open and pluralistic in the running of the Assembly." By the end of the month Labour had released its timetable for devolution: summer 1997, referendum bill and act; autumn 1997, referendum; spring 1998, devolution bill; autumn 1998, devolution act; spring 1999, elections to the Assembly. It was a challenging timetable. By December, a number of Labour MPs had declared their opposition to PR, among them Ted Rowlands, Denzil Davies and Allan Rogers. Llew Smith had already declared his Opposition to devolution *per se*. Ted Rowlands sought, but failed, to change the Labour Party's new disciplinary code to allow MPs to campaign on their own individual consciences in the referenda. By this time, it was clear that the Labour Party's Commission was heading in the direction of a form of electoral reform.

The debate in the Labour Party had an impact on the launch of Yes for Wales. Peter moved to head off potential antagonism from the Welsh Labour Party establishment. He invited someone he trusted, the union leader and Welsh Labour Executive member Terry Thomas, to dinner at the House of Commons and got his private support to give the campaign a fair wind but only on the basis that no Labour MPs were publicly involved. Thomas believed that it would be badly received if a Labour MP were to line up with the cross-party campaign publicly in advance of the report from the Labour Party Policy Commission and the debate at Labour's Conference in March 1997. If he did so, others might come out and form a No-campaign. The Labour Party in Wales was very nervous of disunity – and felt that the involvement of prominent party members with people from other parties would be provocative for those hostile to devolution. There was considerable discomfort that the campaign was to be launched before the election. Peter's strategy was to neutralise opposition before trying to recruit support.

The Conservatives were largely united in their opposition, though one of their candidates, Glyn Davies, while denying that the Assembly was the answer, nevertheless said that the Conservatives had to accept that Wales was a different country. The Conservative Party however said that the Assembly would cost £34 million a year.

In 1979, the County Councils, except Gwynedd, opposed devolution. However, the new unitary authorities seemed to be coming out in favour, with a paper from the Welsh Local Government Association which assumed that local government would support the Assembly provided there was a partnership between the Assembly and local government. It took the view that there should be crossover of membership between the Assembly and local councils.

Business was another of the opponents in 1979. Indeed, the Welsh CBI had provided much of the funding for the No-vote in that campaign. In July, Elizabeth Haywood, Director of the Welsh CBI, had laid out the organisation's views in a speech. She said that economic progress was one of the criteria by which the Assembly would be judged, and set out the CBI's opposition to tax-raising and law-making powers. Nor were the CBI absolutely convinced by Labour's plans for its economic powerhouse. Despite the efforts of academics at University College Cardiff to change business minds at a conference in September, which drew out the admission that CBI members might change their minds if they could see what positive economic benefits would result, business opinion seemed firmly fixed against reform. A further survey for the CBI published in November confirmed this position. The CBI published twenty questions it wanted the Labour Party to answer, to which Ron Davies responded in December, agreeing that the impact on the economy would be the most important test for the Assembly. The Cardiff Chamber of Commerce found opposition amongst its members too, though it did take the step of circulating material from all the parties. A further survey of Welsh business opinion by Deloitte Touche for the *Western Mail* confirmed the 2:1 opposition.

The Institute of Welsh Affairs' research group had published its report, *The Road to the Referendum*, in October. It called for the Welsh referendum to be held after the Scottish poll, on the grounds that in 1979 there had been virtually no attention given to Wales. The report stated that a simple majority should be enough. It called for the distribution to each home in Wales of a summary of the government's position; free mailshots by the parties; and Party Political Broadcasts which should be transmitted across the UK. It also called for national declaration of the results rather than local declarations.

Not all devolution campaigners were optimistic. The Parliament for Wales Campaign in particular was depressed by the referendum. Its leading lights held the view that there was no way the referendum could be won as Labour would campaign half-heartedly and the other parties would not campaign for Labour's proposals.

It was therefore in an uncertain political atmosphere that the Yes for Wales Campaign held its first Steering Committee on 20 December in the offices of Harrison Cowley. Less than a mile away, at Transport House, the Wales Labour Party was having its annual Christmas party. Some of those attending that bash would have been apoplectic if they had known that their own Shadow Secretary of State was attending the meeting and speaking at it. Ron Davies had stolen away so successfully from Transport House that he was already present at the meeting when one of his shadow team, Rhodri Morgan, phoned to say that the Shadow Secretary would be half an hour late!

Sixteen people attended that first meeting, which was chaired by Peter Hain. They were Alun Wyn Bevan, Mari James, Eleri Carrog, Alun Jones, Angela Pulman of Community Enterprise Wales, Ron Jones, myself, Eluned Morgan, Geraint Stanley Jones, Peter Polish, Huw Roberts, Kevin Morgan, Derek Gregory, Daran Hill, Ron Davies and Peter Hain. There were apologies from Hywel Francis, Val Feld and David Waterstone.

Peter welcomed people and explained the confidential nature of the meeting. It was essential that the presence of Ron Davies was not discussed outside the meeting. There had to be confidentiality if people from different positions were to work closely together. "To be involved in some clandestine pre-organisation meeting, that was a bit of an adventure," recalls Eluned Morgan. Peter stressed that the campaign was non-party and had one aim only, to secure a Yes-vote, in what was the only opportunity in a generation to make such a change. He explained that some planning had gone on behind the scenes, and introduced Daran Hill and myself. He then invited Ron Davies to speak.

The Shadow Secretary began by drawing people's attention to an HTV poll about to be released which showed 50% in favour of devolution. He said that the lessons of 1979 had to be learned. This time Labour was firmly committed. He forecast that the Wales Labour Party executive would adopt the report of the Policy Commission in December and also support an element of PR. This would make it easier for the other parties to come on board. He said that the Referendum Bill would be the first Bill presented in May. Scotland's referendum would be held first. Following his contribution there was a wide-ranging discussion around many of the issues.

Yes for Wales was agreed as the title of the campaign. My paper on the purpose of the campaign was agreed. A discussion on the launch took place. Peter Hain indicated the preference for a launch of business supporters of devolution in advance of the Yes campaign itself, on the grounds that business organisations had sharpened their opposition and it was important to demonstrate business support. This would be timed to take place after Labour's Commission had reported. Peter was due to appear on HTV on the 19 January and could trail the launch. Ron Jones agreed to draft a business statement. A number of people agreed to take responsibility for identifying celebrity supporters who could be announced at the launch. The funding of the office was explained. There was some discussion about the size of the budget, mainly focusing on a large amount suggested for advertising and research. It was agreed to test arguments informally with small groups of people and to start on rebuttal arguments. I presented the logo designs to the meeting, beginning with the one I liked least, which showed a daffodil. This was generally felt to be too close to the 1979 design. Splash! had come up with more modern designs, working through a blend of abstractions of people and dragons, in green and red, though people felt that they were too sharp. One of the designs was however quite close to the option eventually chosen.

At the end of the meeting, Peter thanked everyone for coming. He announced that he would not be able to be at the following meeting, and asked me to take the chair for it. Peter said he felt it better if others took over and that he withdrew into the background.

Peter and I spoke by phone the next day. I was worried that some of those at the meeting had not seemed to understand how much we had to do, nor the necessity for adopting modern campaigning techniques such as advertising and polling. Peter was much more relaxed. He pointed out that we had presented a number of *fait accompli*, and it was important to allow people to air their feelings. The Yes for Wales campaign was born, but was still to remain secret for another two months.

Two: An Idea of Wales 1979-1987

Littering the path to the 1997 referendum was the debris of the 1979 campaign. On 1 March 1979, the people of Wales voted against devolution by 956,330 to 243,048. Welsh Secretary John Morris acknowledged the scale of the defeat: "When you see an elephant on your doorstep, you know it's there."

John Morris's elephant rolled over, expired and blocked the way forward for nearly two decades. Whenever the '79 referendum was mentioned it triggered gloom and memories of division and defeat amongst advocates of devolution.

Plaid Cymru activists remembered delivering Labour leaflets because many Labour Party members wouldn't touch them. They wouldn't be taken in again. Dafydd Elis-Thomas remembered picking up leaflets from Whittington's printers in Neath and driving them to North Wales for Plaid members to distribute. There were different leaflets for different party supporters in the appropriate party colours. One leading Plaid activist of the time, now prominent in the Welsh media, confessed to me in 1997 that he had distributed Conservative Yes leaflets in the 1979 referendum. "It was a desperate campaign," recalls John Osmond.

Gwynfor Evans stated in his autobiography, "As a rule it was only Nationalists who canvassed for the Assembly." That is an exaggeration. In 1997 we found many activists from other parties who had worked hard for victory in 1979. Mari James recalls the temporary inspiration – it didn't last long – of working together with people from a range of parties. "It was very inspiring for those starting out on political careers in Wales to be in meetings where people might disagree on all sorts of things but were joining together to work for an Assembly."

Even some of the younger generation of today's politicians have memories of that campaign. In 1979, Eluned Morgan had only recently started at the Welsh language secondary school Ysgol Gyfun Glantaf in Cardiff. She remembered "going round Ely, the estate in Ely, trying to campaign for the Yes-vote then, when I was 11 years old, and going to school with stickers on, and of course the school was very much in favour and Ely was very much against."

Hywel Francis, then a member of the Communist Party, was Treasurer of the Yes Campaign in West Glamorgan. His father Dai Francis was a key spokesperson all over Wales. Hywel remembers "in this valley, they couldn't get a local Labour Party person to chair a public meeting." He didn't realise how bad things were before the result. "On the day the local Plaid Cymru councillor loaned me his megaphone. He wouldn't do it, so I went up and down the valley with Mair and the kids out of school and the response was cold and hostile."

Kim Howells, then undertaking part-time teaching on the Miners' day release Course in Swansea and also then a member of the Communist Party, remembers "as a result of my friendship with Hywel Francis I'd become involved in the devolution campaign and I'd addressed a few meetings and delivered leaflets and generally experienced the shambles that was the Labour Party in South Wales in the late '70s." Howells wasn't surprised when devolution was "soundly trounced" as he put it. "It was a bit like I'd experienced the decade earlier in '68, we assumed that the workers were on our side, but the workers weren't on our side, you know."

Alun Michael was Shadow Chair of Planning on Cardiff City Council. A strong supporter of devolution since the 1960s, he had edited the Labour publication *Wales Radical* and been criticised by George Thomas, then Secretary of State for Wales, for being too pro-devolution. In 1979 he remembers "a big divide within the Wales Labour Party – one that was very deep and damaging." Other Labour members remembered the division within the party and the vicious internecine warfare of the campaign. In his autobiography, James Callaghan, Labour's Prime Minister at the time, and Michael's predecessor as MP for Cardiff South and Penarth, bitterly recorded: "Among the Labour dissidents were some who were most self-righteous in condemning the government if it ever failed to regard Party Conference decisions as immutable."

From the Labour Conference of 1976 to the vote in March 1979 the issue publicly divided two people (and their constituency parties) who were close friends and who within a short time were to succeed Callaghan as Labour Leader. Neil Kinnock, who led the Labour opposition to devolution, and Michael Foot, one of his mentors, argued continuously about the subject. Donald Anderson, another of the gang of six Welsh MPs opposed to devolution later said that "the devolution distraction" had been forced upon the party by "zealots". "Few Constituency Labour Parties actively campaigned during the Referendum," he recalled.

Given all the problems of the past, why had devolution – with or without a referendum – returned to the political agenda in the 1990s? Why indeed, despite eighteen years of a Conservative government out of kilter with the vast majority of Welsh people, did the movement for greater Welsh autonomy survive? To find the answer, we need to look at what happened to Wales after the referendum defeat in 1979.

For socialists, nationalists and other radicals in 1979, the referendum was the first part of a two-stage defeat. The failure of the Welsh referendum, and the modest victory in Scotland, led directly to the vote of no-confidence successfully tabled by the Thatcher Opposition, and from there to the 1979 Conservative election victory in Britain as a whole. Though Labour again won overall in terms of votes and seats in Wales, the Conservatives achieved their best performance since 1874, gaining three seats to hold eleven overall and increasing their share of the vote to 32.2%, a gain of 8.3%. They did particularly well in rural and Welsh-speaking areas.

The Liberals lost Emlyn Hooson's Montgomeryshire to the Conservatives, a seat they had held without a break since the nineteenth century. As John Davies has written, "Henceforth, it was possible to travel from Holyhead to Chepstow without leaving a Conservative constituency." Plaid suffered particularly badly. Their leader, Gwynfor Evans, lost his Carmarthen seat to Labour, largely due to an astonishing 18% increase in the Conservative vote. Plaid's average vote per seat was lower than when they had fought the 1959 election. Labour lost two seats to the Conservatives, Anglesey, where Elystan Morgan, Chairman of the All-Party pro-Assembly campaign was the candidate, and Brecon and Radnor. Labour's twenty-one seats were its worst performance in Wales since 1935.

The election result gave evidence of three different kinds of groups in Wales. Denis Balsom, Senior Lecturer in Politics at Aberystwyth, came up with his now-famous 'Three-Wales model', developed from the Welsh Election Study survey. This saw Wales divided into Y Fro Gymraeg, the traditional Welsh-identifying and Welsh-speaking areas; Welsh-identifying non-Welsh-speaking Welsh Wales, taking in most of what historians would largely call South Wales; and the remainder, British-identifying British Wales.

A detailed political history of the period has yet to be written. All that can be done here is to sketch out some of the main features of the period, and some of the phases of argument over self-government and devolution. In the late twentieth century, in a very real sense, Welsh politics has been about a clash of cultures, and the contest between different narratives for ownership of the story of Wales. It is largely a story of Opposition political cultures, since the Conservatives themselves were absent from the devolution debate.

Devolution did not return to the political agenda in any meaningful way until after the Conservatives' third election victory in 1987. But that did not mean that Wales became completely absorbed into a British politics with no significant Welsh dimension. In fact, in the period 1979-1987, there were very significant battles fought which contributed in part to the maintenance of a distinct concept of Wales, notably the battle for S4C and the specific characteristics of the miners' strike within Wales.

But the immediate period following the double defeat was one of considerable introspection within Wales, leading to a lengthy debate over Welsh identity amongst Welsh intellectuals, but also arguably amongst a wider range of people. A minor Welsh Identity industry was created, its products a stack of books, tracts, articles and cultural magazines. At an intellectual level, the Welsh debate went through all the phases common to debates in most cultures after a moment of defeat: despair; self-disgust; pessimism; historical and cultural analysis of imagery and icons; attempts to disentangle national feeling from state-identity; desire to create a more progressive and usable national identity; demands for political and cultural reform. The main participants in this debate were socialists and nationalists, though it impinged on others as well. For intellectuals on the Left, the shock of the Conservative victory challenged major pre-conceptions they had held about Welsh identity and Wales' place in the UK. John Osmond recalls having to re-cast the themes of the book that became *The National Question Again* as a result: "The first working title for the book was 'Socialism, Nationalism and Internationalism: a Welsh Perspective', then, in March 1979 the devolution referendum was held and all previous assumptions about Welsh politics and indeed Welsh identity itself, seemed fatally undermined. For many of the contributors the event was a personal, political and even professional trauma." As a result, other political formations would have to be discussed, and Welsh identity debated, not assumed. The writer Ned Thomas closed his magazine *Planet* in early 1980. The decision, he wrote in its last issue (before it was re-born five years later) "was taken well before 1 March, 1979, though with one eye on that day. Had a Welsh Assembly materialised, a different kind of magazine would have been necessary." But in defeat, he didn't think there was a place for the kind of militant reformism *Planet* stood for. He saw a need for a more populist response.

Supposedly, that response came with a fortnightly magazine called *Arcade*. Having left Wales in 1979, I remember how *Arcade* kept me in touch with the Welsh politics of the early '80s. Its editor and founder, John Osmond, recalls: *"Arcade* was a deliberate attempt to address, in the best way we could, the aftermath. There was a desert in Wales in terms of debate. I think what we did in that couple of years with *Arcade* was help rebuild an agenda. To some extent we had to find ways of addressing the wider Welsh audience which is fundamentally English-speaking."

Famously, the historian Gwyn Alf Williams, a nationalist and follower of the Italian Communist martyr Gramsci, delivered the first sustained intellectual response to the 1979 defeats. His BBC Radio Wales Annual Lecture, broadcast on 12 November 1979, was entitled 'When was Wales?' Williams said that the Welsh were difficult to identify. "The frontiers of a Welsh nation had rarely coincided with the frontiers of a Welsh people. Nations are not born; they are made." People invented "a usable past to inform an attainable future." Britain was now unravelling: "The British nation and the British state are clearly entering a process of dissolution, into Europe or the mid-Atlantic or a post-imperial fog. Britain has begun its long march out of history."

With a degree of hyperbole that now doesn't bear examination, he declared:

> How ironic it seems then, that in Referendum, General Election and European Election during 1979, it was the Welsh who registered their country as the most passionately and totally British of all the regions of the United Kingdom and about a half of Northern Ireland. We Welsh look like being the last of the British. There is some logic in this. We were, after all, the First.

What defined the Welsh, in the end, he said, were the English. The Welsh were a nation with no historical memory, surviving "in the interstices of other people's history". The Welsh had survived by being British. "Welsh identity has constantly renewed itself by anchoring itself in variant forms of Britishness." He gave a warning against a narrow nationalism based on the Welsh language: "The application of a strict Welsh linguistic nationalism today, of course, would mean instant death to the Welsh people as a distinct people." He then looked ultimate defeat in the face: "No wonder we are being driven to ask when was Wales? When did we begin?

We are living through what may be our end. The end of Wales and the Welsh as distinct identities." In keeping with the spirit of defeat and the contemporary left-wing debates already underway on the collapse of the Labour government, he moved into apocalyptic language.

> It is apparent that Wales and the Welsh, as distinctive identities, cannot survive the capitalist mode of production in its present historic phase. A tiny Welsh nation may survive in a marginal and impotent bunker; a vivid Welsh-language culture should survive if only in aspic. But the continuous reproduction of Wales and the Welsh over generations requires the elimination and the transcendence of the capitalist mode of production. If capitalism in the British Isles lives, Wales will die. If Wales is to live, capitalism in the British Isles must die.

Nearly twenty years on, living in what David Marquand has called, in his book *The New Reckoning*, "a world of multiple capitalisms" and in a Wales that is certainly not dead, it would be easy to chastise Gwyn Alf Williams posthumously for his error. His assumptions were typically reflective of the debates that Wales was about to embark upon, and which would intensify after the second Conservative victory in 1983. (Indeed, Williams and most others on the Left would sound even gloomier after that.) But the peroration of his lecture moved away from the pessimism of the intellect to an optimism of the will:

> Wales is now and Wales has always been now. Wales is not an event, it is not a moment, it is not a mystical presence ubiquitous through our history like some holy ghost. Wales is none of these things.
> Wales is an artefact which the Welsh produce; the Welsh make and remake Wales day by day and year after year. If they want to.
> There is no historical necessity for Wales; there is no historical necessity for a Welsh people or a Welsh nation. Wales will not exist unless the Welsh want it. It is not compulsory to want it. If we want Wales, we will have to make Wales.

After 1979, the political debate in Wales swung sharply Left. Dafydd Elis-Thomas wrote in *Arcade*: "The political argument in Wales is about what kind of socialism we have." The Callaghan government was widely seen as having failed. It had failed to implement the Labour manifesto and its conference pledges. It had compromised on devolution. It had failed to take forward the debate on the language, and on broadcasting. It had been responsible for the closure of factories and steelworks. To appease the

IMF, it had made cuts in spending on health, housing and education. The Labour Party across the UK entered a period of soul-searching that would see its first major split for decades. Against expectations, Michael Foot was elected Leader of the Labour Party rather than Denis Healey, who was too closely allied to the Callaghan government's rejection of Keynesian economics. As the party swung against the EEC, against nuclear weapons, and against the mixed economy, a New Left emerged in control in the constituencies and the town halls in the metropolitan centres of England. That New Left – prone to infiltration in some areas by the Militant Tendency and the International Marxist Group – found its champion in Tony Benn, who narrowly lost the Deputy Leadership election in 1981 to Denis Healey.

While most Welsh Labour MPs voted for Denis Healey against Foot, Foot's own campaign was co-ordinated by the Bedwellty MP Neil Kinnock, now prepared to reconcile his opposition to devolution with Foot's support for it. Meanwhile, the debates over the future of Labour in Wales were as bitter as anywhere. As Labour's 1979 candidate in Barry, the historian Peter Stead wrote, again in *Arcade*: "It was inevitable that the disillusionment of Labour's committed activists would be reflected in Conference decisions and equally inevitable that Labour's archaic constitution would have to be amended." But he warned that alongside the re-selection of MPs – the issue for which the Left in the Labour Party and particularly the pressure group the Campaign for Labour Party Democracy was focusing much of its campaigning – there should be a real attempt to breathe life into moribund constituency Labour Parties and to recruit new members. Instead, he feared, "Labour has turned in on itself. It has become [an] ideologically pure and closed sect." He forecast correctly that Benn himself would distort the political debate. That was what happened. A major rally against unemployment in Cardiff became the focus of an attack on Healey.

Kinnock's Bedwellty constituency was at the heart of the battles. The constituency supported Benn for the Deputy Leadership. Kinnock voted for John Silkin and then abstained. Kinnock supported Foot on the Labour Party National Executive against the hard Left. After a bruising debate his constituency supported the Kinnock opposition to the International Marxist Group's Tariq Ali joining the Labour Party, and endorsed the rejection of Peter Tatchell as the candidate for Bermondsey. But the local party initially opposed Kinnock over the instigation of an enquiry into the Militant Tendency. Kinnock was challenged for his seat but won comfortably. According to his biographer, Robert Harris, "the most credible challenger would have been Ron Davies", but Davies, who had voted 'No' in 1979, decided to stay in the race for Caerphilly.

At this point, the debate within Labour was occurring largely within the context of the British state, and the idea that what the Left needed to do was to capture the state and achieve socialist policies through the state machine. One of the seminal texts of the period, published in *Marxism Today* in January 1979 before Thatcher's victory, by the New Left academic Stuart Hall, projected a clear and striking analysis of Thatcherism and its effect on British politics without once acknowledging the real political debates over the nature of the British state then actively underway in both Wales and Scotland. It would take the British Left almost a decade and three lost elections to engage with constitutional change, imprisoned as it was, noted Gwyn Alf Williams in the same publication in 1982, "in the myth of the Westminster Parliament, in social democracy or, for dissidents, in the bastardised British Gaullism of many Bennites."

In the nationalist movement, the result of the 1979 defeats produced a range of reactions. Some saw the referendum result as the rejection of Welshness. Gwynfor Evans called on the Welsh working-class to "show their loyalty to Wales". Dafydd Elis-Thomas and others saw the defeats as in part the failure of Plaid Cymru to engage more clearly with a socialist analysis. "To us," he wrote in *Arcade* in 1980, "1926 must always mean more than 1536." He grounded his analysis in his recognition that the Welsh economy had "the largest public sector and the smallest native capitalist sector outside Eastern Europe. Ours is already virtually – in terms of who employs us – a nationalised economy. The unreal choice between state capitalism and multi-national capitalism stares us in the face." Elis-Thomas said that Labour "had frozen the working class into a state of subservience and inactivity." Plaid must ally itself with the unions.

There emerged in Plaid, in the words of Gwyn Alf Williams, in his 1985 book *When Was Wales?*, "a libertarian-Marxist style" whose members "tried to establish contact with ecological, peace and women's groups". Some would see it as a form of pseudo-Leninism. The National Left, as this group was called, succeeded in getting Plaid Cymru to change its constitution by a two-thirds majority at the Party's Carmarthen conference in 1981, to seek the establishment of a Welsh decentralized socialist state. "What we were looking for was a formulation which combined National, without being nationalist, with Leftism, without being obviously infantile Left or whatever Left," said Elis-Thomas. He felt that one of the risks for Plaid after 1979 was that it retreated into a limited form of nationalism. "I think it was very important to save the Party from nationalism. I regard myself as very much in the Saunders Lewis tradition of saving the Party from nationalism in order to establish a more realistic intellectual base to the practical politics." Cynog Dafis saw the National Left as enabling Plaid to be more practical "coming down from the intellectual heights, getting involved in the nitty gritty of life".

Even Gwynfor Evans supported the endorsement of decentralized socialism, though some members of Plaid fought it and eventually a number left. Indeed, much of the argument, particularly around the peace agenda which grew in importance on the British Left as a whole in the early eighties, with the campaigns against cruise missiles and the Falklands War, had been central to Plaid for some decades, though it achieved a new kind of intellectual credibility as the resistance thesis. "What was new," wrote John Davies, the nationalist historian in his essay in *The National Question Again*, "was the emphasis upon class". By 1985, however, even Elis-Thomas was admitting that the strategy had deficiencies. There were some gains in local elections in the Valleys (just as the Liberals achieved some local election strength in Cardiff and Swansea). It helped gain members but some traditionalist Plaid voters found temporary solace with the Alliance and the Conservatives. The historian Dai Smith has noted in his essay on Raymond Williams: "the National Left was, down to 1984-5, able to win attention in left-wing Labour circles in England by aligning itself with the potentially disruptive movements of feminism, neutralism, communalism and anti-racism." One of those who noticed the development was Peter Hain, in his book *The Democratic Alternative*. Hywel Francis recalls Dafydd Elis-Thomas on a platform at Coleg Harlech in the middle of the Falklands War. Someone in the audience said he agreed with Dafydd's speech but Dafydd was clearly in the wrong party. "Quick as a flash, Dafydd came back and said 'yes, I think we all are, aren't we'."

Outside Plaid, the reaction to the defeats was in some cases more violent. On December 12 1979 the first holiday cottage was burnt. A variety of shadowy organisations came into existence, "little groups with big names" as Gwyn Alf Williams described them, like Meibion Glyndwr, Guardians of Wales, Workers Army of the Welsh Republic, some of whom had links with other terrorist organisations. The arson campaign directed against a variety of targets, including Conservative candidates, gave rise to a range of police actions which alarmed civil libertarians of all kinds, particularly when this ostensibly sought to implicate organisations such as the Welsh Republican Socialist Movement who, though far to the Left, certainly did not support violence as a form of activity. There were even absurd attempts by some in the police force to implicate Elis-Thomas, according to John Osmond, in his book *Police Conspiracy*.

The election of 1983 confirmed the overwhelming sense of defeat. With new boundaries the Conservatives won 14 seats (up 3). Labour dropped to 20 (down 1). Plaid and the Liberal Democrats took two each. Labour slumped to 37.5% of the popular vote, only slightly ahead of the Conservatives on 31% with the Alliance on 23.2% and Plaid on 7.8%. The Bennite battles within the Labour Party had caused the defection of many MPs, including three in Wales, Tom Ellis (Wrexham), Ednyfed Hudson Davies (Caerphilly) and Jeffrey Thomas (Abertillery) to the SDP. The SDP and the Liberals in Wales were to take 23% of the vote in Wales in the 1993 election: their high point. Though Davies left Wales to fight Basingstoke in Hampshire, Ellis came close in Clwyd South-West and Thomas performed respectably in Cardiff West. With the Liberals, the SDP MPs in Wales provided a grouping which continued to advocate devolution. However, the turmoil of developing an Alliance left them little time to enter the wider intellectual debates on the nature of Wales. The Liberals and the SDP suffered similar problems to those which would also beset Plaid. They recognised a need to do well in Labour areas to have any hope of becoming pan-Welsh parties, but their urban campaigning was often a pale imitation of their core support in rural Wales. Neither of the Alliance parties had many members in Wales, but they performed better than Plaid in both the general elections of 1983 and 1987. After the Brecon by-election of 1985, won by the Liberal Alliance's Richard Livsey, Plaid recognised the "considerable danger posed to us by the Alliance". At a Parliamentary level, between 1983 and 1992, the Liberals enjoyed more influence and strength than Plaid, and recorded higher general election votes. Elis-Thomas in particular saw Plaid's traditional supporters as representing "a kind of Welsh liberalism". The Alliance did make determined attempts to get Welsh speakers selected for seats, and

Liberal community politicians like Rev. Roger Roberts and Mike German campaigned hard in seats like Conwy and Cardiff Central. But there was always the danger of a maverick candidate, such as Felix Aubel in the Cynon Valley by-election, who later left to join the Conservatives and re-surfaced in the No Campaign in 1997. The Welsh SDP had some difficulties with its more centralist national committee when, in 1985, the Welsh SDP negotiated a successful seats deal with the Liberals, contrary to the views of the National Committee, David Owen hauled the Welsh SDP Chairman Gwynoro Jones over the coals. Frank Leavers, who worked in Cardiff for both Alliance parties, was frequently called to London to account for the Welsh deviations from the line. Owen's stance in the miners' strike would do little to help the Alliance parties in Wales.

The Conservatives were too busy governing to worry about identity. The character of Conservative rule during this period – indeed throughout the whole 1980s – gave rise to a paradox. Though the party was implacably opposed to accountable devolution, its own actions helped strengthen the case for it, by ensuring devolved powers continued to be strengthened within the Welsh Office and within the quangos. The Conservatives even created new Welsh quangos in some areas, such as housing and education. This helped ensure that there was a highly devolved Welsh civic society, even if there were no directly accountable public institutions. As Elis-Thomas put it: "The existence of the Welsh Office, itself brought about by a Welsh political discourse, then calls into being a whole series of semi-autonomous pressure groups and national lobbying organisations in the voluntary sector to lobby itself." Conservative Secretaries of State made good use of what powers they had to maintain some autonomy from England, acting as Governor-Generals: keeping the Welsh Development Agency, ultimately coming to support the creation of S4C, later creating the Cardiff Bay Development Corporation, the Valleys Initiative and the Welsh Language Board. They were able to buy off a section of the Welsh middle-class in the arts and cultural sectors with their grants and patronage, ensuring a divide and rule strategy to ease the difficulties of governing a country in which they were in a minority. Clive Betts says they were able to do this because the language issue was not a problem in the constituencies which they themselves held. Betts notes that "the Tory vote is far larger and more faithful than revealed by the Party's see-sawing number of MPs in Wales." Between 1979 and 1992 their vote declined by only 3%, from 32% to 29%. As Plaid feared, some of its traditional support would respond to action in support of the Welsh language.

Intellectually during the period 1979-87, there was a striving for a deeper understanding for the defeat than orthodox politics could give. Debates over identity are never far from the core of Welsh politics. The tense, anguished reconsiderations of Wales and Welshness were in a way a substitute for a politics of devolution. They were largely debates amongst intellectuals. Though some party members were involved there were plenty of other, more urgent political struggles to preoccupy the political parties of the Left and the pressure groups, from Cymdeithas to CND. But the interest in identity did on occasion more deeply involve the general population. Geraint Talfan Davies, now Controller of BBC Wales, then Head of News and Current Affairs at HTV Wales, recalls the series HTV made for Channel Four, *The Dragon Has Two Tongues*, which featured Gwyn Alf Williams and Wynford Vaughan Thomas debating Welsh history. "It was a 13-part series. We published document packs to go with it and amazingly we had something like 120-130 discussion groups around Wales meeting every week to discuss that week's episode." This involved 2,000 people.

Fears that Wales was dying underpinned many of the interventions on the theme of Welshness. In *Arcade* Hywel Francis wrote that Wales was "potentially the biggest mausoleum in the world". His concern that Welsh popular history was being turned into some caricature of itself – "some kind of sickening entertainment" – was a common one across the UK in the 1980s. Major industrial manufacturing regions were widely seen as being turned into a museum culture which both stripped out the politics from the history and portrayed the people as victims without organisation. Francis, and other Welsh historians such as Dai Smith and Gwyn Alf Williams, tried to reconnect the people with the politics, and rescue the Welsh people from what Edward Thompson, writing about the English working class, had called "the enormous condescension of posterity". Wales had had *A People and a Proletariat*, according to one of Smith's books. The historians reclaimed the history of the South Wales miners in *The Fed*. They had already established a new journal, *Llafur*, to reclaim Welsh Labour history. They made real connections between Wales as it was and Wales as it is. Raymond Williams, reviewing two of their books in *Arcade*, noted "Every reader of this new history will find, at some point, a moment when his own memory stirs and becomes that new thing, an historical memory, a new sense of identity and relationships....

The personal memory, local and specific, is then suddenly connected with the history of thousands of people, through several generations. As the particular and the general, the personal and the social, are at last brought together, each kind of memory and sense of identity is clarified and strengthened. The relations between people and 'a people' begin to move in the mind." A new generation of feminist historians opened up new insights into the history of women in Wales. This was a political process: in the ruins of Thatcherism, Wales was licking its wounds, recovering resources of hope for the struggles ahead.

Sentimental representations of Welshness and nationalist mythology were targets of much of the writing. Dai Smith devoted a book *Wales! Wales?* to attacking simplistic national fantasies. In a short, tough article in *Arcade* Kim Howells took aim at "the myth that the Welsh are a race of hymn-singing, blinkered rugby fanatics" focusing his fire on Max Boyce in particular. Howells' complaint was that the Welsh were laughing at "an externally manufactured" image of themselves – one that was sustained by the rootless professional Welsh who pass themselves off as arbiters of taste and national identity. Howells' complaint paralleled that of Francis about the St Fagan's Folk Museum: South Wales and its history was being stripped of its politics.

This recovery of a history of English-speaking South Wales by historians closer to the Labour movement than to nationalism nevertheless overlapped with the directions in which some nationalists were trying to take Plaid. Gwyn Alf Williams noted "the objective denial of Welshness to the English-speaking Welsh". In *A People and a Proletariat* Dai Smith wrote that Wales "had been a plurality of cultures": Gwyn Alf Williams and Dafydd Elis-Thomas were coming to a view of Wales "as a community of communities". This historical recovery was, at one level, part of trying to understand the longer-term reasons for the defeat in the referendum. Smith wanted something "deeper than politicians' guesses" about the history of the people of Wales "whose experience, albeit patterned, cannot be summed up by the preciosity of words like 'community' or 'nation' nor by the flag-waving of phrases like 'inferiority complex' or 'class consciousness'." His own desire was to recognise the validity of the English-language and British Welsh experiences as part of the making of Wales, an inclusivity in contrast with the linguistic nationalism of many in Plaid and amongst the *crachach*, a term that has come to represent the largely Welsh-speaking cultural establishment.

Gwyn Alf Williams expanded his thinking on Wales into a book, *When Was Wales?* He wrote in the language of near-despair:

> Small wonder that some, looking ahead, see nothing but a nightmare
> vision of a depersonalized Wales which has shrivelled up into a Costa
> Bureaucratica in the south and a Costa Geriatrica in the north; in
> between, sheep, holiday homes burning merrily away and fifty folk
> museums where there used to be communities. This is without doubt
> a nightmare. Some human society will obviously survive, though what
> kind it will be, no one can tell.

Williams looked to history as providing some salvation:

> In that Welsh making and remaking of themselves, a sense of history
> has been central. The Welsh or their effective movers and shapers
> have repeatedly employed history to make a usable past, to turn a
> past into an instrument, with which a present can build a future. It
> was once done in terms of myth, it has been recently and can be
> again done in terms of history.

But, he said, in the time of Chernobyl, the Welsh people "are now nothing but a naked people under an acid rain".

To the extent that participants in the debate on Welshness had political affiliations, they tended to be members of Plaid, the Communist Party or Labour. The debate drew, to a degree, on the thinking of New Left intellectuals who had posited the notion that nations were imagined communities and traditions were invented. One book, *Wales, the Imagined Nation,* drew many of those themes together. The book's editor, the poet Tony Curtis, said that the volume tried to answer the question "How do we imagine ourselves to be Welsh and where do we imagine Wales to be?" The essays ranged over literature, including poetry and the novels of the industrial hinterland, to the cinema, theatre and television, the visual arts and landscape, and to the treatment of women in the imagery of Wales. Poems, such as Harri Webb's 'Synopsis of the Great Welsh Novel' were also included. Underlying the writings of the different authors were major political differences: what united them was the recognition that there was no single Wales or Welsh experience, but that the plural Welsh experience was important and distinct.

If these debates were predominantly academic, contemporary sociological research has identified a clear sense of Welshness as distinct from Britishness in a variety of communities. Opinion polls continue to show a strong self-identification as Welsh by a majority of the population. One of the clearest changes in Wales' self-image however has been the changing role of women. This is not simply a consequence of the feminisation of the workforce (though Gwyn Alf Williams noted in 1982 "during the 1980s the Welsh working class will become, both numerically and in strategic terms, a female working class"), nor the decline in traditional male industries such as coal and steel. It was also a strong characteristic of social movements in Wales during the 1980s, including the peace movement, the miners' strike and the language movements. "Within weeks of the strike starting," wrote Kim Howells, in the book *Digging Deeper*, "South Wales women threw off all that garbage about being 'behind' their men and began occupying coal board offices, blockading steel-works' gates and touring Europe putting the case for the defence of their communities."

However, the first assertion of Welsh identity after the 1979 defeats came in the battle for a Welsh fourth channel. The struggle for a Welsh-language television channel was a long-standing objective. Its most explicit political expression originated in a campaign by Cymdeithas yr Iaith Gymraeg begun in 1968 and spelt out in detail in the society's manifesto of 1972, drafted by Cynog Dafis, who had been the society's second chairman. By 1979, the objective had the support of all the political parties, and could not be considered the preserve of nationalism only. However, the Conservative Government's decision not to go ahead with the Welsh fourth channel, announced by Home Secretary William Whitelaw at the Royal Television Society in September 1979, had the ultimate effect of identifying the campaign with Plaid Cymru. The following month, the party's conference established a fund into which those who opposed the government's plans could pay their licence fees. In November, three academics, Dr Ned Thomas, Dr Pennar Davies and Dr Meredydd Evans switched off the Pencarreg TV transmitter. Six months later, on 5 May 1980, Gwynfor Evans announced that he would fast to death unless the government reinstated the plan. On 17 September, the government capitulated.

In historical memory, those bald facts are the ones now remembered. But this was the campaign of more than one person. As one Cymdeithas yr Iaith activist, Angharad Tomos, recalled in the book *What's This Channel Four*? "Sianel Pedwar Cymru was not the result of extensive debates and government reports and committees. It was the prize of a tooth and claw battle all the way." In fact, in the latter stages, debates and government reports and committees (Crawford, Siberry, Annan) did play their part. And it was a campaign in which both Labour and the Liberals also played their part, and one supported by English-speaking people as well. Cymdeithas yr Iaith Gymraeg's campaign for a Welsh channel had from the start a nationalist dynamic although it received the support of thousands who were members of other parties and of none. It was a long campaign of refusal to pay licence fees, occupation of transmitters, damage to television property, vigils and demonstrations, culminating in 1976 in the damage to the BBC's Blaenplwyf transmitter and the subsequent conspiracy trial. The campaign had been underway in earnest for over ten years before the government's capitulation, and was a major focus of Cymdeithas action in the 1970s, with many individuals arrested, fined and imprisoned.

Within six months, Plaid had 2,000 people paying into their licence fee fund. By July, the first of those refusing to pay their licence fee were being gaoled. The Pencarreg Three were fined substantial amounts. Cynog Dafis played an active role and was involved in direct action himself. He remembers: "I think we bought a television in order not to pay the licence in the end." That month the government announced a Welsh Language Television Committee, to review the situation and if necessary make changes. Two visits by Prime Minister Margaret Thatcher to Wales were disrupted. In Swansea, she had to leave a conference by a rear door. In Anglesey, her car was surrounded and shaken by protesters shouting "Save Gwynfor". At the Eisteddfod in August, there were angry protests when Nicholas Edwards arrived as Secretary of State. Gwynfor Evans reaffirmed his intent to fast. "Television crews and reporters choked the lanes around his home in Llangadog" wrote the BBC's Patrick Hannan. He embarked on a farewell tour of Wales with an opening rally in Cardiff attended by 2,000 people.

By September, the government was worried, fearful of the possible reaction if Gwynfor Evans did carry out his threat. A delegation of three elder statesmen, Lord Cledwyn, the Archbishop of Wales G.O. Williams, and Sir Goronwy Daniel, met the Home Secretary on 10 September to reinforce the message, urging the government to set up the Channel, at least as an experiment. Michael Foot, despite their political differences a friend of Gwynfor Evans, had also arranged to see Whitelaw that day, having dined with Evans a month before. On 17 September, the government gave in: that evening, Gwynfor Evans renounced his fast.

As John Davies has noted in *Broadcasting and the BBC in Wales*, "unlike the government's policy on steel, its decision on the Welsh fourth channel was not central to its strategy." Cultural matters could be determined without much dislocation or too much public money. One Welsh-language campaigner put it like this in 1998: "it's as though Welsh-speakers are being given their own reservations: broadcasting, the arts, the language. We're allowed to do what we like in these areas as long as we keep away from everything else: the economy, social policy and so on." Nevertheless, it was the Conservative government's first U-turn.

For Gwynfor Evans, it became a personal triumph. "The astute politician milked it for all it was worth", noted Patrick Hannan. "There was more than a gleam in his eye when he explained that he was glad to be able to explain to the Marxists that one man really could influence history." In his autobiography, Evans confesses that his objective was "the renewal of Welsh Nationalists' spirits". "I gave 5 October as the date when the fast would begin because the months of October and November would be a good time for the campaign to reach its crescendo. Furthermore, Parliament would be returning at the beginning of October and Plaid Cymru's Annual Conference was to be held at the end of the month." He expressed his disappointment that the government gave in so quickly: "If only we had been given five or six more weeks of excitement and national awakening, Plaid Cymru – on which the nation's future completely depends – would have been established in an unassailable position." Aled Eurig, then working for Plaid's Parliamentary party, remembers the party was looking for issues with which to fill the vacuum. Elis-Thomas had some concerns about Plaid's involvement with the campaign. He wanted Plaid to be seen as more than a linguistic campaign: "I've always held strongly to the view that the job of a political party was to be a political party, it's not to be a movement or a campaign."

If the struggle for S4C was evidence of the enduring strengths of Welsh language culture under Thatcherism, the miners' strike of 1984-85 was evidence of the enduring strengths of Labour culture in South Wales. For much of the eighties, South Wales felt like it was the target of the Thatcher government. The counter-point is telling. As John Davies records in his history of Wales, "in the early 1980s the making of Welsh programmes was virtually the only kind of employment which was expanding." Unemployment in Wales was 12.8% in 1980 and 16 per cent in 1983, and varied between 15% and 19% to 1987. Steel and coal were two of the worst hit industries. Steel-making ended at Shotton, Ebbw Vale and Cardiff. There were 25,000 miners in Wales in 1983: there had been

34,000 in 1973. In steel, there were 19,199 in 1983, compared to 65,981 in 1973.

The leading role of the miners in the Labour movement in Wales has been well-documented. If it is the 1921 and 1926 strikes and the campaigns against means-tests in the 1930s which are the best known, what is not often acknowledged is the miners' contribution to Welsh culture as a whole. Hywel Francis wrote at the time of the strike, "The miners' union in South Wales has a record second to none over many decades in its concern for its communities, the cultural and educational heritage of Wales and for all those who struggle for peace and justice throughout the world."

The South Wales miners led the action which forced one of the earliest U-turns, after the S4C decision, of the Thatcher government. The National Coal Board announced plans to close between 20 and 50 pits in Wales in 1981. There were spontaneous strikes in South Wales, followed by action in other coalfields. Hywel Francis attributed this to the campaigning by the South Wales NUM after the closure of the Deep Dyffryn colliery in the Cynon Valley in 1979.

The background to the strike in South Wales in March 1984 was that government plans for the coal industry would leave South Wales with only three pits. 20,000 jobs would go and a further 20,000 would be lost in related industries. Unemployment in Wales would rise to over 20% and in mining communities over half the male population would be out of work. "The valleys of South Wales would be nothing more than industrial museums inhabited by dying communities," wrote Francis in 1985. The people of Wales knew that this was an attempt to destroy the NUM; and that there had to be a saner energy policy.

There can be little doubt now that the Conservative government had prepared very carefully for the miners' strike, nor that they had seen this battle, years before, as almost inevitable. The appointment of Ian MacGregor as Chairman of the NCB, after his period at British Steel, in September 1983 was the precursor. This was shortly followed by the notice of a scheme of pit closures in October. The actual detonator of the strike was the closure of Cortonwood Colliery in England announced on 1 March 1984.

Kim Howells, then an NUM Wales Research Officer, working for the NUM Wales leader Emlyn Williams, recorded the early moments of the strike.

A large section of our twenty-one thousand miners and cokemen were in no mood to take the lead once again in confronting a national government. South Wales had led every major coal stoppage since the balmy days of the mid-1970s: the fight to keep Deep Dyffryn open in 1978/79; the temporary defeat in support of the steel-workers in 1980; the successful opposition to Thatcher's first pit hit-list in February 1981; the bitter campaign in 1983 to prevent the board closing the Tymawr/Lewis Merthyr mine.

Howells said that too many miners in South Wales had bad memories of travelling throughout Britain to obtain support against the closure of the Tymawr/Lewis Merthyr pit.

In fact, he said "most pits struck spontaneously on the first morning or within the next twenty-four hours. A couple had stragglers who were picketed out. But once stopped, there was no strike more solid anywhere in Europe."

His account is worth quoting at length:

By May 1984, South Wales pickets were operating as far north as the Heysham nuclear power station near Lancaster. They were in the coalfields of Lancashire, Derbyshire, Staffordshire, Warwickshire, Nottinghamshire and Leicestershire. They were covering the Wash ports, helping out in the Essex ports, picketing cement works and power stations in Cambridgeshire, Birmingham, Oxfordshire, Hampshire, Devon, Cornwall, and in all of the counties bordering on Wales as well as in the whole of Wales itself. At one time, our pickets were camped twenty-four hours a day, seven days a week outside twenty-two power stations: coal-fired, oil-fired and nuclear, from Sizewell to Pembroke and from Wylfa to Fawley. The cost was astronomic and the effort enormous. For month after month, the coalfield despatched an average of four to five thousand to these various targets.

They had, said Howells, to learn new campaigning tactics; evaluating targets, gathering intelligence, deciding which targets to hit, which to avoid.

Howells noted the support for the Welsh miners came from all over Wales (indeed, from all over Britain):

for the first time since the industrial revolution in Wales, the two halves of the nation came together in mutual support. Pickets from the south travelled to the nuclear and hydro-stations in the north. Support groups in the north brought food, money and clothes to the south. Friendships and alliances flourished; old differences of attitude and accent withered and out of it all grew the most important "formal" political organisation to emerge during the course of the strike – the Wales Congress in Support of Mining Communities.

The Wales Congress was set up on the initiative of the South

Wales NUM. It was backed by Labour MPs and officers, by Plaid Cymru and the Communist Party, and embraced organisations such as the Wales TUC and Cymdeithas yr Iaith Gymraeg. At its launch, according to John Osmond, "the South Wales miners' leader, Emlyn Williams, said that when he had been first told about the movement he thought it was intended as some kind of surrogate Welsh Assembly." Williams said that had Wales had devolution, the miners would have had a voice. Hywel Francis recalls: "we brought together all these disparate elements across Wales and outside Wales which were supporting the miners. What we were trying to say was that Wales was united and they were embracing the miners and so we were creating a sense, a perception, that the miners, as the Cymdeithas slogan said, are fighting for Wales." Francis wrote at the time that the strike was creating a sense of Welsh identity that transcended language and regional differences.

Kim Howells saw the Congress as opening up "the possibility of mutual action to defend and strengthen communities, whether their life-blood is coal or farming or engineering or oil refining." The strike had given people confidence, provided a new collective spirit and revived community life, re-awakening in ordinary people the understanding that it was possible "to take the first concrete steps towards creating a more humanitarian and socialist society now, in the dreary midst of Thatcherism, and that it was idiotic to assume that such steps were only possible after some special kind of electoral victory or a triumph on the barricades. With no prompting from *Marxism Today*, the *New Left Review* or *Labour Weekly*, the people of the coalfields created the basis for a new politics which grew out of experience and necessity." For Hywel Francis also, the Welsh Congress "did raise some fundamental questions about democracy and accountability which go far beyond a Parliament for Wales." And it is interesting looking back at how many other people who would be involved in the 1997 Yes Campaign, from Tyrone O'Sullivan of Tower Colliery, to union leader Terry Thomas, were centrally involved in the strike.

The most obvious long-term effect of the strike within communities was the more prominent role of women, coming to terms with new forms of organisation which later excluded men, and organising their own activities. Women were free of the bureaucratic and hierarchical structures of the union, which gave them more freedom to manoeuvre, according to some observers. But they also had to overcome patronising and sexist behaviour, particularly in the earlier days of the strike, when they were seen as appendages of the men. Sometimes it was hard to get the lodges to support women speakers and respond to requests from outside for women speakers. Some of the Welsh women quoted the example of the women at Greenham, using peaceful protest. "On a picket-line at Port Talbot," one told Beatrix Campbell, "we turned four lorries away. We used persuasion – and asked them to respect the picket-line. It was lovely." There were many accounts of women speaking in public for the first time. "I don't make a speech, I just speak from the heart. I tell them about life in our little community, the unemployment that's facing our kids. I try to make them understand it's their fight too," Mary Coombes from Mardy told the *New Statesman*. The women raised funds, provided food parcels, occupied pitbaths and picketed. There was no doubt that some miners occasionally found this threatening.

The strike in South Wales, noted Howells, also proved the fragility of the organised structures of the Labour movement, such as the much-vaunted Triple Alliance between the Transport, Steel and Coal Unions. This worked for a couple of months and then disintegrated, leaving the miners with the need to find other imaginative ways of spreading their campaign. The occupations of the massive cranes at Port Talbot and the transporter bridge spanning the Usk were two of the tactics employed. Direct action was returning to industrial Wales as it had to the Welsh language campaigns.

The ending of the strike in South Wales, with the miners marching proudly back to work without a settlement, not crushed, has subsequently been attacked by some on the British Left and some in Plaid Cymru, who have vilified the Labour Party and the Communist Party. In fact, the return to work was widely debated and was the subject of a vote by a delegate conference of the NUM on 3 March 1985.

The strike itself had a wider political significance. Its end signified the beginning of the modernisation of the Labour Party. Throughout the strike the miners had been plagued by the question of why there had been no ballot. In fact, in South Wales it is almost certain that a ballot would have been overwhelmingly supported. The absence of the ballot proved a diversion from the essential issues of the strike and put the miners and their political supporters on the defensive. At Labour's 1985 Conference Neil Kinnock quoted the local lodge official in his constituency, who complained not only that the strike had been held at the wrong time of year, at the end of the winter, but also about the absence of the ballot: "'The fact', he said, 'that it was called without a ballot denied to the miners unity and it denied to the miners the solidarity of so much of the rest of the trades union movement'."

Was the miners' strike an example of a Welsh movement? Clearly it saw new kinds of connections between different movements. Hywel Francis recalls:

> There was this very very strong emotional attachment across the whole of Wales to the miners. I suppose initially it focused around the National Eisteddfod which happened to be on the edge of the Valleys, in Lampeter, within striking distance so to speak. That weekend the funds of the South Wales miners and support groups had been sequestrated. I had phone calls, and this is the first time I ever spoke to him, from Rhodri Williams (then of Cymdeithas, now of Agenda TV) who was willing to do benefits.

Cynog Dafis remembers: "Kim Howells claimed that he discovered Wales at that time, he discovered that there was something beyond Hirwaun, I remember him saying that." Dafis and his wife Llinos were themselves involved: "Llinos went out to deliver a load of milk to Blaenrhondda and the couple that she met were called Taliesin and Dilys, and they called Taliesin Tal. On one occasion Dilys said something about Llin, she said 'I can't get my tongue around these Welsh names', she said. And her name was Dilys, and her friend was Taliesin!"

Dafydd Elis-Thomas was also involved. "There were some interesting moments when you had the farmers protesting the milk quotas, donating the milk to the miners and all that, which was very symbolic for me because they combined two means of production if you like." Elis-Thomas believes that the confidence built up in the miners' strike contributed something positive for the later campaign for devolution. Francis felt that the Wales Congress was a precursor of Yes for Wales in many ways.

Kim Howells remembers the strategy:

> we felt that if we were going to sustain a relatively small workforce then really the basis of our support was going to be that the people of Wales supported us. We worked very consciously at that, we set up the Congress, and you know I worked very closely at the time as one of the movers with Dafydd Elis-Thomas. I didn't like his friends very much, but I always got on with Dafydd, I suspect because he was a socialist and a hustler. I took to him. It was a sort of spiritual thing rather than a political thing, I didn't meet anybody who was opposed to the Wales Congress apart from Tories obviously, who

thought it was all a kind of aberration, and the most unimaginative hatchet-faced Labour bureaucrats, apparatchiks, who just saw any kind of inclusive move as being a threat to their hegemony.

Howells recalls links being made with Blaenau Ffestiniog and parts of Ynys Môn. But looking back, he is less convinced now that it achieved its aim of being an All-Wales movement: "It hadn't become a national struggle, it had become very much a South Wales struggle. We'd made great friends with people in North Wales and even some in mid Wales but we'd envisaged some kind of all-Wales' miners' movement."

For Howells, the strike raised two key questions about Wales. The first was the nature of identity:

It strengthened my resolve to see Wales not just as a sort of caricature single image place, it kind of taught me that it's a very complex place and that the notion that somehow there's a blanket Welshness is as daft as the notion that there's a blanket Scottishness or Englishness.

The second was the need for political structures and institutions:

The big lesson for all those of us who thought about it was that syndicalism didn't work and we needed political power, and we needed forms of political power that didn't exist at the time, and one of those forms of political power was going to be devolved political power.

That raised for Howells the question of "how the hell do you become involved in devolved politics, in a new form of politics, without succumbing to the dubious appeals of nationalism."

Three:
The National Question Reborn
1987-1995

It was not until the third Thatcher victory that devolution returned to the Labour agenda in Wales. In the 1987 election Labour saw off the Alliance challenge once and for all. In Wales Labour defeated a number of Conservative MPs, regaining seats like Newport West, Cardiff West and Bridgend. This election also began a process of changing the character of Welsh Labour MPs. Though the term Welsh-identifying is often used in a cant way, the reality was that 1987 saw a number of younger MPs elected who were more at home with the Welsh language. There had always been Welsh Labour MPs actively involved in supporting Welsh language initiatives. Ted Rowlands and his wife Janice had been highly active in getting the first Welsh language school off the ground in Merthyr, for example. 1987 saw the election of a number of Welsh-speaking or Welsh-learning MPs, such as Rhodri Morgan, Alun Michael and Paul Flynn.

Labour still faced a Conservative Party with a substantial majority in the House of Commons. But the length of Conservative rule, the impact on industries in Wales, particularly the mines, and the assault on local government, all combined to put devolution back onto the agenda. By the autumn of 1987, John Osmond, writing in the re-launched *Planet*, identified a number of former Labour local government opponents of devolution who had swung round. "The most significant change of heart has been that of the Labour leader of Gwent County Council, Lloyd Turnbull", wrote Osmond. He quoted Turnbull as saying: "I chaired and spoke at most of Neil Kinnock's anti-devolution meetings in this county in 1979. But I've changed my mind and would now campaign the other way."

Osmond also cited other former opponents of devolution such as John Allison, former leader of West Glamorgan and David Lewis, mayor of Torfaen. An explanation was given by Anita Gale, the new General Secretary of the Labour Party: "Because it was so divisive, devolution has been a taboo subject since 1979. Now it's creeping back onto the agenda."

It is from 1987 that Ron Davies dates his own conversion to devolution. Interviewed by John Osmond in 1995 for his book *Welsh Europeans*, Davies said:

> Like everyone else I was pretty deflated by that result. I felt the future was bleak. We had delivered in Wales, winning seats like Cardiff West and Clwyd South West. If England had performed as well we would have won the election. There was a very strong feeling that democracy was being undermined. This question of democracy – the question of Welsh representation – confronted me as a political reality which we had to address.

Support for the idea of a Welsh Assembly began taking an organised form in 1987 when the Campaign for a Welsh Assembly (CWA) was formed. The campaign began in the Cardiff Central constituency amongst members of several political parties shortly after the 1987 election.

All the Opposition candidates in the constituency, which had been held by the Conservatives, supported devolution. The Labour candidate Jon Owen Jones and the Plaid Cymru candidate Siân Caiach convened a meeting at the Great Western Hotel. The Liberals were also involved, though the battle for second place in the constituency between Labour's Jones and the Liberals' Mike German had been bitterly hard-fought. A survey was carried out in the Cardiff West constituency to gauge opinion. After this a public meeting was held. John Osmond became Secretary, with Jon Owen Jones as Chairman. Others who became involved included Frank Leavers, who would later become the Liberal Democrat candidate in the Vale of Glamorgan by-election, Bert Pearce of the Communist Party and Siân Edwards of Plaid. They held between 20 and 25 meetings across Wales over the next year or so: "Every other Sunday evening," recalls Leavers. The campaign said that the election results of the 1980s had "produced a groundswell of feeling that there is a need for urgent debate about the nature of our democracy when Wales is ruled by a government supported by a minority of the Welsh electorate."

The CWA's first strategy paper said that "merely attacking the present regime at the Welsh Office and its policies of economic development, without an alternative vision of how the Welsh state bureaucratic structure can be organised and directed, is to ensure failure. Any alternative political programme must start from the reality of the Welsh bureaucratic state as it exists." The Welsh Office needed to be accountable to the Assembly.

The CWA took heart from the existence of the Campaign for a Scottish Assembly, established in 1980, which it noted now planned to establish a Constitutional Convention to draw up a blueprint for a Scottish government and to agitate for a Scottish Assembly. They also noted that Northern Labour MPs were calling for a Northern Regional Assembly. They called on Labour's 24 Welsh MPs to join in. But there was considerable resistance from the Labour Party, not least in Parliament. Though Neil Kinnock had shifted his own position, the Shadow Welsh Secretary Barry Jones (Alyn and Deeside) was largely indifferent and his successor Alan Williams (Swansea West) was still opposed to devolution. The priority was party unity. Paul Murphy, Treasurer of the Labour No Campaign in 1979 and now MP for Torfaen, was a member of the Front Bench team. Alun Michael, who joined the team in 1988 and had been active in the 1979 campaign, was the most pro-devolution member. Michael recalls arranging for the Front Bench team (himself, Murphy and Jones) to visit West Germany, to learn about the relationships between the Lander and the Federal Government. "Those people in the Lander and at Bonn were absolutely clear that the Lander was the powerhouse of economic regeneration in Germany and our idea that there was an automatic, inevitable conflict between national government and local government and regional government, they didn't accept."

Within the Wales Labour Party, the campaign was largely ignored at first. Some were hostile to it, though a number of local party bosses like Jack Brookes, leader of South Glamorgan County Council, supported it. Kim Howells was one of the speakers at one of the early Cardiff meetings arranged by Jon Owen Jones. By the autumn of 1988 the CWA claimed groups in Cardiff; Newport (Gwent); Ogwr; Merthyr; Aberdare; Rhondda; Rhymney Valley; Swansea; Llanelli; Carmarthen; Narberth; Lampeter; Aberystwyth; Brecon; Llandrindod; Mold; Bangor and Blaenau Ffestiniog.

The CWA held an open seminar in April 1988. It recognised that one of the key problems of the 1979 campaign had been that "far too little and too late was done to carry the argument in detail to the people. Before, we did not do enough to deepen the people's understanding of the issue. In particular we did not sufficiently link the issue of an Assembly into every major question of jobs, industrial closures, social service cuts and the rest which could have made it a real-life bread and butter issue for all." The campaign acknowledged that polls showed consistent support for an Assembly in the run up to the 1987 election, and that support increased if Scotland was to get its own Parliament. It set out a series of policy objectives for an Assembly, from environmental and ecological planning to universal child care and education, and set out "to demonstrate in words and in action the relevance of the Welsh Assembly to every major issue affecting the lives of the people and the future of Wales."

An all-party campaign, it held its first conference in Merthyr on 26 November 1988, with speakers including Llanelli MP Denzil Davies, Merthyr MP Ted Rowlands (both Labour), Geraint Howells, Liberal Democrat MP for Ceredigion, and Gwyn Alf Williams. Williams noted the developments in the Soviet Union: how whole peoples were now regaining their nations, their flags and their citizenship. He called for a Welsh Perestroika. He referred to the new regionalism in the EU, with only Britain standing against it. "We are unique in Europe. We are the only country in Europe now where there is no sovereignty of the people. The people are not sovereign in this country; sovereignty resides in the Crown-in-Parliament which is a constitutional fiction to mask the real, almost untrammelled power of an oligarchy." The Conservatives were undoing what Labour had done and what Lloyd George had done before them. In Wales people should make their campaign alongside the Scots and alongside other Europeans. He noted "we in Wales face a more difficult job. We do not have the independent history of the Scots; our history has been a history of division, internal fragmentation which has left us helpless." He set out a call for Welsh people to work together to achieve reform:

> We have a border in Wales (Act of Union). No-one proposes to make it a Berlin Wall, but it exists. Everything West of that line is Wales, everyone west of that line who commits herself or himself to Wales is a member of the Welsh people; I don't care what language they speak, I don't care what colour their faces are. I don't care where they come from. If they live in Wales and commit themselves to Wales, they are Welsh people. And it is the elementary democratic right of that Welsh people to take possession of its own country, to elect in full democracy an assembly which will take over the Welsh state which already exists in embryo and will exercise as much self-government as is humanly possible within the new Europe in which we will take our place.

He called upon people to focus on what united them, not on what divided them.

Coming shortly after the SNP won the Govan by-election, the Conference noted that devolution was now firmly on the agenda again, and that this had been recognised by the Shadow Secretary of State for Wales, Barry Jones. The CWA also noted that other pan-Wales bodies interested in serious issues had been launched since the 1987 election, notably the Institute of Welsh Affairs and the St David's Forum. Thirteen Welsh Labour MPs had signed a Commons Early Day Motion backing a Welsh Parliament. They included Gareth Wardell, Brynmor John, Ted Rowlands, Ray Powell, Alun Michael, Rhodri Morgan, Martin Jones, Win Griffiths, and Ron Davies. Four others who held Front Bench responsibilities (which meant they couldn't sign the Motion) were also thought to be sympathetic. The CWA quoted Ron Davies as explaining his own reasons for changing his mind: he quoted "a slogan painted on a railway bridge in his Caerphilly constituency: 'We voted Labour – we got Thatcher'."

The CWA also noted that the Campaign for a Scottish Assembly in Scotland had now published its document *A Claim of Right for Scotland* and a Scottish Constitutional Convention was expected in 1989. Meanwhile the European Parliament had recently called for elected Assemblies in Europe's regions.

That same month, another constitutional campaign, Charter 88, was launched on the anniversary of the Glorious Revolution with a statement published in the *Guardian,* the *New Statesman* and the *Independent,* attacking assaults on civil liberties and making the case for a written constitution. Though its early draft ignored the specific interests of Wales and Scotland – which led to considerable criticism at an early Charter 88 open meeting in 1989 from Scottish representatives – grouping them under support for regional assemblies, the campaign provided an English dimension for constitutional reform, right at the heart of the Metropolitan Left, as John Osmond put it in *Planet* at the time.

It was not however enthusiasm for a Welsh Assembly which drove the movement for constitutional reform in the Labour Party in the period 1989-92. Hostility to nationalism, particularly after the bitter by-election in Pontypridd in 1989, won by Kim Howells, where Plaid pushed its vote up to 25%, brooked few moves in the direction of an explicitly Welsh agenda. Organisationally, it was Charter 88 and the Scottish Constitutional Convention which led the way. Politically, Labour's success in the 1989 European elections, and Jacques Delors' appeal to the TUC to look at the benefits of Europe provided a wider context that enabled Labour to rethink its dependence on the strictures of the British state. But local Labour resistance to the CWA remained. In 1989 Jon Owen Jones was selected as Labour candidate for Cardiff Central. John Osmond had become more actively involved in Charter 88, and felt that the CWA could make no headway unless Labour's position moved significantly. Within Labour, Alun Michael and others were trying to create a united position on devolution for the Party. Michael was surprised at the preparedness of Neil Kinnock to rethink his own position. Michael's calculation was that devolution could ultimately only be delivered by a united Labour Party. That meant respecting the views of those who differed, and overcoming their fears of what they perceived as a strident pro-Assembly minority within the Party which was too close to Plaid. Hywel Francis, who joined the Labour Party in 1991, took a similar view. He felt that the important task was to convert the Labour Party to the project, not working from the fringe. Devolution found its way back onto Wales Labour Conference agendas. First, after a year-long Commission of Inquiry, came a commitment to a Welsh Regional Council: by 1992, a commitment to an Assembly, at the same time as reorganisation of Welsh local government.

In 1991, the Campaign for a Welsh Assembly was in a position to expand. Osmond became involved again. With the support of the National Union of Civil and Public Servants, who provided an office and funds, he came up with the idea of a pre-election advertisement in the *Western Mail*. Over a thousand people paid for their names to be included. The advertisement called for an all-party conference on devolution after the election.

After Labour's fourth successive defeat in 1992 (despite more gains in Wales, such as Delyn and Cardiff Central) Ron Davies took over as Shadow Secretary of State for Wales following Ann Clwyd, herself pro-devolution, who had moved the debate on. Davies believed that Labour could no longer be half-hearted about the issue. Two days after the election, Peter Hain, elected in the April 1991 by-election as MP for Neath, wrote an article in the *Western Mail* advocating a Constitutional Convention. The Wales TUC also passed an emergency motion at its conference calling for a Welsh Constitutional Convention. So did the Liberal Democrats. But the Wales Labour Party Executive and the Wales Parliamentary Labour Group rejected this outright. The Wales Labour Party set up a Policy Commission to discuss the issue. It was not to report finally until three years later, though an interim report, *The Welsh Assembly: The Way Forward*, was published at the Party's 1993 Conference. Davies himself was already, however, speaking in terms of a democratically-elected Parliament, and talking about the direct relationship between the Welsh economy and a new Welsh democracy.

This was also the term which the Campaign for a Welsh Assembly had begun to embrace. In 1993, it polled members on a name change, and they overwhelmingly endorsed the name Parliament for Wales Campaign (PFW). The Campaign sought legislative and financial powers for the Parliament.

It held a conference attended by 250 people (huge in Welsh terms) in March 1994 in Llandrindod Wells. The people who attended represented a wide variety of organisations – churches, unions, students, cultural organisations, disabled people's groups, women's organisations, green groups, councils and political parties. The conference was addressed by MPs from all parties, including Alex Carlile, Peter Hain and Cynog Dafis. Jonathan Evans spoke for the Conservatives against it. Carlile and Dafis confirmed the positions of their two traditionally pro-devolution parties. Hain told how he had seen a sea change in his constituency in favour of devolution. He identified three principal reasons: the Conservatives' attacks on democracy in Wales; the importance of Europe; and the knowledge that it was economically more sensible to devolve. He brought a commitment from Ron Davies that an incoming Labour Government would legislate for a Welsh Assembly in its first year of government – the first time this had been said in public. He warned that opponents of devolution were resurrecting the idea of a referendum to delay change: "I'm not really interested in a referendum, but I am not afraid of one either." Hain spoke as a Labour MP and also as the Welsh Parliamentary Labour Party Campaign Officer with Ron Davies' covert support. However, his appearance provoked angry criticism within the Party establishment. MPs like Allan Rogers (Rhondda) attacked him. He and Jon Owen Jones, MP for Cardiff Central, and Paul Flynn (Newport West) who also spoke, were summoned to the Wales Labour Party executive to be ticked off. A 'Democracy Declaration' was debated and then adopted at the PFW's AGM in Aberystwyth. Advertisements supporting it were placed in the *Western Mail* and *Daily Post*. Some, such as Ned Thomas, questioned why it had not had a greater public impact. But the CWA and then PFW had clearly moved the debate on.

That year had also seen the reorganisation of local government. As Mari James, then the National Coordinator of the Parliament for Wales Campaign, argued in the book that grew out of the Parliament for Wales Conference, "One effect of the Local Government (Wales) Act has been to promote the case for a Welsh parliament and to bring about some of the conditions that are required for a new political settlement." In 1979, the County Councils had been some of the key funders of the No Campaign. The new unitary council structure, creating many smaller councils, flagged up all the difficulties of having no all-Wales tier of government, and the democratic deficit at the all-Wales level. This time, Council leaders were less likely to be hostile to the creation of an Assembly or Parliament, and many were incensed at the apparent gerrymandering of boundaries. Ron Davies had been working patiently to get agreement between the local authority organisations on the Conservative Government's local government proposals. Davies recalls "meetings after meetings after meetings" to reconcile the warring districts and counties. But he knew this was an opportunity to take forward the devolution debate. The line on which he was able to get agreement was that Labour would not agree to local government reform unless there was an All-Wales dimension. He produced a paper called 'No Devolution, No Deal' which spelt this out.

It was in this context that the Wales Labour Party's Policy Commission published its consultation document on a Welsh Assembly, *Shaping the Vision*. Six consultation meetings were then held in Aberystwyth, Caernarfon, Cardiff, Llandrindod Wells, Mold, and Swansea. But these events were overshadowed by the death of Labour leader John Smith in May. The tragic death at a relatively young age of a politician thought to epitomise honesty and humanity produced a state of national mourning which had not been felt for a generation, certainly not for a politician. A Scot of a different political persuasion, Neal Ascherson, recorded "when John Smith died it suddenly seemed unbearable to lump him with 'all the others'." It was, said one commentator, really the end of the eighties, the end of the politics of self. For supporters of devolution, it was a grave loss. Smith was not only personally committed but passionate about reform. He had been Michael Foot's deputy during the agonised debates on devolution in the 1970s and believed devolution was "unfinished business".

Tony Blair's leadership platform had promised political renewal, and had committed him to the Welsh Assembly, "with power over Welsh affairs". As Labour's new leader, Tony Blair made an early visit to Wales in November 1994, where he warned that the constitutional debate had not penetrated as far into England as it had into Scotland and Wales. But he demonstrated an open mind on the issue of devolution.

Blair appointed Kim Howells to the Front Bench constitutional role. Howells believes Blair's views on devolution were shaped by his experience as a politician in the North-East of England "and its equally unique relationship with Scotland" – a difficult relationship in some ways where some in the North-East viewed Scotland as being granted opportunities by Labour which their own region would not enjoy. Howells believes Blair knew "I was a bitter opponent of nationalism."

In his early days as Leader, Blair often spoke of his 'project'. He is a strategic politician, carefully carrying out reconnaissance and assembling his position before identifying routes forward. His one-nation, inclusive, modern, tolerant New Britain philosophy was carefully targeted at Middle England, not at Wales and Scotland where the concept of "one nation" itself raises spectres of Greater England. From the start, Blair declared that there would be no "no-go areas" for Labour, even in Southern England. He attacked the pessimism of left-wing intellectuals in England about the possibility of political progress there, and sought to broaden Labour's appeal beyond its traditional heartlands. One of his chief lieutenants, Jack Straw, as Shadow Home Secretary and constitutional spokesperson, wrote in 1995, "It is time to end the right-wing ghetto in which public feeling for England has too long been corralled". Yet England's importance to Blair was obvious: England accounts for 80% of the Westminster Parliament's seats.

Even before Blair's election, Labour was already enjoying considerable success in England. The June 1994 European elections saw extraordinary results there for Labour. But Blair demonstrated a personal appeal to voters in England as well as Wales and Scotland which few Labour leaders before him had ever enjoyed.

The focus on England, Blair's campaign to drop Clause Four, and his modernisation strategy, unsettled many in Wales, and may itself have cemented support for devolution within Labour, as well as for Wales within the UK. In the autumn of 1994, Ron Davies prepared a paper to be submitted on behalf of the Wales Labour MPs to the Policy Commission. This called for an Assembly with tax-raising powers, primary law-making powers, and all the powers of the Secretary of State. It would be elected by PR. While the debate on Clause Four rolled on, the Wales Labour Party's Policy

Commission was making progress, and would be ready to publish its final report for the May 1995 Wales Labour Party Conference.

Opposition to devolution had, however, already surfaced in the Wales Labour Party. On 16 January 1995, Llew Smith, MP for Blaenau Gwent, published a paper attacking the idea of an assembly or a senedd. *The Welsh Assembly: Why it has no place in Wales* argued for a referendum and claimed that "much of the popularity for an assembly lies more in the unpopularity of the present government rather than for devolution of power in Wales". Smith said he believed that devolution would ultimately lead to a separatist Welsh State. He linked his opposition to an assembly in part to his hostility to the EU and to the Maastricht Treaty. His paper called for devolution through industrial democracy, and defended Clause Four as being about devolution in industry. Smith referred approvingly to Labour's 1983 manifesto (described by Gerald Kaufman MP as "the longest suicide note in history") as representing the kind of politics he wanted. The Paper also argued for more devolution to local government, warned that devolution would mean the ending of the post of Secretary of State and a reduction in the number of Welsh MPs, and opposed proportional representation.

There were two very tense meetings of the Labour Party Policy Commission in early 1995. At the first, in Transport House, Cardiff, in March 1995, Kim Howells was present for the first time. According to some of those present he raised objections to the size of the Assembly (100 members), the question of legislative and tax-raising powers and the nature of the desired electoral system. The question of whether there should be a referendum also came up, but was dismissed. A further meeting held at the South Glamorgan County Hall in Cardiff Bay a month later was described by Davies as "one of the nastiest meetings I've ever been in." There had been a leak of one of the Commission documents shortly before the meeting, and some saw Davies as the source. This put him on the back foot from the start. Davies, Rhodri Morgan and Gareth Hughes battled to protect a commitment to giving the Assembly powers to reform the quangos. Davies felt that in the absence of primary powers he had to have a commitment to special powers to reform the quangos, for education and for the Welsh language. He got a commitment to a phrase allowing that there might be a case for special powers after arguing long and hard with Wayne David, MEP for South Wales East, over lunch. But he lost on PR. Aside from this, Davies, Howells and others were involved in a series of meetings in Westminster to try to knock Labour's overall constitutional programme into shape.

When Labour's proposals leaked out, on 9 May 1995, it became clear that the Party was proposing a more limited Assembly than many wanted. It would take over the existing responsibilities of the Welsh Office. It might have limited law-making powers – for restructuring the quangos – and no powers over taxation. It would be funded by central grant from the Treasury. The Assembly would have 80 members. The draft that was leaked suggested two options for their election: first past the post with two members from each of 40 constituencies, or a form of Proportional Representation (the Additional Member System). In fact, as the final report made clear, PR had been explicitly rejected at the Policy Commission and at Labour's Executive the previous month. The report also recommended measures to support better gender balance. The *Western Mail* detected the fingerprints of Kim Howells on the document. Interviewed by the paper, Howells said he hoped the Assembly wouldn't be stuffed full of local councillors. He defended the first-past-the-post system on the grounds that it was better than the additional member system offered as an alternative, saying he wouldn't have had a problem if a proper PR system had been on offer. Howells himself believes that the Policy Commission was a valuable forum, which argued out in private many of the issues which would come to be debated in the referendum campaign.

The report was officially launched by Ron Davies three days later. The revised *Shaping the Vision* document stressed that devolution was meant to strengthen the Union, not weaken it. Devolution to Wales was part of a new constitutional settlement for the UK as a whole. The plan rejected separatism. It said that Wales and Scotland had different traditions, and therefore different forms of devolution should apply.

At the Wales Labour Party Conference on 19 May, Tony Blair called on all Labour MPs to support the plans. This was seen as a coded attack on Llew Smith and Allan Rogers, at that stage the only two identified critics. Blair said: "It is a serious policy put forward by a serious party and I expect MPs to be serious and disciplined in promoting it."

The following week, the first signs of dissent emerged. One newly-elected member of the Labour Party's Wales Executive, Gareth Hughes, who had been a member of the Policy Commission, announced plans to campaign for a strengthening of the proposals. He wanted to see primary legislative powers, tax-raising powers and PR. Meanwhile the Liberal Democrats published an analysis of the Labour electoral system, which they called *Stacking the Votes*. They said that the system chosen would produce disproportionate results.

At the National Eisteddfod that year, Gareth Hughes announced the backing of about 60 party members for Wales Labour Action, which would campaign for stronger powers, powers of taxation, PR, and gender balance. David Morris MEP and Sue Essex, former Leader of Cardiff City Council, were both named as prominent members. Hughes said a number of MPs were sympathetic. Also at the Eisteddfod, Labour launched a document called *Bonfire of the Quangos*, announcing plans to make all the quangos accountable to the Assembly.

Responses came at the Party Conferences that autumn. The Liberal Democrats called on Labour to agree to join a Constitutional Convention, along the lines of that in Scotland. Alex Carlile said that there should be cooperation on those issues where the parties agreed. The Party passed a resolution calling for proportional representation for the Assembly. Peter Black, the Liberal Democrats' Welsh Chair, called Labour "autocratic, anti-democratic and illiberal". Martin Thomas QC attacked the "dinosaur element" in the Welsh Labour Party.

Plaid Cymru, meanwhile, demanded a referendum to be called by the Conservative Party before the General Election. In a pamphlet entitled *A Democratic Wales in a United Europe*, Plaid Cymru Leader Dafydd Wigley called for a pre-election multi-choice referendum to allow people to indicate their preference between the status quo, an elected parliament with limited powers, or full self-government within the EU. He called Labour's Assembly "a waste of time". The Conservatives denounced Labour's plans as marking the break-up of Britain.

Within the Labour Party, Ron Davies was working hard to strengthen the proposals on the quangos and to keep alive the PR option. With union support he got the Welsh Executive to re-open the Commission. Then he began producing a series of papers that autumn for the Commission, arguing the case in more detail.

By the end of 1995, the battle-lines for the election were set. After almost two decades, devolution was back on the agenda. At this stage, there were no grounds for expecting a referendum. Davies still had to get final agreement to the actual inclusion of powers to reform the quangos. That was one of the key achievements which he would obtain at the May 1996 Labour Conference. Davies now had something on which to build a wider consensus. Both he and Tony Blair spoke of the need for inclusivity in undertaking constitutional change. Davies told the conference that Labour had to be inclusive and reach out to other parties:

> If you are embarking on a project of reconstructing a democracy, of building a new society, there's a lot of common sense in seeking agreement and making compromises.

It was just as well the matter of inclusivity was raised. It would provide a basis for bringing electoral reform back on to the agenda. By this time, the argument on the referendum was underway in earnest within the higher reaches of the Labour Party. Within two months, the referendum would be announced. Then there really would be a need to seek agreement and make compromises.

Four: Launching the Yes Campaign

The Wales Labour Party Executive finally approved the overall plan for devolution on 13 January 1997. The decision was not unanimous but the package would be put to the Party's conference in March. It included the element of PR which Ron Davies had been working for. He saw the agreement on electoral reform as necessary to get both the Liberal Democrats and Plaid Cymru to join a Yes Campaign. Davies had discussed the possibility of an Assembly with sixty members with Alex Carlile, then leader of the Welsh Liberal Democrats and the party's only Welsh MP. Forty would be elected by first past the post, and twenty on the basis of a form of PR in multi-member seats, based on the Euro-constituencies across Wales. The two sat together on the Joint Labour/Liberal Democrat Consultative Committee on Constitutional Reform. Davies believed he had achieved an agreement that the Liberals would campaign and that they would sign up to these proposals. He outlined the discussions to his Front Bench team at a weekend strategy meeting in Newport early in the New Year. The Joint Labour/Liberal Democrat Consultative Committee had also agreed that the Scottish referendum would be held before that for Wales.

Immediately, Labour dissidents Allan Rogers and Ray Powell showed their hand, adding to the opposition already expressed by Llew Smith. They declared their opposition to PR and consequently to Labour's devolution proposals. As one Welsh journalist saw it, "Ron did make some people stand on their heads and they didn't forgive him."

Plaid Cymru also saw the plans as unacceptable though for different reasons. Dafydd Wigley stressed once more that if there was to be a referendum then it should include several options. He also had reservations about the number of seats proposed for the Assembly, believing that there would not be enough members to do the work. And he was concerned about whether the proposals would ensure gender balance. Welsh journalists tried to press him about the circumstances in which he would vote No, and Wigley said that if he thought the Assembly plans would undermine local government he would vote No. Plaid Cymru MP Cynog Dafis remembers "we had a very fraught meeting of the National

Council." He recalls people saying "we're not going to allow '79 to happen again."

Yes for Wales observed these developments with some concern. What we feared was that the division amongst the political parties who supported devolution – and division within the likely next government party, Labour – would alienate voters from the over-all devolution project.

The Campaign had to press on with its own initiatives. The campaign's first activity, the launch of a business grouping, was due to take place shortly after Labour's Executive met on 13 January. Ron Jones, Chairman of the TV company Agenda Productions, had agreed to draft the statement. Peter and I and the new organiser Daran Hill, now in post in the Campaign's office in 7 St Andrew's Place, worked feverishly to get names to sign up to the statement. Daran recalls being on the phone to me many times a day at this stage. Peter identified some potential supporters in his own area. The one name we wanted was John Elfed Jones, former Chairman of Welsh Water and HTV, and a former Chairman of the Welsh Language Board. Jones thought carefully about participating. He had a number of conversations with both Peter and myself, and even made some amendments to the draft statement that was to be issued. After this, both of us were confident he would sign up. But the day before we were to release the statement both Peter and I received phone calls from Jones saying he had been advised not to make his position clear before the election by a prominent Labour member of the House of Lords. We were both disappointed. His name at that stage would have been a significant coup. In the end, the statement was too orientated around the media industry and the valleys of South-West Wales. But we hoped that it might help to neutralise disquiet among business, and undermine the claim that it was solidly against the Assembly. The statement issued by the Business Forum was endorsed by Geraint Stanley Jones, now working in TV production, Ron Jones, Mike James, Chairman of BJ Construction and of Swansea Rugby club, Jack Pearce of John Pearce Ltd the haulage company, and Rhydian Davies of Consolidated Coal. The most prominent business supporter was David Waterstone, former Chief Executive of the WDA and Chairman of Ansaldo plc and many other companies.

Despite this set-back, on 17 January 1997, the *Western Mail* front page was headed 'Tycoon Forum backs fight for Assembly'. The Business Forum on Devolution took much of Wales by surprise. It took the broadcasters a while to track down spokes-people for the campaign. Ron Jones fielded several interviews during the course of the day. Early warning had been given several days before to the *Western Mail*'s editor, Neil Fowler. I had briefed Fowler on both this and the forthcoming Yes for Wales launch. The *Western Mail* would be given exclusive coverage in recognition that exclusivity would be likely to guarantee prominence. The campaign's thinking was simple. Though the *Western Mail* was not the most widely-read newspaper in Wales, being beaten by the *South Wales Echo* amongst other Welsh papers and by the Welsh circulation of London-based tabloids, it was actively interested in the devolution debate and read by opinion-formers. We also believed the paper would help to set the agenda for the broadcasters.

The statement, drafted largely by Ron Jones with input from David Waterstone and John Elfed Jones, said that the Business Forum believed that devolution would be "a positive force for the Welsh economy". It went on "we believe that devolution gives Wales an opportunity to address some of the deficiencies of the present structures and institutions of government. We should help government help business by taking a positive role in the devolu-tion debate. We can work together to make devolution a plus for business." Ron Jones told the *Western Mail* "Wearing my business hat, I don't think Wales has been well-served by a centralised form of government." Jones played a critically important role in taking on the bulk of interviews. Behind the scenes, he also helped the campaign by arranging a short-term loan.

The initiative was welcomed by Ron Davies, who said he was confident that the Assembly would be able to enter a partnership with Welsh business and commerce. The Business Forum state-ment attracted considerable media attention, with a feature and an editorial in the *Western Mail*, as well as broadcast coverage. Yes for Wales itself was delighted that the exclusivity given to the *Western Mail* had resulted in real prominence for the announcement. The statement heartened longstanding devolution supporters. Ioan Bowen Rees, former Chief Executive of Gwynedd County Council saw it as "the most significant development in Welsh politics since the creation of the Welsh Office in 1964". Significantly, the Business Forum launch was welcomed in Tony Blair's office. Peter had tipped them off that it was coming. The Labour leader referred to it as a positive development when he attended a Wales Parliamentary Labour Party meeting in Westminster at the end of January.

At the same time as the Business Forum was launched, Plaid Cymru launched its campaign for self-government within Europe. The campaign had two aims: to boost Plaid's election vote, and to force Labour to add a further question, on self-government in Europe, to the referendum ballot form. Plaid leader Dafydd Wigley warned Labour that internal division in their party could cost Wales devolution.

Following the Business Forum launch, *Wales on Sunday* was given a hint about the planned Yes Campaign launch. The leak appeared on 19 January, to coincide with Peter Hain's interview planned by HTV for that day. The story ran "A 'rainbow coalition' of Welsh devolution supporters ranging from bishops to sportsmen is expected to reveal itself within weeks." On HTV, Hain welcomed the business launch and hoped that this could be built on. He said it was a shift of opinion and that a broad-based campaign was needed. The leak was carefully planned: perhaps too well planned, as very few noticed it. But Hain hinted at the new campaign and made it clear that there would be developments very shortly.

The second meeting of the Yes for Wales Steering Committee took place on 24 January and did not pass unnoticed as the first meeting had done. Clive Betts recorded in the *Western Mail* the next day that a group had met to consider launching a Yes campaign. Betts was given a specific quote in line with the agenda that Yes for Wales was starting to focus on: "Members of the group believe that devolution is too important to be left to the political parties alone". Betts returned for more on Monday, 27 January, and was briefed on the outcome of the meeting. He was able to report that, unlike the Business Forum, the Yes Campaign would not be run by "bi-lingual media folk" and that the group had decided to reject the demands by Plaid Cymru and the Parliament for Wales Campaign for a multi-choice referendum. Soon, the story was starting to gain currency around Wales. The Welsh-language weekly *Golwg* carried a feature on 31 January, with quotes from a Yes Campaign spokesperson that a campaign would be launched shortly on the basis that unity was essential. The same theme was projected: that the progress of devolution was being held back by debates between the political parties over the merits of particular forms of devolution. *Golwg* professed to believe that Labour Party 'fixers' had been actively involved in putting together the all-party campaign and the Business Forum. In fact, there was considerable concern within the Labour Party itself about the Yes Campaign launching in advance of the General Election.

Planning for the launch, to be held at City Hall, Cardiff, occupied most of the next three weeks. The Campaign was determined to get celebrities on board. Alun Wyn Bevan focused on sports celebrities. Eluned Morgan went after the pop groups. "I remember phoning up a number of different groups trying to get hold of the Manic Street Preachers, and actually getting through to one of them and being terrified when they answered the phone!" she recalled later. Morgan found that though there was general support, only a few such as Cerys Matthews and Catatonia, the Super Furry Animals and the Stereophonics did much that was practical. Morgan recalls "I did speak to Cerys Matthews, she was enthusiastic, she was very happy to put her name forward." Eluned was delighted and rang me immediately. It was what we had wanted right from the start. The Yes Campaign needed to be close to popular youth culture and now we could claim it.

The actual launch of Yes for Wales was carefully prepared. The editors of the *Western Mail* and the *South Wales Echo* and the Political Editor of *Wales on Sunday* were carefully briefed. Each was promised something different: though the three publications occupy the same building, there is considerable rivalry between them. Broadcasters were also put on notice.

The plan was to set out the basic case for Yes for Wales in an Agenda-page article in the *Western Mail*, in the name of Professor Kevin Morgan. He may not have been aware of it at this point, but Morgan was emerging as the favourite to be Chairman of the organisation. Articulate, sincere and identifiably from the Valleys Labour heartland, Morgan was an effective and original media performer. The article would be followed with a story in *Wales on Sunday* that would identify some of the celebrities who would be involved. Separate interviews would be granted for the *South Wales Echo*. North Wales' celebrities were also identified and the *Daily Post* tipped off.

Yes for Wales was determined to ensure that the key message that devolution was too important to be left to the politicians was communicated throughout its launch and through all the publicity which followed. The Campaign also wanted to make the point that the new campaign was different from that of 1979. The *Western Mail* headlined the article in Morgan's name 'The People's Cause' but gave it the sub-heading 'Devolution is too vital to be left to the politicians, says a new non-party group'. Its headline for the Yes Campaign's launch was 'Devolution is far too important to be left to the politicians'. By the end of the week, the paper had adopted virtually the same line itself. Its editorial the following Saturday was headed 'Devolution is bigger than the politicians'.

Morgan's article revealed that the Campaign would focus on the principle of devolution, "rather than wrangling over the details". Campaigners understood that there were real issues involved in the details, but they were worried that the overall case was going by default. The new campaign was supported by people from all over Wales with different views on different aspects of devolution but who recognised the dangers of division in the face of what would be a united No campaign. "Unless we win the referendum, there will be no chance even to debate the details of devolution we want. Without a Yes-vote, the whole project is doomed. This is the last chance Wales has to decide its future for at least a generation." The Campaign looked on the referendum as an opportunity, not an obstacle. There was an entire generation – over 600,000 people – that had been too young to vote in 1979. This was the generation that had given rise to the most invigorating popular music culture Wales had ever known. It was a generation comfortable with the diversity of Wales and Welshness. The article also revealed that the group had been behind the Business Forum. The Campaign said it also expected several Conservatives to emerge as supporters in due course.

The *Western Mail* announced that the group had taken up an office in Cardiff and appointed a full-time organiser. Daran Hill had been working hard with our Steering Committee members to produce a long list of endorsements for the Campaign. "I spent about two weeks just telephoning people," he recalls. "As a result I was able to give *Wales on Sunday* the name of Tyrone O'Sullivan, one of the leaders of the Tower Colliery miners' buyout, as one of the prominent Welsh people who would be declaring themselves for devolution the following day." On the Sunday, the broadcasters began to cover the story with a number of early evening interviews.

Cardiff City Hall was then thought likely to be the home of the Assembly. Its Council Chamber was organised to show off the new Yes Campaign logo revised by Roger Fickling of Splash! from the designs earlier submitted to the Steering Committee. Still short of cash, the campaign had had to borrow display boards from Alun Jones's union NAS-UWT. Daran Hill felt it made "a visually poor spectacle". The platform for the launch was to be Kevin Morgan, the Archbishop of Wales Alwyn Rice Davies, the broadcaster Mavis Nicholson, and Eluned Morgan. We were anxious to ensure a gender balance in the public personalities and a balance between English- and Welsh-speaking Welsh people. Not all went as planned, however. When the Archbishop arrived, he said he was there to observe not to join the platform. He was very supportive personally, but felt restricted by his position.

The objectives for the launch were to obtain substantial coverage for the organisation and to demonstrate broad-based support. The list of names announced as supporters of the Campaign was reasonably impressive. It included the first Permanent Secretary of the Welsh Office, Sir Goronwy Daniel, sports stars such as cricketers Tony Cottey and Steve Watkin, hockey player Linda Watkin, rugby player Stuart Evans and boxer Steve Robinson, former rugby international Ray Gravell, Secretary of the Welsh Rugby Union Vernon Pugh, actors Siân Phillips and Philip Madoc, playwrights Ewart Alexander and Elaine Morgan, and the rock group Catatonia. As journalists and guests arrived, Catatonia's album *Way Beyond Blue* greeted people attending the press conference. The Campaign also published its statement of purpose, a barely-changed version of the paper that I had written the previous August.

We had rehearsed in detail many of the questions we might be asked. Daran had drawn up a series of questions and answers. We expected to be asked why we were launching prior to the election and were bound to be asked why we had chosen the same name as the main 'Yes' slogan in 1979. The charge of being a Labour front was particularly sensitive. Kevin Morgan was frustrated with what he saw as the cynicism of the media. "We are what we seem," he told journalists, meaning this was simply a group of people who cared about the devolution argument. To ensure cross-party backing, the Campaign had arranged that Alex Carlile would issue a statement of support, and the Liberal Democrat Peer Lord Geraint was one of the supporters. Carlile's statement promised that the Liberal Democrats would work closely with Yes for Wales, which he saw as an important step forward. His colleague Richard Livsey saw it as an important initiative, and believed that it was the right time to launch it. Eleri Carrog, an active member of Plaid Cymru, was in the audience at the press conference and declared her support, as did others who were not members of a political party, such as the Rev. Dewi Eurig Davies, the former President of the Welsh Congregational Union. Even so, the BBC's *Wales Today* that night suggested the campaign was Labour-dominated. The Conservatives fielded their Welsh Office Minister Gwilym Jones who said the Campaign members were a collection of "has-beens and never-weres". The Campaign responded that: "The Minister has demeaned his office by his petty, personal attacks on a wide range of Welsh figures far more distinguished than himself."

At this stage, in advance of the General Election, the Campaign had not yet won over all of those seeking greater powers than Labour was prepared to deliver, and this was reflected in some of the coverage. *Golwg* expressed scepticism about the preparedness of New Labour to deliver. Cynog Dafis remembers wondering about the Campaign, "to what extent it was a Labour front organisation, you know, suspicions of that kind, and noting that Eluned Morgan was sitting on the platform, why should she be there, and that kind of thing."

The campaign launch achieved widespread broadcast coverage on radio and television on the day before the launch and the day itself, with most media outlets in Wales running the story, including BBC Radio Wales, BBC Radio Cymru, BBC Wales TV, S4C, Swansea Sound, and Touch FM. HTV however ran the item very low in their bulletin. Newspaper coverage was extensive all over Wales. Daran Hill recalls "in terms of media management, we were particularly successful at that stage because there was nothing in the media apart from what we wanted to be in the media, and bear in mind we were coordinating the names of 140 people by the time we did go public. That was no mean feat."

For some people, the announcement of the Yes Campaign was just what they had been waiting for. Kevin Brennan clearly remembers this. "I immediately signed up because to me it was exactly what was needed and exactly what I had been preaching to colleagues in the Labour Party and others who were supporters of devolution, namely that we were getting very close to midnight and here people were still quibbling over the numbers."

The Welsh language newspaper *Y Cymro* also welcomed the launch unequivocally:

> It was about time that somebody gave a focus to the movements in Wales around the simple concept that we need a positive vote for devolution in the referendum which the Labour Party has promised. There is a need to crystallise people's minds around this notion in the wake of the signals which illustrate that the nightmare of the last referendum might repeat itself.
>
> There is already bickering within the Labour Party, and between it and the Liberal Democrats, and between Plaid Cymru and everyone else. Plaid has even threatened to campaign against the Assembly

promised by Labour on the grounds that Wales is being offered less than that which Labour has pledged to Scotland. The only people who benefit from such division are the Tories – the only political party which has a policy against an assembly of any sort.

But Kevin Brennan's response was not altogether shared in the Wales Labour Party. Its suspicions had not been helped by Hywel Francis inadvertently briefing Labour Party figure Ken Hopkins about the Campaign at an early stage. Ron Davies told Francis, "You've been having some interesting conversations, haven't you?" Francis recalls "Peter [Hain] rang us and gave us a bollocking." Paradoxically some saw the Yes Campaign as a Plaid front and continued to do so until much later. Eluned Morgan remembers the first Wales Labour Party Executive after the launch of the Yes Campaign where it was discussed. "There was a very firm No from our Labour Party Executive, they thought that it wasn't the right thing to do, but it could also be damaging to the Campaign if we were to join." In a later Executive however she felt that people did open up more to the idea, recognising that the Campaign could be valuable in non-Labour areas.

By now the political debate on devolution was well underway. At the end of the week of the Yes Campaign launch, the Conservatives met for their Annual Welsh conference. The Prime Minister, John Major, attacked Labour's plans for an Assembly, posing questions about the inter-relationship of the Assembly and other institutions, and widened his attack to the party's overall plans for constitutional reform. He claimed: "A thousand days of Labour government could ditch a thousand years of British history." The Conservative Party Chairman Brian Mawhinney said that the Assembly would cost £34 million in salaries. The Secretary of State for Wales, William Hague, contrasted Labour and the Conservatives: "They offer an expanding Welsh Assembly. We offer an expanding Welsh economy." But away from the platform rhetoric, Hague said something more interesting. Interviewed on the BBC's Radio Five Live, he stuck to the party line of opposition, but said that the Conservatives would have to respect the result of a referendum.

But by March 1997, Wales Parliamentary Labour Party Referendum Coordinator Don Touhig MP was worried that not enough had been done to get the Labour campaign into gear. "If a referendum on a Welsh Assembly was held today, I believe we would lose it!" he told colleagues in a paper. He said that devolution did not excite the electorate. More importantly for this stage, he found that most Labour activists and councillors, as well as groups in the community, were ignorant of Labour's proposals. He was also concerned that the Labour referendum organiser Andrew Davies would not be starting work until April and that there had been only one meeting of Labour's campaign team. Touhig was concerned that people were taking the result of the referendum for granted. "A Labour victory at the General Election is no guarantee of a YES vote in the referendum," he wrote. He believed from his travels that Labour voters didn't want more government, but better government, and the Party had still to develop the ideas and arguments to convince people to vote Yes. It also needed to ensure proper staff resources during the campaign. He knew that most Labour staff were focused on the General Election but felt the need to take them outside that frame of reference briefly so that certain key decisions could be finalised. He had asked Andrew Davies to begin to cost key campaign tools including focus groups, posters and literature.

The idea had been that Andrew start work in the autumn. Labour had already agreed to such an appointment in Scotland but the Wales Labour Party was not convinced the campaign needed an extra resource from outside. Hain and Ron Davies were worried that the focus on the General Election could leave the Party unprepared for the referendum campaign. After a great deal of internal wrangling, which Ron Davies found deeply frustrating, the job was advertised. Davies was interviewed alongside six others for the job, re-interviewed and eventually offered it, after the intervention of Davies, Touhig and Labour's General Secretary, Tom Sawyer. This explained the delayed start.

Labour unveiled its plans *Representing Wales* prior to its conference at the end of February. Some of those opposed to Labour's devolution proposals, including some prominent in local government, believed Tony Blair didn't really want devolution and had persuaded themselves that he certainly wouldn't come to Wales to campaign. As Rhodri Morgan put it, "I think there was a general feeling that certain senior councillors, who shall be nameless, were waiting to see which way the wind was going to blow. If they thought that Tony Blair was going to push for devolution in a big way, they were going to be for devolution." Some of them believed devolution would not be won, and were toying with the idea of being involved in the campaign against devolution. They thought Blair would be advised not to come to Wales during the referendum campaign. Yes for Wales had picked up some of these feelings, and had passed them back to Hain and Davies, urging them to ensure that Blair emphasised he would be coming back to Wales to campaign when he spoke at the conference on Friday 28 February. Whether that pressure worked or whether it was already intended, Blair announced: "I promise you we will legislate for a Welsh Assembly in the first year of a Labour Government. And I promise you in the referendum that precedes that legislation, I will be with you, here, in Wales, campaigning for a Yes-vote. And let us have a united party in Wales behind that campaign."

His promise to come back to Wales was the sound-bite used by the media that evening. Interestingly, in the light of the later White Paper title, Blair also called for the Assembly to be "a strong voice for Wales". Ron Davies and Don Touhig had been working hard to obtain backing for Labour's devolution plans from all Labour Council/Group Leaders in Wales at the same time. They had visited the different Labour groups to make the case. Even the most sceptical of Council leaders signed up to the statement, albeit in their own words. That was a significant triumph.

The Liberal Democrats were also in conference in Conwy just along the North Wales coast from Labour. Unlike Labour, where there had been total unanimity, there was a real debate as to whether they should campaign for the devolution proposals in the referendum. Their activists, including Swansea Councillor Peter Black and Cardiff Councillor Jenny Randerson, were worried about the party supporting Labour's proposals. Randerson had gone on record as saying "If we do not challenge Labour's devolution plans, they may prove unacceptable to electors in Wales in a referendum." Alex Carlile had to fight hard to protect his line and the Joint Constitutional Committee proposals. He made a speech saying Labour must review the electoral system. Ron Davies told BBC Wales that he would be prepared to look at that – a move that was interpreted by journalists as Ron helping Alex out of a difficult position.

There were other encouraging signs too. The Welsh Economy Research Unit at the Cardiff Business School suggested that the cost of the Assembly could be as little as £5 per head of population. On St David's Day itself, Yes for Wales felt one of its early goals had been achieved. The *Western Mail* came out in favour of devolution, though it wanted the Labour Party to give Wales more details before people voted in the referendum. The paper ran a very long editorial setting out the reasons for its support, which concluded "The right type of Assembly, which makes Wales fitter, stronger and prepared for the challenges of the Twenty-first Century, will be worth the nation's support." This was in contrast to the situation in 1979, when the *Western Mail* had been at best half-hearted in its support. A few days later, the Joint Labour/Liberal Democrat Consultative Committee on Constitutional Reform published its report. For the campaign, the most important statement in the document concerned the timing of the referendum: "Both Parties agree that a short time should be allowed to lapse after the Scottish referendum in order to ensure the debate in Wales, with its distinctive form of devolution, is not overshadowed by the process in Scotland."

One of the important triumphs for Davies in this committee was that he had won support for powers for the Assembly to reform quangos, despite the opposition of Jack Straw. The powers had already been written into the *Road to the Manifesto* document and had been approved as Wales Labour Party policy the year before, and were endorsed in the Joint Consultative Committee Report.

Sadly, however, some remained in defeatist mood. "A defeat for the Welsh Assembly in a referendum is likely because the Labour Party will be telling the Scottish electorate that an assembly is second-best," wrote the Press Officer of the Parliament for Wales Campaign in a letter to the *Guardian* on 22 February. Yes for Wales' supporters were infuriated. Only the previous day, the Steering Committee had discussed the need for a cordial relationship with the Parliament for Wales Campaign. Indeed, many of the most prominent Yes for Wales activists were members of Parliament for Wales. By March, it was clear that the Parliament for Wales Campaign would not decide on whether to campaign for a Yes-vote until June. PFW representatives met with Daran Hill on April 11th. The meeting was positive, though the PFW leaders said that as things stood they would be unable to campaign for a Yes-vote if Labour won since the Assembly did not go far enough. It mattered little. By now, Yes for Wales believed that it had virtually taken over the leadership of the non-party pro-devolution campaign.

Yes for Wales was launched: but it was now election season. The Steering Committee agreed that it would take a back-seat between its launch and the General Election. The Campaign's role would clearly and necessarily be less visible in the run up to the election. It would comment on articles and letters in the press but would not make any political comments about any of the parties. It was time to review the organisation's strategy, and develop the plans necessary to deliver the Campaign after the election. Yes for Wales had four issues to focus on: Money; Mobilisation; Media; Materials. Of these, the most pressing was money. On 17 March Yes for Wales ran its first advert asking for funds in the *Western Mail*, with others following in different papers. It launched its internet website the same day, and mailed its supporters and potential supporters through the mailings of other organisations. Small sums were coming in, and pledges were being given. But the officers of Yes for Wales knew that they needed far more. Already, by mid-March, £10,000 had been spent, on salaries, rent, phones, a computer and printer, design and printing, and postage. If they were to run an effective advertising campaign during the Campaign, major investment would be needed from somewhere. (A sum of £250,000 was being talked of, with more for polling.) There would also be a need for publicity for local groups. The Campaign had a mailing list of 1500 and a further 2000 were mailed through other organisations. "I'd never had so many paper-clips in my hands in my life as preparing those letters," said Daran. A proposal from a professional fundraiser was examined but put on hold until after the election. A second member of staff was seconded by NUS Wales for a few months.

The Steering Committee agreed a strategy paper at its 21 March meeting. This reviewed the success of the Campaign so far, noting that a number of its objectives had been achieved and messages communicated. It was highly conscious that, as yet, the Campaign had not penetrated the tabloid press aside from local papers. It recognised that the campaign would need to speed up after the election. This would require extra staffing and clearer lines of responsibility for the Steering Committee members. The campaign would also need to clarify its relationship with the new Government: "a reappraisal of our role as a complement to the work being done by Government rather than political parties." The paper saw the Campaign's role to the end of June (the expected date for publication of the White Paper was early July) as focusing on fundraising, recruiting celebrities and establishing the infrastructure of the campaign, with local groups in particular. The paper envisaged a November poll with the official campaign launch in October. It predicted that the period from the White Paper to the official launch would involve expanding the base of support through growing the mailing list, establishing active local and sectoral groups. The publication of the White Paper would require persuading people to make the change from supporting the principle of devolution to supporting the devolution package on offer. Polling should be underway by the summer, as should the development of the case for devolution for different groups. Women – who seemed more sceptical than men – should be a particular target with clear understanding of why devolution would address issues of concern to women. New celebrity names would be released gradually over this period to encourage supporters and achieve tabloid coverage. Rock bands would, it was hoped, cut a campaign CD and perform a concert. The final phase would require a high-profile media campaign, advertising, polling, and mailings. There would need to be extensive co-operation with pro-devolution political parties. The Campaign also planned two National Forums, one in May after the election, and one in early October at what was expected to be the start of the campaign. By April this had come to be called a National Conference and the date changed to July 12-13. Mailings were planned to councillors, trades unions, arts organisations, and other Welsh national organisations.

The Committee decided on some key tasks to be accomplished before the election. These included preparing guidelines on setting up local groups and sectoral groups; planning for a post-election press conference on May 5th; planning for a National Forum meeting, intended to be wider than the Steering Committee, which would be held between the election and the publication of the White Paper; targeting more celebrities; managing relationships with the political parties and the Parliament for Wales Campaign during the election; developing a campaign timetable for the post-election period; and re-organising the Steering Committee, which had grown significantly, into more effective working groups.

We saw local groups working in the communities of Wales as key to getting the message across to ordinary people. Pre-election, tasks of local groups were identified: to ensure a high profile for the campaign locally as well as nationally, dealing with local media and encouraging local debate on the benefits of decentralisation; to mobilise activists to campaign for a Yes-vote; to act as fundraisers and recruitment agents; and to provide a non-party and cross-party forum for people from different political parties to come together. It was recognised that nationally-produced material would be needed for many groups though some would produce their own. The Committee also broke its supporters down by sector (business, arts etc.), and gave out responsibilities for getting sectoral groups off the ground. It also drew up a detailed list of Wales-wide events between the election and the expected referendum date.

The Steering Committee was working relatively well for a group of people who had been drawn together from a wide variety of backgrounds, and despite its relaxed attitude to people who were invited along for no other reason than that they knew someone on the Committee who had thought they might be useful. There were occasional tensions about what the Campaign should say about the political parties or the Parliament for Wales Campaign. Some wanted to start early, getting public leaflets and car-stickers available as soon as possible. Others felt that this would undermine the major impact needed post-election. Some were cynical about more modern campaigning techniques such as private polling, focus groups and campaign advertising. Occasionally, there was a need to remind people that if there were a change of government, the Yes Campaign would have friends in high places. It would be a waste of energy to develop campaign materials and the precise key messages too early on, before even a White Paper on the Assembly was published.

What was important now was identifying more activists and big-name supporters who could be used to front campaign activities later. Eluned Morgan was excited to be involved but also felt frustrated at times by meetings she attended: "There was a lot of enthusiasm but actually not that much action. I remember the debates and trying constantly to close down debates about what kind of assembly we should have." Val Feld joined the campaign at its second meeting: "I thought is there a Chair, is somebody leading this, is there a structure, what's happening and where do I fit in?" Peter had asked me to chair the second meeting. I chaired the meetings through to the election, though that had not been my plan originally. I was managing Daran Hill day to day, and was also the closest point of liaison to Hain. I found myself both having to chair meetings and explain and defend the Campaign organisation. This was not ideal. In any case, I had not been back in Wales long enough to be convinced that I could carry the role through effectively. I made it clear that I wanted someone else to take on the role of chairing meetings, and to spread the tasks around between members. Like Eluned, I was also finding it frustrating that though things were agreed at meetings little was being done in between them. "People used to swallow the paper that was given to them without committing themselves to do anything much themselves," Daran Hill felt at this stage.

The Steering Committee was growing in size. Meetings of sixteen people were not uncommon, though they were not always the same people, and this meant difficulty in getting consistency of decisions. In reality, the decisions right up until the election were being taken by a small group involving myself, Mari James and Daran Hill, with Kevin Morgan consulted on issues where a public face was needed for a response. I wanted Val Feld and Hywel Francis, both of whom had recent experience of campaigning across Wales, to become more involved. It was clear to me that many on the Steering Committee had not grasped the scale of the task. Val Feld admitted this later: "I could see we had to do a campaign but it didn't occur to me the scale of what we had to do. I'd done lots of campaigns but I'd never done anything of that particular nature before." But there were also huge areas of uncertainty. It was not clear at this point how involved the political parties would be. Nor was it clear to what extent there would be government money for the Yes and No campaigns. The Campaign was moving forward with many areas unresolved. By now, I was additionally aware of another factor that was not known by other Steering Committee members. Huw Roberts, who had been attending Steering Committee meetings from the start, was likely, if Labour won the election, to join Ron Davies' team as a Special Adviser. This meant that the campaign would have a close link with the Welsh Office.

Devolution did not have as high a profile in the General Election as Ron Davies had hoped. The delay in appointing its referendum organiser was one reason. Davies had wanted to make Labour's devolution plans an essential part of the Labour election campaign in Wales. He believed that if the Party had fought the Election raising the profile of devolution it would have helped to create a better idea of what devolution was about. Instead, Labour in Wales had to follow the Millbank election grid. "If the issue of the day was education, we in Wales had to say 'us too'. If the issue of the day was health, we in Wales had to say 'and us too'," said Davies. Davies had to fight to get the commitment to devolution included in Labour's pledge cards. Labour had five pledges which were set out on the pledge cards and then featured heavily in Labour advertising. Four of these related to devolved matters like education, health and the environment. One related to crime and punishment, which was not a devolved matter, but one for the Home Office. Davies wanted devolution included. First, Davies was told there could not be six pledges, and so the card was printed without the Home Office pledge but with the devolution pledge. Then he was told after all there were to be six pledges in Wales, including the Home Office pledge.

The other parties clearly had no such constraints. Plaid and the Liberal Democrats both made devolution a feature of their election campaign. Perhaps that accounted for the *Western Mail* poll in the election campaign itself, which initially worried supporters of devolution. The poll showed that support for devolution had fallen to 34%, and that 37% were opposed, 30% didn't know. Privately, Yes for Wales felt that this could be attributed to the fact that it was Labour's views that were being judged, and Labour was under fire from all three other parties in Wales on its plans. Yet devolution was not getting a high profile from Labour itself, so its own case was not being defended. Davies and others were deeply concerned about the performance of the Wales Labour Party headquarters during the election. Davies brought back his own Shadow Cabinet researcher John Adams to work on a number of issues for him and also asked Huw Roberts to join him in the campaign, assisting with Davies' own personal press relations. Roberts had originally been approached by Rhodri Morgan MP, a close personal friend, to see if he might be available to act as Special Adviser. Davies was interested in Roberts' experience as a civil servant, as someone who had worked in the private sector and who was a highly professional press spokesman, having served as Director of Public Affairs for both Independent Television News (ITN) and SWALEC, before setting up his own company. Roberts had also worked in the Welsh Office, in the Department of Energy and at Number Ten. He was very involved alongside Davies in the election campaign, and joined Ron Davies in Caerphilly for his count, where he found the atmosphere surprisingly downbeat initially, as people were still under strict instructions not to be complacent about the result. He then went back to Cardiff for the Labour election party there. On his way home later his car nearly left the road when he took both hands off the wheel and cheered on hearing on the radio that Michael Portillo had lost his seat.

The scale of Labour's victory stunned most people in Wales, as it did elsewhere in Britain. In Neath, Peter Hain celebrated an outstanding result, the biggest majority for Labour ever seen there. He spoke to Hywel Francis in Neath's Bear Hotel during the celebration party after the count, telling him that the Yes for Wales campaign would need branches quickly. Peter wanted Neath to be underway quickly and wanted Hywel to lead it. Hywel promised he would get it moving.

Five: Phoney War

Huw Roberts hadn't been in Downing Street for twelve years. Now, on the afternoon of Saturday 3 May 1997, he accompanied Ron Davies to his appointment with Tony Blair at Number Ten. As they walked along the short distance from the security gates to the centre of government itself, Roberts remembers "the usual shouting across the street from the hacks." Journalists were throwing questions at them. "What do you think you'll get, Mr Davies?"

They had arrived in London mid-morning, having been driven from Caerphilly by the Leader of Caerphilly Council, Graham Court, and his son-in-law. Their instructions were to be there by noon. Arriving well before the appointed time, they hoped that they would be able to wait in the Welsh Office, just a short walk across Whitehall from Downing Street. Davies rang his soon-to-be Principal Private Secretary June Milligan and said "Look, I've got to be in London, I'm going to look daft sitting outside in the car, can I come and wait in the waiting room?". Protocol was against them. "We were told in no uncertain terms we couldn't even wait in the waiting room of the Welsh Office," remembers Huw. "He wasn't even allowed to sort of cast his gaze on the place." In his office in Gwydyr House almost a year later Davies remembered: "We couldn't go in the waiting room at five to three, five past three there was a bloody car waiting to bring us across here."

Instead, they adjourned to Davies' old office in 7 Millbank. They had to stay there watching television as other new appointees arrived at Number Ten to get their instructions. They were hungry and thirsty, but no-one wanted to leave the room in case the call came from Number Ten. Eventually, around two o'clock, they had a call which told them to expect further a call later. At this point, Graham Court volunteered to go out for some fish and chips.

The call to attend Number Ten finally came. Court volunteered to drive Davies and Roberts to Downing Street, but Davies said he'd prefer to walk and asked Roberts to accompany him. Court and his son-in-law went to the Welsh Office to await their arrival. "I want to be the first to congratulate you," said Court.

Inside Number Ten, they were told that the new Prime Minister was in the Cabinet Room and to go and wait outside. Roberts had worked in Number Ten as a Press Officer under Bernard Ingham, and led the way. Outside the Cabinet Room was Sir Robin Butler, the Cabinet secretary. Roberts had met him years before but doubted Butler would remember. He re-introduced himself: "It did mean we weren't completely the boys from the sticks, every little bit helps in terms of establishing yourself." Tom Clarke, MP for Coatbridge and Chryston, who had served as Shadow Minister for Disabled People's Rights, was also waiting. Messengers offered them tea. Roberts remembers "a sense of the Winter Palace about the place." Young people were rushing around, unfazed by their surroundings. Cherie Blair was standing in the connecting door to Number Eleven, talking to Derry Irvine. On their right was the press room, where the new team had just walked in and started work. It was "the inexorable progress of the Blair machine," recalls Roberts.

Roberts chatted nervously to Davies who was rather quieter. "It's not unnatural that Ron was fairly quiet at that stage, it's a long way to have stepped like that." Soon Davies went in to see Blair alone. When he came back, he said to Roberts, "Well, he's asked me to do it." By now, Gavin Strang, Shadow Agriculture Secretary, had arrived for his meeting with the Prime Minister. They all chatted for a few minutes.

Outside Number Ten, journalists threw questions at Davies. His car had arrived. Roberts opened the near-side door and walked around to the other side. The driver was the first to call Davies Secretary of State. Then the car pulled across Whitehall the two hundred yards or so to the Welsh Office. They were greeted at the door by June Milligan.

In the Welsh Office, Davies was handed a folder titled 'Briefing for Incoming Ministers'. Inside, he found a guide to the Welsh Office and its departments, and a list of key actions necessary to get the devolution process underway. The Civil Service had been busy. Devolution was top of the agenda. A draft White Paper accompanied the folder. Davies found that the Cabinet Office expected a paper by lunchtime that Monday on the way forward for the devolution legislation. The paper would go to the Legislation Committee on the Tuesday and to the Committee on Regional Policy on the Wednesday. The government machine was looking to the publication of the Referendum Bill on 15 May.

Davies and Roberts worked through some of the paperwork and

agreed to meet officials in Cardiff the next morning. They wanted to celebrate. A bottle of wine was found in a fridge somewhere in the Welsh Office. "Memorably they couldn't find a cork-screw anywhere in the Welsh Office," recalls Roberts. Eventually they found a wine-shop in Kensington as they were being driven back to Wales, where they bought a cork-screw. "It now sits in pride of place in the Welsh Office." They drank the bottle in the back of the car.

Meanwhile, John Adams, Ron Davies' researcher for nearly two years, was tying up loose ends in Cardiff. By Monday he was working for Davies again as the second Special Adviser.

Over the weekend, Yes for Wales learned that there was pressure within the new government for the two referenda to be held on the same day, rather than the Scottish Referendum preceding the Welsh one. We were asked if we could ensure that our press conference on the Monday referred to the Joint Labour/Liberal Democrat Constitutional Committee Agreement which had called for the two referendums to be staggered. We were able to do more than that. I was writing an article for the *Western Mail* Agenda page on Monday and redrafted it to refer to this.

On the Sunday, Huw Roberts organised his second photocall since the election. The first had been in the Café Quarter in Cardiff on Friday morning, when as many new Labour MPs as could be gathered had been entertained to a working breakfast. On Sunday, Ron Davies arrived at the Welsh Office to be met by the Permanent Secretary, Rachel Lomax. There was a round of interviews for the main broadcasters and the press, then down to business, working on the Welsh Office input to the paper to go to the Cabinet Office.

Yes for Wales had prepared carefully for the post-election period, booking space in the *Western Mail* and other newspapers for advertisements under the heading: "You've changed the government, now you can change the face of Wales," on Bank Holiday Monday. The purpose was to recruit more activists and raise more funds. A press conference was also planned for that day. Yes for Wales had three objectives: to welcome the result and the election of a government pledged to devolution; to warn that the election result did not necessarily mean the referendum was won; and to call for a single united Yes Campaign on the principle of devolution.

The Yes for Wales case was set out in my article in the *Western Mail*. This stressed the key themes to be outlined at that morning's press conference. First, it noted that Labour's devolution plans had received a majority in England as well as Wales. It called on the government to honour the commitment to holding the Welsh referendum after that for Scotland. It suggested that Conservatives might come on board the Yes Campaign, and revealed that Edward Heath had told the Campaign that devolution was compatible with the union. The article argued that a multi-choice referendum would lead to two Yes Campaigns arguing their positions in the media and on the doorstep against a united No Campaign. The article pointed out that bickering between devolution supporters would alienate the uncommitted. It suggested that the poll that appeared during the election campaign showing the Yes-vote falling behind was evidence of that.

At the press conference, addressed by Kevin Morgan, Mari James and Derek Gregory, Welsh leader of the public service union, Unison, and myself, the campaign reiterated that it did not believe that a Yes-vote was a foregone conclusion. We would have to work for devolution. Derek Gregory spoke of his own personal support, and that of his union. We announced we were holding a rallying conference in July and had invited the new Secretary of State to speak. We appealed to pro-devolution Conservatives to take note of the election result and come into the open. The Campaign stressed the importance of two referendums happening on separate days: a point that was further emphasised by Hywel Francis in a letter to the *Western Mail* a couple of days later.

As the Yes for Wales press conference was assembling in Cardiff, Peter Hain took a phone-call at his home. The Downing Street switchboard found him in the classic manner. A couple of clicks, and the new Prime Minister was on the phone. He chatted briefly with Peter, then told him that he would like him to go to the Welsh Office as a Minister. Peter was staggered. He'd been led to believe that there was a possibility that he might be a Minister but had assumed he would be likely to stay on in David Blunkett's Employment team. He wondered aloud whether this was in addition to the Welsh Office team which had been operating in Opposition. He was told that an element of substitution was involved, which left him none the wiser. Blair told Hain that winning the Referendum Campaign was very important to him, and he wanted him to help deliver that.

Almost immediately, the Downing Street machine started briefing about Hain's appointment, one of a number of what were seen as "inside left" appointments within the new Government. At this stage, neither of the two deputies in the shadow Welsh Office team, Cardiff West MP Rhodri Morgan or Bridgend MP Win Griffiths, had heard from Downing Street. Within an hour Hain found friends phoning to congratulate him. According to the press reports, Downing Street was saying that Hain was to be in charge of the Referendum Campaign. Hain tried to find Ron Davies to talk to him, and had to go through the security man in the Welsh Office, the only number he had. Eventually he got through, and made arrangements to see Davies. Meanwhile Jon Owen Jones, MP for Cardiff Central, a Shadow Whip, whose first task post-election had been to compile biographies of all the new Welsh MPs in two hours on Friday morning, was confirmed in his Whip's position.

Yes for Wales activists heard of Hain's appointment after returning home from the press conference. I took a call from a senior figure in the BBC who said he took it as the first sign that Blair was serious about devolution. Shortly afterwards I heard from Peter himself. I was delighted. Hain's appointment meant that the Labour government's commitment to the devolution project could not be doubted by anyone in Wales. Peter's reputation as a campaigner, and as someone known within the political parties to have been actively involved in getting Yes for Wales off the ground, would be a positive message. One of his first actions was to phone Hywel Francis to get the Neath group up and running. Now he was in the Welsh Office it was even more important that his own patch should be at the forefront of the campaign.

That evening, I spoke to Huw Roberts. He was depressed. He was a long-standing friend of Rhodri Morgan, and it was now clear that Rhodri would not be joining the government. This left the Ministerial team without a Welsh-speaker, but more importantly at a personal level Huw was devastated. He had never expected this. Morgan had approached him in Opposition to see if he would be willing to serve as a Special Adviser. He shared a flat with Rhodri in London, and they lived in adjoining houses in the Vale of Glamorgan.

At a political level there was some good news, however. The paper going to the Legislation Committee would now contain a recommendation that the Scottish referendum should be held before the Welsh vote. Davies had been able to point to that morning's *Western Mail* article as showing that there was pressure within Wales to keep to the Joint Lib-Lab agreement. Two days later, Roberts was able to tell the newspaper that the government was moving at supersonic pace to deliver its referendum bill. The plan was to hold the referendum in advance of Labour's autumn conference.

The election had dramatically changed the context in which Yes for Wales was working. As well as making good on its own plans to establish an infrastructure around Wales, it had to work out its own relationship with the Government and in particular the Welsh Office. Peter Hain felt there was a real feeling of excitement there. He thought that the Welsh Office had never really been treated properly under the Conservatives over the previous twenty years. It had been seen as the end of the Whitehall machine, very much the last to be consulted, the add-on. The professionalism of the Welsh Office civil servants was not being engaged.

Yes for Wales was concerned that the overwhelming Labour majority might undermine the enthusiasm for devolution. This was a widely-held concern, but one that had been publicly articulated only occasionally. Yes for Wales did not have the resources for opinion polling, but the Campaign was aware of research carried out in Scotland for the emerging Yes Campaign there. This suggested that even in Scotland, where there had been a much higher-profile all-party Constitutional Convention for some time, there was a very low level of understanding of the way in which Scotland was currently governed or the meaning of devolution itself, let alone the new government's proposals. In the second week of May I presented a short paper to Peter, 'Winning the Yes-vote'. This argued that there was a real danger of extrapolating from the election result. "We would be deluding ourselves if we concluded that 1 May can be automatically translated into a Yes-vote in September." The paper pointed out the absence of real research. "We do not know in any scientific way what are the real feelings of voters – their hopes and fears, the things that will drive them out to vote one way or another." I argued for research by the Welsh Office, and for resources for advertising. The Welsh Office would need to run a basic information campaign on the government's proposals. The Yes Campaign would need resources for advertising for a positive campaign about the benefits of the Assembly, and for a negative campaign about the opponents of the Assembly, tying opposition to the Assembly firmly to the Conservative Party.

The same day at a meeting of the Yes for Wales Steering Committee, Professor Kevin Morgan was formally appointed Chairman of Yes for Wales – intended as a public role – and other officers were also appointed. Morgan, a well-known academic from the Cynon Valley, was Professor of European Regional Development at University College Cardiff. "I was very flattered to be asked, but secondly shocked as well. I'd always been the academic commentator as it were, and then I had to think how this would change things in terms of my role in Wales. On reflection I thought, well this is an enormous responsibility, but that it is also an honour."

Yes for Wales had calculated that both the Parliament for Wales Campaign and Plaid Cymru would continue to argue the case for a multi-choice "preferendum" for a few months longer. A few days later, the Parliament for Wales Campaign attacked Yes for Wales as having been "spawned by Labour's campaign managers". Kevin Morgan reacted to the letter on behalf of the Campaign. "They were pushing for the much more maximalist version of the Assembly, and frankly my only concern was to get the Assembly up and running."

The launch of the Referendum Bill on 15 May was an important event in the calendar. The Bill was launched at a press conference at the Welsh Office before a specially designed backdrop. Coverage the next day was largely good, aside from the front-page of the *Daily Post*, which said that Ron Davies had threatened MPs opposed to devolution. Davies had certainly told the press conference: "I don't believe it is appropriate for any Labour MP to take any course of action which would include, for example, associating with others in opposition to our campaign or indeed publicly campaigning on their own behalf against our proposals." But at that stage, there was little to suggest the degree to which this issue would dominate the debate for the next month. Behind the scenes, there was one element of concern. The wording on the ballot paper was felt to be very tortuous. Hain wanted to amend the draft Bill for it to say just Yes or No. Welsh Ministers later tried to persuade their Scottish counterparts to agree to move an amendment changing the wording at the Committee Stage, but they were not prepared to do that.

However, the first signs of a No Campaign were beginning to be felt. In the Rhondda, two women activists, one a former Chairman of the Wales Labour Party, declared their opposition. An unnamed senior Conservative spokesperson in Wales said that there would be an all-party No Campaign launched during the summer.

Organisationally, Yes for Wales was starting to get moving. The Wales TUC privately declared its support and agreed to join the

Steering Committee. The first local Yes group was launched in Neath on 19 May 1997. A public meeting was held in Caernarfon in late May to provide momentum in North Wales. By the time of the 23 May Steering Committee meeting Yes for Wales had pinpointed local launch plans for sixteen areas of Wales.

Meanwhile, though Plaid Cymru would not determine its policy until 26 July at its special conference, Plaid Leader Dafydd Wigley had already indicated that Plaid would only oppose Labour's plans if they offered no increase in devolved power. Plaid Cymru Peer Dafydd Elis-Thomas said he would be prepared to compromise and back the plans, as long as Labour campaigned for its own proposals. In the interim, Plaid continued to run its 'parity with Scotland' campaign, avoiding attacking Labour's plans but stating that Plaid wanted more. They held a bicycle tour from Machynlleth to the Valleys and a petition campaign. At the end of May, Yes for Wales held its formal first meeting with Plaid Cymru. Plaid had always had a good relationship with Ron Davies, and Peter's appointment as a campaigner was helping to persuade them that Labour was taking the campaign seriously and investing in the campaign. Cynog Dafis and Ieuan Wyn Jones, who were leading Plaid's campaign organisation, had been privately briefed by Labour Ministers. The two MPs were anxious that Plaid should not come on board too soon, believing that this would play into the hands of any No Campaign which would represent Plaid's support as demonstrating that the Campaign was in the hands of the nationalists. There was a group of Plaid activists arguing that Plaid should stake out a radical position so that Yes for Wales should be seen as moderate. To Dafydd Elis-Thomas and others this would have meant confusing the message. Cynog Dafis recalls "I recognised the fear that if we warmed too much to the Campaign and began to be too active in it, Labour activists might withdraw." But Dafis thought that Plaid support would be an asset to the Yes Campaign.

Although Plaid would not take a final decision on whether to support the campaign until after the White Paper was published, they would be able to have a speaker at the July Yes for Wales Conference who would attend on the basis of asking questions about the White Paper's content. They were also in favour of holding a joint press conference with the Liberal Democrats and the Greens. They proposed to canvass by telephone in the four seats they held and their next best four and wanted to know what Labour would be doing. When Plaid did come on board Yes for

Wales they would deliver leaflets as Yes for Wales, rather than as Plaid. However, Dafydd Wigley personally kept very distant from the Yes Campaign, ensuring that when Plaid people were involved they were people other than himself, "not because of any antagonism to the Yes Campaign, obviously" but because it was necessary for Plaid to be seen as separate from it. Wigley believes that Plaid could have put more people and more resources into the Yes Campaign earlier had the Labour involvement in the Yes Campaign been more obvious early on. "There needed to be enough Labour people in it to be creating the flavour for us to be in half a step behind and not taking the high ground. The fact that Labour people were not going in but rather were running their own campaign because there were some people who didn't want it to be cross-party, that made it more difficult for us to get in sooner and to a greater extent." Plaid's organisation was supervised by Cynog Dafis and Ieuan Wyn Jones and implemented by General Secretary Karl Davies and Research Officer Dafydd Williams, who produced a paper arguing for the campaign to do more to get the issues of jobs across. Throughout this period, Labour Ministers held regular private discussions with Wigley, Dafis and the Liberal MPs Richard Livsey and Lembit Öpik.

The Liberal Democrats said they would campaign for a Yes-vote if Labour consulted on the question to be asked. They were now informally represented on the Yes for Wales Steering Committee. Their leader, Richard Livsey, was heartened by Labour's determination to hold the referendum early. "The general principle they were pursuing I was very much behind," he said. In the middle of May, the Welsh language magazine *Barn* published quotes from a series of interviews undertaken with Conservative activists which indicated even some Conservative candidates and councillors were rethinking their position. Glyn Davies, candidate for Montgomery in the General Election, had already called on the party to rethink its position on devolution and had said he would be happy to be a member of the Welsh Tory group in the Assembly.

The Labour campaign was also now moving into gear. Andrew Davies, the organiser, had raised similar concerns about the need for research as had Yes for Wales. He was anxious to clarify what central budgets would be available; what the Welsh Office would legally be allowed to do in terms of information, polling and publicity; and what the lines of communication would be between the Welsh Office and the Wales Labour Party. Hain had similar issues on his mind and during May had gone to Labour's campaign machine at Millbank to try to get support for a private opinion poll. The initial view was that they couldn't afford one. But there was a widespread view developing that additional resources would have to be provided to both the Welsh and Scottish devolution campaigns. Worn-out after the election, the party officers at Millbank had not immediately realised that the referenda were to be that autumn. Labour's Deputy General Secretary – then General Election coordinator – Margaret McDonagh had assumed that they would be a year later. They needed experienced organisers to assist in both referenda. Alan Barnard, a key organiser in most of Labour's recent by-election successes in opposition, was told very soon after the Election, in May, that he would be needed in Wales. Barnard, who had worked flat out for months, could see his summer holiday disappearing.

Andrew Davies and Wales Labour Party General Secretary Anita Gale attended a meeting of Labour's National Referendum Unit on 19 May. It was the only meeting that the Unit had. Millbank was clearly given the message that the result in Wales could not be taken for granted. The meeting was important in defining the level of Millbank's organisational and financial commitment. In the terms the Labour Party had been using to define its General Election strategy, Scotland was the safe seat, "the majority seat" and Wales the "key marginal". Welsh Office Ministers argued strongly, and ultimately successfully, that the bulk of Labour referendum spending should be in Wales and not Scotland. Andrew Davies remembers David Hill, Labour's Chief Press Spokesman, making a further important contribution to Labour's strategy. "What we've got to do," Hill said, "thinking about a referendum, is think about what Harold Wilson did for the European Referendum in 1975. He ran it as a Prime Ministerial, presidential-style campaign and appealed to the electorate over the heads of the party, and I think that's what we've got to do with this." On the ground, Labour had confirmed the plan set out by Don Touhig before the election that Labour had to target its voters in its heartland areas, particularly in South-East, West and North-East Wales. They would mail their members direct, providing briefings and mailings. Andrew Davies made the point early on that it would be difficult to get to voters in the areas of Wales likely to be tuning into TV stations in England rather than Wales.

Millbank would not, however, let go of its control of the purse-strings. Barnard was given clear instructions that he was in charge of the budget, thought to be close on £250,000. Andrew Davies says he never knew what the budget was. Others in Wales found this frustrating, though it is difficult to see how central resources could be allocated without accountability. It was a problem that Barnard had had to face before on several occasions, when he was Head Office's man in by-elections, arriving with the authority of the Party Leader, and understood the sensitivity of the position.

The message about the need for fundamental research had got home. Labour's polling guru, Philip Gould, was asked to undertake some focus groups on 5 and 6 June. A major quantitative polling exercise was also undertaken from 19-21 June. Gould, a former advertising executive who had played a major role as an adviser to Labour in its Shadow Communications Agency for the best part of a decade, was very important to Blair's New Labour project. His work enabled Labour to gain a clearer understanding of the aspirations of the electorate.

Andrew Davies accompanied Philip Gould to the focus groups. Millbank wanted a second opinion on the views expressed. The initial experience was quite depressing. There were two sets of focus groups, held in Maesteg and Wrexham, in each case with a male group and a female group of Labour supporters over the age of 35. Davies believed that the Maesteg group would be more optimistic than that in Wrexham. He recalls Gould walking round and round the Maesteg Sports Centre after the first group, saying "They just don't want us". "We were depressed after the Maesteg one," said Davies. "Partly because many of the guys were unemployed. The female group was very different, much more buoyant, much more outgoing." Few of the participants knew much about the plans for a referendum.

Gould found the Wrexham group more positive. "He thought we could win this one,' recalls Davies. "The crucial factor was that the people there felt neglected emotionally... and that they needed a voice." Gould asked Davies what he thought about the slogan 'Wales Deserves a Voice'.

Gould's detailed findings were very important. Overall, he found that people in Wales were less confident, felt more neglected and were more nervous of change than the rest of the UK:

> The word which best sums up the national mood in Wales is fragility. They think that, at last – with a new Labour government – things are going to get better, but the slightest thing could put this at risk. Their underlying mood tends to be that something is about to go wrong.
> People in Wales feel neglected. Politically, socially, economically,

Phoney War

they feel deprived. They do not feel they get a fair deal, and they
don't think anyone much cares.

Their response to neglect is not to demand aggressive change but
to want improvement blended with security. They want safe, secure
change.

"All this," he said "leads to an ambivalent Welsh identity. People
do feel Welsh and proud of it. But people also want the security,
support and comfort of being part of Britain." North Wales felt a
double neglect.

Gould found that people in Wales were as enthusiastic about the
new Government as people anywhere, probably more so. They
were also as supportive of Blair and New Labour. They were no
different from people in England in terms of their concerns about
the NHS and schools. The Conservatives, he found, were totally
written off in Wales, but he also found that people liked William
Hague, who was seen to take Wales seriously. Hague benefited by
not being John Redwood and had become more popular the more
people saw of him.

People were in favour of the Assembly in principle but had little
enthusiasm for the project and many reservations. On the positive
side, they saw an Assembly as giving them a bigger say, a stronger
voice, allowing more recognition for Wales, more democracy and
involvement and more chance of inward investment and jobs. It
was part of Tony Blair's vision, part of getting Britain moving. The
referendum was the first test of the Labour Government and the
first opportunity to support it. On the negative side, an Assembly
meant red tape, cost, and it could lead to separatism and isolation.
There was also an ambivalence about timing – why do it now when
a new government had been elected? They were also worried that
it could be a step back for Wales, meaning old-fashioned ideas and
old-fashioned politicians. It could slow down change, taking power
away from Tony Blair and the new Government and give power
to less efficient, effective and able politicians. It was an unnecessary
upheaval.

Gould argued that rational arguments for the Assembly could
not be separated from the emotional pressures. People tended to
want it, but wanted to be certain about it. The most powerful
advocacy would be Tony Blair coming to Wales and arguing for it.
He said there should be four key communications elements: benefit
(NHS/Education/jobs); emotion (Wales deserves a voice and
recognition); security (strong voice in a modern Britain); and re-
assurance (Tony Blair takes it seriously).

NOP was commissioned to undertake an opinion poll of 1500 people. It found that initially, when asked about their views, people split 35.5% Yes; 25.8% No; and 34.5% Don't Know. When asked a series of questions designed to pick up on key issues, and then asked their general view again, support rose, with 48.8% saying Yes, 27.4% saying No and 20.3% Don't Know.

One of the first tasks for Andrew Davies was to talk to the Labour Party membership and its activists, to try to get them onside for the campaign. He came up with the idea of a briefing pack to be sent to Party members, and then set up ten meetings around the country. Davies and Barnard knew that there was some ambivalence amongst the party's membership. They needed to get the membership motivated. The party phone banks were used to talk to members directly to explain the Party's thinking. Gareth Thomas, the party's newly elected MP for Clwyd West, was appointed coordinator of the campaign in North Wales. He found there were doubts to be overcome. "A lot of the party members, I think, were lukewarm to the idea of devolution and I spent quite a bit of time persuading party members that they should help with the campaign. There was a general feeling of exhaustion and do we really have to fight another General Election?"

The meetings went well, by and large. "In a way, they were misleading," says Davies. "It was difficult to tell whether people were genuinely enthusiastic. The Cardiff one was overflowing, there was standing room only, and I think in a way that may have been misleading because I think we thought there was tremendous interest. Well, I think people just wanted to come along and find out." But Davies was encouraged by the interest in Labour constituencies. He spoke to dozens of Labour branch meetings. "We had lots of requests from branches and constituencies to go and speak about the Referendum." A clear presentation was developed, explaining Labour's strategy and messages for the referendum. Things were different from the General Election strategy: Labour areas were now key areas. They had to maximise Labour turn-out. They would need high profile activities, street stalls, blitzing, leafleting, summer show stalls, letters to local press, radio phone-ins, and public meetings.

Andrew Davies presented the details of the campaign to the Wales Parliamentary Labour Party meeting on 18 June. He had undertaken a SWOT (a Strengths, Weaknesses, Opportunities, Threats) analysis of the campaign, and was intrigued to find that it was very close to what the focus groups found. In his view, the strengths of the campaign included: the momentum deriving from the election victory on 1 May; the popularity and trust enjoyed by Tony Blair; the commitment of Labour MPs and most political parties in Wales; the absence of a major figure to lead the No Campaign; the support of local government and a highly professional party organisation. But there were also weaknesses, which included the fact that the Party was largely ignorant of the detail of the proposals; the electorate was largely unaware of the plans and likely to be unenthusiastic about change and fearful about separatism; there were limited resources for the campaign and the prospect of some division within the Party. The main threats were that the No position would be easier to put over; that the party would be seen to be divided as in 1979; and that there might be a low turn-out. Davies saw significant opportunities in bringing the Prime Minister and members of the Cabinet to Wales to project the message. They could focus on the Tories as the opponents. The positive message would be the need for a strong voice for Wales, exploiting the feeling that Wales and its people had been neglected. Labour's MPs were encouraged to lead their local campaigns, to help with rebuttal, and to motivate local members.

Within the Wales Labour Party, there was a degree of tension between Transport House in Cardiff and the Welsh Office. Andrew Davies found himself caught in the middle. The Wales Labour Party Executive had set up a sub-committee to organise the campaign. Officials had assumed that the sub-committee would be chaired by the Welsh party's Chairman Terry Thomas, but in a carefully planned pre-emptive move Ron Davies took the Chair at the first meeting on June 6th. The committee became known as the Secretary of State's Referendum Campaign Strategy Group. There was a long discussion at the meeting about the party's relationship with Yes for Wales. It was agreed that it was OK for Labour Party members to join the Yes for Wales Campaign, and that it had an important role to play not least in areas where Labour was weak. It was felt that party officers locally should be involved in the Labour campaign however. The Welsh Office team saw the committee as extremely unwieldy. Davies said there should be a smaller task-force to run day-to-day campaigning. The Task Force included the Secretary of State or his nominee, Alan Barnard from Millbank, the Party's General Secretary in Wales Anita Gale, Andrew Davies, and Terry Thomas. Harry Jones, Leader of Newport Council representing local government, played a critical role. John Adams or Brione Huish acted as secretary.

One senior Labour figure believed "there was never any proper chain of command, to be honest, in the Labour campaign." Hain found himself having to broker agreements between Millbank, Transport House and the Welsh Office. Davies' PPS, Nick Ainger, took the chair at meetings when Davies himself couldn't be there. The task-force met more or less weekly up to the referendum. Andrew Davies had a draft timetable in place for the campaign. June would be a matter of getting the campaign structure in place. July would see the White Paper and the launch of the Labour campaign. There would be visits to shows and a 'Rolling Referendum Roadshow' through August, and a more intensive campaign during September, and a re-launch in the last week of September after the Scottish result.

By the end of June, Yes for Wales was planning to find ways of using volunteer staff. By now, the Campaign had over 500 supporters. It had also allocated responsibility for getting sectoral groups off the ground. Christian Ministers Say Yes was launched at the end of May. ("It's the Yes Ministers," joked Professor Hywel Francis, by now the Convenor of the Steering Committee, when he heard the news.) It had the backing of the Archbishop of Wales and the Bishop of Bangor. A statement drafted by Cardiff Minister Aled Edwards said "as Christian Ministers we deal on a daily basis with people's lives in terms of health and education and jobs. In a non-party political way we would support any constitutional development which offers a new prosperity to the people of Wales." Students Say Yes was launched on 21 June. We also decided to prepare, post-White Paper, different statements of the Case for Devolution (the education case, the housing case and so on). Meanwhile the Wales TUC came out in favour of devolution at the beginning of June. Kevin Brennan, of the Cardiff group, published a paper arguing that the costs of the Assembly might be lower than previously supposed.

But money was still short. The Yes Campaign budget was only £43,000. However, on the fundraising front, Yes for Wales received some better news. On Friday 6 June I attended a conference called by the Rowntree Trust in London to discuss the new Government's constitutional programme. There were representatives from Charter 88, Liberty, Scotland Forward, and a number of MPs. I warned the conference that the Welsh result could not be taken for granted. Privately, I urged the Rowntree Trustees to bring forward the second year of the Yes for Wales grant now that it was known that the referendum would be in 1997 not 1998. I

The Guardian Debate in Cardiff

Ron Davies explains the White Paper at the Yes for Wales Campaign reception at Cardiff Castle

One of the many Yes for Wales press conferences

Kevin Morgan at the Yes for Wales Conference

Academics Say Yes – playwright Ewart Alexander and Hywel Francis

SWS Says Yes – Stifyn Parri explains the electoral system to Siân Lloyd

Women Say Yes

The two Mary Lloyd Jones banners shown off by Ann Clwyd MP, Mair Francis, Ron Davies MP, Wayne David MEP and Hywel Francis

Yes For Wales Campaign Stall in the Valleys

Unveiling the new campaign ad – Mari James, Kevin Morgan, Val Feld, Eluned Morgan MEP and Hywel Francis

The A-frame van is vandalised

A final message – but where's the plane?

The Park Hotel as the Carmarthen result comes in

Inclusive singing of *Hen Wlad Fy Nhadau* – Rhodri Morgan MP, Dafydd Elis-Thomas and Kevin Brennan

The author enjoys a first drink after the result

Ron Davies arrives at the Park Hotel party

was promised a hearing for the suggestion at the Trust meeting in the next couple of weeks if an application was received in time. The Trust had originally sanctioned grants over two years, since there had been scepticism as to whether the referendum would come so early. Now there was a possibility that the Campaign could get all the money, providing matching monies were raised, during the summer.

Within our own Campaign not all was rosy though. While I was leaving the Rowntree Conference, I took a call on my mobile phone from Hywel Francis, who told me that in launching the TUC's own document, David Jenkins, General Secretary of the Wales TUC, had attacked Plaid Cymru and their "narrow nationalist agenda". Francis was livid. In Cardiff a Yes for Wales Steering Committee was meeting. It was one of the most fractious meetings we had, with deep disagreements on a number of organisational and strategic issues, including even whether the Campaign's conference, scheduled for mid-July, should be cancelled. That weekend, Francis, Mari James (one of two Vice-Chairs) and Val Feld, who was now the Treasurer, and myself, had extensive telephone conversations. It was clear that the Steering Committee had become too large to function effectively. Not all members were able to get to every meeting. This meant that the conclusions could change each fortnight depending on who was there. We resolved to put together a paper for the next Steering Committee meeting to be held at Llandudno, and try to create a more disciplined structure. We would also need to involve the local groups which were now springing up around Wales in some kind of forum. Nine more groups launched in June: Cardiff, Ceredigion, Newport, Bridgend, Blaenau Gwent, Rhondda, Port Talbot, Ynys Môn and Torfaen.

The potential slogans for the Campaign were now being tested out. Peter Hain made a speech at an Institute of Public Policy Research lunch at the Copthorne Hotel in Cardiff. His press release was headed 'Peter Hain says "Don't Get Left Behind"'. The slogan 'Wales must not get left behind', used in his speech to demonstrate what could happen if Scotland and London voted Yes, had been suggested to me by a business supporter. It was to feature prominently later in both the Yes for Wales and Labour campaigns.

As rumours circulated about the prospects for a No Campaign, there was concern about the way in which the media would cover the campaign, and the broadcasters in particular. Kevin Morgan reported to the Yes for Wales Steering Committee on 6 June on his meeting with the BBC's Chief Political Adviser, Ann Sloman, which he had found disturbing. He was very concerned that an inactive No Campaign would receive as much coverage as an active Yes Campaign on grounds of 'balance'.

The organisation paper was put to the Yes Campaign Steering Committee at the Wales TUC in Llandudno on 20 June. The officers were now clear that there were three further phases to the Campaign. Though the date for the referendum had not yet been finalised, it was expected to be in mid to late September. The 'Campaign Proper' was expected to begin after the August Bank Holiday. There would be something of a phoney campaign through August, never the best time to campaign on anything. A burst of activity would follow around the White Paper launch, which would signal the start of the campaign as a whole. The period until the White Paper must be concerned with getting the campaign infrastructure (local groups, campaign materials etc) up and ready. The Campaign identified the need for extra staffing resources and a range of campaigning materials, from balloons and stickers to T-shirts and adverts. Some of the local groups were now taking up green and red ribbons as symbols of the Yes Campaign.

We also finally managed to address the issue of unity within the pro-devolution movement. On 14 June, with interventions coming from a number of Yes for Wales Steering Committee members, the Parliament for Wales Campaign agreed to campaign for a Yes-vote. Ron Davies spoke at the PFW conference and praised the "marvellous" Yes for Wales Campaign. An amendment was successfully moved by Yes for Wales Vice-Chair Eleri Carrog to drop PFW's call for a multiple choice referendum, on the grounds that it would be divisive and would lead to the media reporting disagreements in the pro-devolution campaigns. Eleri was backed up by Mari and myself.

The Wales TUC, the following week, was one of the first events where the political parties spoke to each other and appeared together. Dafydd Elis-Thomas was there for Plaid and Rev. Roger Roberts for the Liberal Democrats. Daran Hill, Yes for Wales' National Organiser, remembers at the beginning of the conference Terry Thomas, the Labour Party Chairman and trade union leader, refusing to take a Yes for Wales sticker on the grounds that it was a nationalist front. This was a common view initially, with delegates thinking that Yes for Wales were Plaid or Liberal Democrat fellow travellers. Daran Hill, Hywel Francis, Val Feld and Mari James all talked to delegates, explaining what the

Campaign was. But the turning point was the arrival of Ron Davies. Davies wore a Yes for Wales sticker when he addressed the Congress. By the end Terry Thomas was handing them out himself. He stuck one on Davies' lapel. "Terry, you don't know how much this means to me," the Secretary of State told him. Peter Hain and Eluned Morgan were also wearing the stickers. Unions that were not affiliated to the Labour Party, like the banking union BIFU and the broadcasting union BECTU also came on board Yes for Wales. The Yes for Wales activists watched transfixed at the spirit of inclusivity that was breaking out. "I remember the moment when Dafydd Elis-Thomas kissed Anita Gale and Hywel and I sort of standing back and saying 'we're making history here'," said Val Feld.

The Liberal Democrats' Welsh Executive had agreed to support the Yes Campaign and the very next day, the Liberal Democrats decided on their support for a Yes-vote at their special conference. The Plaid Cymru Council however deferred a final decision until the White Paper was published. There was considerable anger within Plaid, many of whose activists believed that they were being frog-marched towards support for Labour's Assembly. Dafis presented a paper with a series of options to Plaid's June Council meeting. Within Plaid there were clear tensions. Plaid came out of the General Election with morale high. Their MPs felt that they could come on board a Yes Campaign. But according to Ieuan Wyn Jones, they faced a generational problem. Many who remembered 1979 were very wary. The leadership had to persuade them that things were different now, but they had to move carefully. Younger and newer members did not have the same baggage. The June Council was basically used to gauge opinion. Some heated views were expressed. At that meeting it was agreed that Plaid members could work through Yes for Wales if asked. Also they took the in principle decision that if Plaid was to be involved in the devolution campaign it would do so through Yes for Wales rather than as Plaid. In the end Cynog Dafis recalls "we would maintain our distance until the end of July and particularly until we were convinced that Labour were serious about their own proposals because we were not convinced about that." The Plaid mood was in general pretty pessimistic. Dafis wrote to me: "at the moment the publicity is bad and the mood increasingly pessimistic – a strengthening sense that a No-vote is likely if not inevitable. PC members in the Valleys believe Labour is being at best duplicitous and at worst working against a Yes."

Sectoral groups were now being launched. Yes for Wales was particularly concerned that women voters seemed less supportive of devolution than men. A letter was handed to the Secretary of State at the Welsh Office by Women Say Yes on 23 June, calling for fair representation for women. Neath became the first local authority to support the Campaign. The Campaign was also able to announce an all-party platform for its conference to be held in July. Across a wide front momentum was growing.

July began with further good news for the Yes Campaign. The first opinion poll since the election appeared to show a falling away of those opposed to devolution. A *Western Mail* poll showed that those planning to vote No had dropped from 37% to 27%, while those planning to vote Yes had increased from 34% to 39%. Taking account of a likely differential turnout between Yes and No voters, that gave the Yes camp 43%. 28% were undecided. Most encouraging was the level of support in the Valleys, where most of the anti-devolution MPs were concentrated. The Yes for Wales Campaign welcomed the poll, but privately noted the high number of don't knows. At this point the Labour Party announced that the Prime Minister would be writing to all Labour members in Wales, and that meetings would be held all round Wales in the week of the White Paper, expected to be the week beginning 21 July. On 4 July, new Yes for Wales groups launched in Carmarthen, Monmouth and Swansea. Further Rowntree monies meant we now had more materials to offer them. A journalism student, Kate Stokes, joined the office at the beginning of July to spend her vacation acting as the Campaign's Press Officer. Shortly after, Darren Evans, a business high-flier back from a Harvard postgraduate degree, set up shop in Pontypridd, to get things moving in the Valleys. But there was still no White Paper, and the work had not yet been done to fashion the policies, the arguments and the clearest messages. Indeed, until the White Paper was ready, it could not be done.

Six: The Making of the White Paper

At 7.30 on the morning of 3 July, I was in the bath in my London flat when the phone rang. It was Peter Hain. The Government had decided the night before that it couldn't organise a public launch for the White Paper on the Welsh Assembly, as this could count as campaigning. Peter wanted to know whether I thought that Yes for Wales could do so. We were likely to have less than three weeks. I was taken aback. The launch of the White Paper had, I thought, been a key element of the Government's strategy for getting the whole notion of devolution into the minds of the people of Wales. The Yes for Wales office was small. There were three people working there, all busy organising the Campaign's conference just ten days away. Organising a public launch and reception for the 200 people that would be likely to attend would be very labour-intensive. I promised Peter I'd look into what was possible and would phone him back later.

I decided that the only course was to book a professional event-manager. I turned to the PR firm Harrison Cowley who were Yes for Wales' landlords, stressing the significance and high profile nature of the event to barter down their fee. Now I had to find a venue, find the money for the event, and get a list together of celebrities who would be able to attend. That evening, there was a private dinner of the Business Forum on Devolution in Cardiff. I could speak to a number of businesses there and try to raise some money from them. During the day I spoke to Peter again. Peter wanted Siân Lloyd, the Welsh-speaking TV personality, to compere the event, and believed she would be willing. With her on board, it ought to be possible to line up other celebrities. I rang Geraint Stanley Jones, the former Controller of BBC Wales and former Chief Executive of S4C, who promised to phone round a number of people he knew. Alun Wyn Bevan promised to speak to sports personalities, and so did the PR team at Harrison Cowley.

The launch had to be kept a secret at this stage. I was given the name of a promotions agency, RGO, who might also be able to find celebrities, and provide music for the evening. Cardiff Castle was the venue. At this stage it was planned to be an indoor event.

By the evening, I was able to report to Peter that I had secured some money to pay for the hire of the PR company, and that other donations would be forthcoming. I had done this off my own bat, and I knew I needed to ensure that colleagues in Yes for Wales were happy with what I had done. But we still needed to ensure secrecy for the event. Late that night, back home in Cardiff, I decided to phone Hywel Francis, the Convenor of the Steering Committee, and talk it through. Francis was apoplectic. He took the view that a celebrity-driven 'luvvie' event was entirely the wrong image for the Campaign. We argued for an hour on the phone about whether the event should go ahead, and if so, what kind of event it should be, eventually agreeing that it would go ahead and would be much more inclusive. Celebrity speakers would be joined by people from a variety of different backgrounds, unemployed people, women returners to work and many others, who would themselves give witness to what a new democracy would mean for Wales. Hywel agreed to keep the event quiet for now and to set about organising other people to contribute.

The extraordinary decision that the Government could not hold its own public launch for the White Paper was symptomatic of arguments behind the scenes. Ron Davies, Peter Hain and Win Griffiths were finding it hard to get an understanding from the civil service of what would be necessary, and every publicity decision they wanted to take appeared to the civil servants to be campaigning and therefore unacceptable for Ministers. "The civil service were incredibly anal about the whole campaign," said one Government insider. Hain sought help from Peter Mandelson MP, the Minister Without Portfolio, charged with ensuring the strategic communication of the government's message. Mandelson was horrified at what he heard. Civil servants were hemming Ministers in. At this rate, there would be no information for voters at all. A special Cabinet Committee was convened by Mandelson to determine the parameters for government campaigning. Welsh Office Ministers found this very helpful. Their officials advised that they would not be able to issue their own summary of the White Paper document to Welsh homes unless it was done in early August, as far away from the poll as possible, so that it couldn't be seen to be influencing public opinion. Hain briefed Mandelson about the problems in advance of the meeting. Mandelson asked the Scottish Office what they were doing about a summary of the White Paper and discovered that they were putting a summary out quite late, whereupon Hain interjected, looking at his officials, that this was not the advice he was getting. "Mandelson was actually very important," said Hain, "in freeing up the Government campaign."

Hain was also concerned to ensure high quality design work for the White Paper. He knew that there were some highly professional people in the Welsh Office's Information Division, who relished the prospect of actually using their expertise properly. The only market research they were allowed to undertake was for the Welsh Office's own information campaign encouraging people to turn out and vote, and for the cover of the White Paper itself. Peter could not get agreement from the Welsh Office officials to sanction government private polling and focus group work as they saw this as being part of the campaign. But he felt they also had to understand the context of the overall campaign. It was arranged that Philip Gould would brief them on the outcome of the research he was undertaking.

Although Mandelson achieved some clarification over what was and what was not permissible, disputes continued to take place over the boundaries throughout the campaign. In turn, Labour Ministers pointed to the Conservatives' privatisation campaigns as examples of controversial government advertising. The answer from the civil service was that this advertising reflected policy incorporated in Acts of Parliament. Once Parliamentary authority was given for the legislation, then money could be spent. In the case of the Welsh Assembly and Scottish Parliament, all that had been passed was legislation allowing a referendum to be held. Parliament had not passed a Devolution Act, so the policy on the Assembly was merely at consultation stage and could be changed. Therefore government money could not be spent promoting it. "The furthest we were advised we could go," said Nick Ainger, "was first of all subsidising the cost of the White Paper, which actually did become a bestseller at one period, and then the mini-White Paper that was going to go into every home."

On balance, the attitude of the new Government, elected in a campaign in which sleaze had been a recurring topic, erred on the side of caution. "It is a very fine line between a government saying this is what is on offer, and this will be definitely absolutely wonderful and good for you," Ainger accepted. The line was that the Labour Party would be campaigning for a Yes-vote, the Yes for Wales Campaign would be campaigning for a Yes-vote and the Government would provide information. Government Ministers were very conscious of the need to ensure that they did not step over the line. John Adams, one of Ron Davies' Special Advisers, saw it as rather more of a clear-cut political decision: "Ron doesn't like throwing money at campaigns. It's just ammunition for our enemy." But Labour officials at Millbank weren't satisfied with the idea of a door-drop of the pamphlet. They would have preferred a video for voters.

If there were debates within government on the campaign, there were also debates on the content of the devolution policy in the Cabinet Committee itself. The full detail of the debates will not be forthcoming until biographies are written and Cabinet minutes published. It is not surprising that in the long grind of committee meetings, starting at 8.00 in the morning and taking substantial parts of the day to work through the details, there were differences. Rhodri Morgan, who remained close to Ron Davies throughout this period, believes that in general "Wales was not in the eye of the storm" during the Cabinet Committee meetings. But it is widely understood that there was significant resistance from the Home Office, led by Home Secretary Jack Straw particularly, during the eighteen committee meetings. Huw Roberts believes that notwithstanding the manifesto commitment "around Whitehall there was opposition across the board. I think they thought it was a dangerous move, un-thought through, fraught with problems." Ron Davies had been concerned that there would be resistance in the Cabinet Committee to the special powers (known as the 'Henry VIII' powers because they gave the Assembly the right to make certain decisions without reference back to Parliament) that the Assembly would be given enabling it to reform quangos. Questions were raised in the Cabinet Committee and Davies explained how the powers would operate, and referred to the Labour election manifesto: "The Welsh Assembly will be specifically empowered to reform and democratise the quango state."

Another area of disagreement was the title to be given to the Leader of the Assembly. It is said that Davies wanted the title Prime Minister of Wales to be given to the Leader of the Assembly. Straw allegedly objected to this, saying that the Welsh Assembly didn't have primary powers, and a compromise was eventually reached of First Secretary. Davies believes that the Lord Chancellor, Derry Irvine, who chaired the committee, did an excellent job. There were compromises and deals struck within the committee but, according to insiders, mainly on smaller issues. Scotland attracted most of the focus, in relation to the extent of the primary powers that the Scottish Parliament would have, for example in respect of the Health Service, and whether it could outlaw abortion.

For Wales, decisions tended to focus on the joint functions and how these would be unscrambled, the issues of the concordats between the Assembly and the Whitehall departments, and the relationship with Europe. It was mainly a case of the departments being territorial about their own powers, said one insider. The Department of Trade and Industry sought to limit the Assembly's powers to hold the regulators such as OFTEL, OFGAS etc accountable. Equally, there were arguments which Whitehall departments lost. It was suggested, for example, that the DTI should have some kind of moderating role, to adjudicate between competing inward investment bids, but this was successfully opposed by Scotland and Wales. There were some changes from Labour's pre-election plans set out in *Preparing for a New Wales*. Bodies set up by Royal Charter, such as the Arts Council of Wales, were excluded from direct control by the Assembly, on the advice of civil servants. There were also extensive arguments over the Barnett formula, particularly in relation to Scotland, where there would be tax-raising powers. It is said that Jack Straw was concerned, in relation to Scotland particularly, that post-devolution it should not benefit both from the Barnett formula and other subsidies and have the ability to levy additional taxes.

Perhaps the strangest intervention, to Welsh eyes, was the suggestion that the Queen would not open the Welsh Assembly. The Welsh Office had hinted prior to publication of the Referendum Bill that the Queen would be invited to open the Assembly. Later, the suggestion surfaced that she would not do so. Confidential papers from the Home Office constitutional unit were alleged to show that the Queen was being advised that as the Assembly was not a sovereign body, she should not be asked to open it. There was a real dispute between Ministers over this, on paper at least. For a time it was exploited by the No Campaign. But Downing Street and Buckingham Palace both confirmed that the Queen would be prepared to open the Assembly.

The first draft of the White Paper was ready in mid-June. A final draft was completed in early July, and agreed. But at the last minute, the Welsh Office team decided that it needed a final re-write, right on the deadline for submission to the Cabinet Office to be distributed to the Cabinet. The draft was seen as "quite boring and long and dull," according to one insider. A team met in Rachel Lomax's office in Gwydyr House, the Welsh Office HQ in London, and worked on the document until the small hours. Lomax, Davies Principal Private Secretary June Milligan, officials such as John Shortridge, and the two Special Advisers, Huw Roberts and John Adams, all worked at the document, with different people taking on different sections at word processors all over the building.

Back in Wales, informal discussion between the Yes for Wales Campaign and the other pro-devolution parties was now occurring regularly. At this stage, however, only the Labour campaign was really underway. Plaid Cymru was still trying to influence the content of the White Paper. Senior Plaid members were still anxious to keep clear space between themselves and the Government, and indeed the Yes for Wales Campaign. On 9 July Plaid began a campaign to persuade the government that the Assembly should have the same powers as Scotland. Ieuan Wyn Jones launched a document arguing that the powers of the Assembly could be strengthened in relation to economic development, transport, education, and the environment.

The degree of preparation involved around the launch of the White Paper went unknown by most pro-devolution campaigners. Those who gathered at Llandrindod Wells for the Yes for Wales conference would have been amazed if they had known what to expect over the next ten days. A further poll for the BBC, released on 10 July, found that positive arguments for the Assembly scored higher than negative arguments, with 71% agreeing that an Assembly would pursue policies better suited to the needs of Wales. However, 50% agreed that a Welsh Assembly would increase the cost and bureaucracy of government in Wales.

On the eve of the Yes for Wales National Conference in Llandrindod Wells, held over the weekend of 12-13 July, news broke that there would be a No Campaign, which was expected to be funded by Sir Julian Hodge. The 'phoney war' was at an end. It provided an extra edge for the Conference. The Yes Campaign had achieved an impressive all-party list of speakers at the conference. Viscount St David, a former Conservative government spokesperson on Wales, had agreed to speak. His tales of how quango appointments were made brought the conference to its feet. "I have to confess that I have sat in a room with a Secretary of State while he has discussed quango appointees, and I can assure you there was nothing politically neutral about it!"

The Conference was attended by 150 people from around Wales, representing many local groups. It was opened in fine style by the Chairman, Kevin Morgan, who addressed himself to the future that the Assembly could bring for Wales and told the Conference that it was time to stop the young people of Wales being faced with the stark message, "If you want to get on, you've got to get out".

The Steering Committee was able to report that over £100,000, including Rowntree grants, had now been raised. The Campaign was seen as the pro-devolution movement. It had mobilised local groups around Wales. And it had produced campaigning materials, including recruitment leaflets, available for local use. The Steering Committee outlined its three-phase plan for the campaign. The Steering Committee acknowledged that it was not the only body campaigning for a Yes-vote, and pointed to the political parties and the unions as having the organisational base capable of delivering the vote on the ground. The Committee looked to involving local groups more in its deliberations.

The first questioner from the floor of the Conference was from Llew Smith's constituency of Blaenau Gwent. He received huge cheers from the audience. There were several other speakers from Blaenau Gwent that day who were also cheered to the rafters. Ron Davies made a powerful speech tracing the development of campaigns for democracy in Wales back to the Chartists. He also declared that the Assembly "must draw in people that perhaps have not been involved in politics before – from the Universities, businesses and industry, the media and arts perhaps." He said merit and quality must come first. Peers, MEPs and MPs should be allowed to stand the first time round.

MPs Richard Livsey, Gareth Thomas, and Ieuan Wyn Jones also spoke. Scotland Forward, the equivalent campaign in Scotland, sent Esther Robertson, one of their main campaigners, as a speaker. The conference engaged in major practical discussions on the Campaign itself: how should it publicise itself, how should it involve women, what the Assembly would mean for the economy, for education, for rural areas. The contributions from the local groups were particularly strong. Cllr Charles Henrywood of the Neath group distributed their question and answer leaflets, and their rigorously-planned campaign timetable, which guaranteed high visibility at all local events as well as organised leafleting and street-stalls. It was extraordinarily detailed, listing a wide range of tasks to be carried out by different members, including stalls at six different summer fairs. Cllr Kevin Brennan explained how Cardiff were organising. There were contributions from Swansea, Ceredigion, Pontypridd, Caernarfon, Pembroke, Bridgend and many other places. Unison pledged financial support to the

Campaign. The Conference also changed the Steering Committee's views on a number of matters, not least about the virtue of a stand at the Eisteddfod. There was a tremendous atmosphere, as the delegates mixed with one another: people from different parties, different places all sharing ideas and enthusiasms. On the Saturday night, the bars were buzzing. The Conference generated significant media coverage for the Campaign, and was an important bonding exercise. Hywel Francis recalls the Conference as being very important in legitimising Yes for Wales. Until then, it was a self-appointed group. The Conference injected a democratic element into the Campaign which enabled people to see it as a national movement. Stirring speeches from Tyrone O'Sullivan and from Eluned Morgan brought the conference to a close.

Campaigners left Llandrindod on a real high, but would have been even more enthusiastic if they had known what was coming. Peter Mandelson had had the idea that there should be a major media blitz around the publication of the White Paper, when there was likely to be real interest from the London papers and media as well as those in Wales. The Labour Party and the Yes Campaign both regarded the *Daily Mirror* as the most important media vehicle for the campaign. Sustaining a campaign over a two month period was going to be difficult, not least during August. Labour, like the Yes Campaign, identified all the campaign opportunities over the summer that it could, but understood that it would be difficult to raise much enthusiasm in the London press – read by more people in Wales than are Welsh morning newspapers.

On Tuesday 15 July, the Yes Campaign was asked to deliver two T-shirts to the Welsh Office. Unknown to the Yes for Wales staff, the T-shirts were intended for a *Daily Mirror* photocall between Peter Hain and the Manchester United star Ryan Giggs. (A photo-call with Ron Davies would have turned up the nostalgic headline 'The Ryan and Ronnie Show'!) This was a coup in which the Number Ten press machine clearly had a hand. At the last minute, however, Giggs' agent got cold feet and pulled Giggs out of the photocall. But it was too late to pull the copy from the *Daily Mirror*, in which Giggs said "I'm fed up of seeing Welsh people treated like a bunch of Sunday reserves. Wales cannot afford to stay on the touch-line a moment longer." Rhodri Morgan was able to raise the matter that day in an intervention in Business Questions, asking the Leader of the House, Ann Taylor: "Will my right Hon. Friend ensure that in next week's debate on the Government's democratic devolution proposals, the Government make it clear that they welcome support from left-wingers, right-wingers, creative midfield controllers and even the occasional striker – as Mr Giggs is, all rolled into one?" (Unfortunately, given the number of Manchester United supporters there, the *Mirror's* special edition did not appear in North Wales, where it would have made even more impact.) The *Mirror* increased its circulation on the day the Giggs story appeared, as it did the next day when it ran a special edition featuring the Prime Minister, who was making his first campaign appearance in Wales.

Blair opened a cancer treatment centre at the Royal Gwent Hospital, then met leading Welsh figures, including several in business, tourism, the media, the unions and local government, over lunch at Llancaiach Fawr, followed by a question and answer session in front of an invited audience. Afterwards he attended a reception for Labour Party members in Cardiff. Blair's visit – his first as Prime Minister – attracted massive TV and radio coverage, on the main evening TV news bulletins as well as the Welsh and national papers. The following day, the *Mirror* once again covered the visit on both its front and second pages, with Blair's message headlined 'Say Yes to New Jobs in Wales'. The message given out in the stories that were printed was entirely in line with the message backed by Philip Gould's research: "the way is open," said Blair in the *South Wales Echo*, "for a new start and a new voice for Wales". This was the kind of media coverage YFW campaigners were looking for: the campaign was really underway now. The only downside was the way in which the Prime Minister was quoted as suggesting that the Assembly would have a role in law and order, which was seen as a gaffe by papers such as the *Western Mail*.

The Yes for Wales plans for the reception to mark the launch of the White Paper in Cardiff Castle were coming to fruition. After the Yes for Wales Conference, I briefed more of our colleagues on the planning for the Castle event, not least because Daran Hill was leaving for a week's holiday. In any case, we needed cooperation on the lists of people to be invited. Geraint Stanley Jones had been very active. He had secured the backing of a number of celebrities for the launch, and guarantees from several of them that they would be there. The attendance list had now gone up to 250, and the decision was taken to switch the event from inside the Castle to its grounds. There would be a marquee in case of rain. The invitations read "Yes for Wales Invites – to a Reception hosted by Miss Siân Lloyd in the presence of the Secretary of State for Wales". Professional broadcast back-up was being provided to ensure the media companies had effective links back to their studios. Media interest was starting to mount as broadcasters and newspapers were given operational warning of the event. As it grew, decisions were taken to scale back on certain items – notably food – to save money. The Welsh National Opera Brass Ensemble was booked to play a medley of songs welcoming guests as they arrived.

Mari James, who was liaising with the Liberal Democrats and Plaid, wanted the Secretary of State to brief the two parties in advance of the White Paper launch. They were said to be fearful that they would not be able to get the balance right between emphasising their own positions, maintaining the freedom to push later for amendments to the eventual Devolution Bill while firmly supporting a Yes vote. They would need time to plan their responses. There were rumours that the White Paper would increase the number of seats in the Assembly from sixty to eighty and also ensure the abolition of some quangos in advance of the Assembly. Plaid was planning for its Special Conference on 26 July and James felt that they should have copies of the White Paper. She was also concerned about whether the Welsh Office would have a presence at the Royal Welsh Show on 22 July and whether the statement could be broadcast there on a large screen. She was conscious that there was an HTV reception in Builth Wells and felt this could be used as an event to mark the White Paper in addition. The Yes Campaign also assumed that the mini-version of the White Paper would be available on the day of the launch and could be distributed there.

Behind the scenes, Welsh Office Ministers were alarmed to learn of a possible delay in publication of the White Paper. The expected date – 22 July – had privately been current for some weeks. There had been debate within the Cabinet committee about the actual date for the launch, and nothing was public yet. Initially, it had been expected that the Welsh White Paper would come out a day after the Scots, but the Scottish White Paper had to be significantly re-written. Indeed, at quite a late stage the *Western Mail's* political correspondent wrongly predicted 24 July when Yes for Wales had been actively planning on the 22nd for some time. The 24th was the date that was in public circulation in Westminster, and the Welsh Liberal Democrats were also planning on that basis. However, the real intention was that Wales would launch first, then Scotland two days later. The Scots were not altogether happy about this, but the argument was put that Wales would not get as much coverage in the London press if its White Paper was launched second, and the London press was critical to the way the proposals were received in Wales. In Scotland, conversely, the Scottish press was most important and would give extensive coverage to the Scottish White Paper whenever it was published. But at a late stage, some in Number Ten began to get cold feet about having the best part of a week's media coverage being dominated by constitutional issues which were believed to be opaque to the majority of the British – and certainly, the English – population. Welsh Office Ministers worked hard to get Number Ten back on board. Hain made several late night and early morning calls to Mandelson and Alastair Campbell, the Prime Minister's Chief Press Spokesperson, emphasising the planning that had gone into the event. With only days to spare, the date was confirmed as 22 July.

In the final day or so before the launch of the White Paper, both Labour and the Yes Campaign continued to create more media opportunities. The date of the Referendum was also confirmed as 18 September. The Labour Party leaked its private poll findings to the *Western Mail*, which showed the people of Wales supported the Assembly by two-to-one. Labour's private poll of 1,550 voters found that 35% supported a Yes-vote and 25 per cent were No-voters. When pressed, however, after asking about the importance of Wales having a voice over education, health and other issues, the Yes percentage climbed to almost 50%. The research also identified a Blair factor, which suggested that the Prime Minister's personal support was important.

Yes for Wales also stepped up its own activities, choreographing a number of other groups to come out in support of the Assembly, including Teachers Say Yes. We finally obtained the public backing of John Elfed Jones, former Chairman of Welsh Water and HTV Wales, who on the morning of the White Paper launch became the most prominent business supporter of the Campaign. The Presbyterian Church in Wales came out in favour. As the London papers looked forward to the publication of the White Paper, Ministers gave due acknowledgement to the importance of Yes for Wales as a popular civic campaign. The *Mirror* also continued its coverage, with an article by Peter Hain on the morning of the White Paper launch. Local Yes groups got in on the act. The Cardiff Yes for Wales Group held a photocall with its banner outside City Hall for the media to use during the day of the White Paper launch. The banner actually read 'Splott Market Says Yes for Wales', but was folded back so that only the Yes message could be seen.

The White Paper on Welsh Devolution, *A Voice for Wales*, was finally launched by the Secretary of State Ron Davies in the House of Commons on Tuesday 22 July. It outlined the creation of a 60-member Assembly, with 40 members elected by first-past the post and 20 by a form of PR. This would deal with "the democratic deficit" in Wales. "Wales could not afford to stand still," Davies said, in the context of other constitutional changes such as the Scottish Parliament and English Regional Development Agencies. The Assembly would take over the powers of the Secretary of State and would have powers to reform the quangos. Some nine quangos and health trusts were to be abolished, including Tai Cymru, the Residuary Body for Wales, the Health Promotion Authority, Cardiff Bay Development Corporation, the Welsh Health Common Services Authority and others. A new economic powerhouse would be created, through the amalgamation of the Land Authority, the Development Board for Rural Wales and the Welsh Development Agency.

The Assembly would have a duty to support and foster local government, and would have the power to transfer functions to local government from quangos, though it would have no powers to remove functions from local government itself. The Assembly would have to consult with business on the cost of complying with most Orders it made. The Assembly would determine priorities for European funding alongside the EU.

Ron Davies told the Commons "Above all else, the Assembly will provide a clear and distinctive voice for Wales." He stressed that he wanted the Assembly "to forge a new kind of politics. The Assembly will therefore be based on principles of partnership, democracy and inclusiveness". He also paid due acknowledgement to issues raised by critics of the proposals during the debates, such as Allan Rogers and Ted Rowlands, referring to them generously by name in his statement. He ended by saying "in this new Britain, Wales will have its voice. The proposals are right for Wales and right for Britain."

The Statement was attacked, inevitably, by the Conservatives, both in the House by Michael Ancram, and at the Royal Welsh Show by William Hague, who said the Assembly would mean "a whole new roomful of politicians, a very expensive room full of hot air". In the Commons, speaking for the Liberal Democrats, Lembit Öpik, MP for Montgomeryshire, announced that "the Liberal

Democrats will campaign for a Yes-vote". For Plaid Cymru, Dafydd Wigley said that his party welcomed a number of aspects of the White Paper. "None the less, it will provide an Assembly that we feel is substantially less powerful than Wales needs." But he accepted that after 1 May the new Government had an overwhelming mandate. Both the Liberal Democrats and Plaid sought assurances about rural areas. Wigley did not confirm whether Plaid would be campaigning for a Yes-vote. Plaid's Special Conference was only four days away. Labour supporters of the White Paper were Ann Clwyd, Rhodri Morgan, Paul Flynn, John Marek, Jackie Lawrence, David Hanson, Huw Edwards and Donald Anderson. Barry Jones asked for assurances for the people of Deeside about rule from Cardiff.

But Labour had its dissidents too. Alan Williams, MP for Swansea West, said that the Secretary of State was offering the people of Wales "the constitutional equivalent of a mystery tour". Merthyr MP Ted Rowlands suggested that not enough quangos were being abolished. Rhondda's Allan Rogers said he thought the White Paper was "a nationalistic, not a parliamentary, response", but said he would be able to support a Bill if he believed it would abolish the quango state. Sir Ray Powell (Ogmore) also urged abolition of the quangos and confirmed he would not vote for a PR system. Dr Alan Williams (Carmarthen East and Dinefwr) was also critical of the proposals related to quangos. Blaenau Gwent's Llew Smith said the quangos could be abolished without an Assembly. Some of these issues surfaced again in an adjournment debate a few days later.

Following the statement, the three Welsh Office Ministers and their advisers rushed to Paddington to catch the train to Cardiff in time to join the reception at Cardiff Castle. It was a glorious summer evening. Throughout the late afternoon film crews had assembled and had started to undertake interviews while the Marquee was being assembled. The WNO Brass Ensemble arrived and started tuning up for the cameras. Behind the scenes all the elaborate planning had paid off. There were 250 guests from the arts, sports and the political parties, as well as local Yes groups. Siân Lloyd took the floor as compere. Geraint Stanley Jones had turned up a wide range of Welsh opera, singing, sports, acting and light entertainment celebrities including Kenneth Griffith, Karl Francis and Max Boyce and the boxers Robbie Reagan and Howard Winston, Beverly Humphries, Margaret Williams, Caryl Parry Jones, Dewi Griffiths, Eleanor Jones, Stuart Burrows, and Huw Ceredig.

RGO had turned up a message of support from Rupert Moon. Hywel Francis and his wife Mair had successfully found their speakers. Guests assembled in good time to ensure a significant audience for the Secretary of State. There was an air of real excitement.

The whole event was carefully timetabled. Mobile phone messages let the Yes for Wales crew know when the Ministers were about to arrive at the Castle. The WNO's Brass Ensemble played a medley of tunes to welcome the Ministers as they walked up the Castle path. At 8.15, Siân Lloyd welcomed the Secretary of State onto the stage in the Marquee. Ron Davies said "The Conservatives – and not just the conservatives inside the Conservative party – realise that what we are doing here is challenging the establishment. This campaign is about the people of Wales saying we have the confidence to run our own affairs."

It was stiflingly hot inside the marquee, but people stayed throughout to hear all the speakers. After Ron Davies, Geraint Stanley Jones introduced the celebrities and read out messages of support. Then came Vaughan Gething, President of NUS Wales, representing young people. He was followed by Mik Standing, speaking on his hopes for what the Assembly would mean for disabled people. Lesley Smith, a women returning to work and study, spoke of her hopes for the Assembly. Philip James, an unemployed miner, explained why he'd changed his mind since 1979. John Elfed Jones spoke for business. Tyrone O'Sullivan brought people to tears as he spoke of his hopes for the Assembly and urged people to demonstrate their commitment to Wales: "Our task is not an easy one. But we have to remember that we are Welsh and that we have always found the courage to climb out of holes." Kevin Morgan as Chair of Yes for Wales then spoke. Finally, Siân Lloyd thanked the sponsors. Ron Davies left for an interview on BBC Wales, and there was a break for guests to chat and take the air. Then, at about 10.20, Siân Lloyd went back on stage to announce the singing of the National Anthem, led by the Opera Singer Beverly Humphries, accompanied by the WNO Brass Ensemble.

Throughout the day Wales had featured prominently in the national television and radio bulletins, and most UK and Welsh broadcasters were represented at the Cardiff Castle event. There was widespread coverage in the next day's papers, with a double-page spread in the *Daily Mirror,* and extensive coverage on that evening's news. It was a clear triumph in terms of news management. Ron Davies was to receive a specific note of congratulation on the coverage from Alastair Campbell. It proved the value of Yes for Wales as an all-party movement independent of Government.

Over the following days, more groups announced their support for a Yes-vote, including the Baptists and the Cooperative Party. Pensioners Say Yes was launched when the executive of the Welsh Pensioners Organisation came out in favour. Even the *Economist* supported devolution. Finally at their Special Conference meeting on 26 July came Plaid Cymru. Plaid's change of position had been hinted at in the Commons the day before by Ieuan Wyn Jones, who said "Wales has a real opportunity to begin the process of constitutional change". But Plaid officials were locked away for hours that week getting a statement together which could be endorsed first by their Executive on the Wednesday and then by their Council meeting. Their President, Dafydd Wigley, was very worried that if there was a No-vote, it could be seriously damaging, even terminal, to Plaid. There were very heated conversations within the Plaid executive and its Council. Cynog Dafis prepared the statement and as Wigley was not at the executive, had to argue it through against its critics.

After the White Paper, Yes for Wales continued to take advantage of the burst of publicity, with more launches. Eluned Morgan's office had been particularly active, identifying potential supporters for a new range of sectoral groups. Farmers Say Yes was launched at the Royal Welsh Show shortly after the White Paper was published. Writers Say Yes was launched in Cardiff by Ed Thomas and Jan Morris. Jan Morris said she was anxious that Wales should not become merely a "poor picturesque region of the English regions with a dying language and a jokey image. This is our last chance. If the majority of the Welsh People don't vote 'yes' in the September referendum, nobody alive is ever going to see true nationhood in Wales." Ed Thomas, the playwright whose film, *House of America*, was out in the cinema, felt it important for writers to speak out. He said, "We are calling for a new Wales, multicultural and bilingual. As a Welsh nation, we've been invisible for too long. A Welsh Assembly will enable us to have a voice to be heard both in Westminster and Europe. It will instill confidence and give us validity."

Ministers took the White Paper out on the road, to gain local coverage on the back of the national coverage already achieved. Meetings were held around Wales to stress the role of the regional committees and the benefits that would be brought to particular regions. Newport Borough Council came out in favour of devolution and the Newport Yes Group was launched. Powys County Council also endorsed the White Paper.

The Labour Party's own campaign was re-launched by Ron Davies on the 28th July in Cardiff. He said that the Labour campaign would see Cabinet and other Ministers out on the road campaigning around Wales. Hundreds of Labour Party members would be out campaigning at the seaside, at street stalls, at summer shows. He urged people to vote Yes for a strong voice for Wales.

Labour's strategy was firmly fixed on delivering its heartland areas, particularly the South Wales valleys. They were very conscious of the Philip Gould research, which seemed to show a very uncertain Welsh identity, that large parts of Wales looked to England – to Manchester, to Liverpool, to London. People in strong Labour areas saw at last, after so long, a Labour government. Did they really need an Assembly? Alan Barnard and Andrew Davies were frustrated that they couldn't simply identify the Assembly with the idea of better schools and hospitals. It was hard to tell the voters what the Assembly would deliver four years down the line. They also had to convert the Wales Labour Party's branches to new techniques and new methods of communicating with voters.

Seven: Just Saying No

According to one Yes for Wales local activist, fighting against the No Campaign was like campaigning against jelly. Though a No Campaign was rumoured to be in the offing for several months, and many people in Wales were approached to lead it, it was not until the day before the White Paper, 21 July, that the No Campaign was actually launched.

The true story of the No Campaign has never been told, and it is unlikely that it ever will be. Some attempt needs to be made to overcome some of the myths about the No Campaign itself. It was never, as its Chairman Robert Hodge alleged, "a people's movement". It always enjoyed extensive Conservative support. And it was never true that there was no contact between dissident Labour MPs and the No Campaign. Some dissident Labour MPs certainly did refuse to have anything to do with Just Say No: very honourably, Alan Williams (Swansea West) for one. But that there was contact has now become clear. What has previously been revealed is the extent to which active contact between the putative official No Campaign and some Labour dissidents – though not necessarily MPs – had existed prior to the establishment of the No Campaign itself, and indeed, prior to the General Election. The No Campaign had several phases. It began in practice before the General Election. There followed the phoney war from the election until the official No launch in July, when the Campaign began in earnest.

Labour faced internal divisions over devolution in Wales. One of its biggest concerns was that the divisions would split the party as sharply as in 1979. Others, notably Plaid Cymru, were worried about the depth of Labour's commitment. The emergence before the General Election of Llew Smith, Allan Rogers and Ray Powell as vocal opponents of the final plans was merely the tip of the iceberg. There were many others within the Labour Party who were believed to be hostile to devolution; some were prominent figures in local government. Conservatives in Wales knew who the sceptics were, and knew also that if the Conservatives lost the election they would need allies to create an all-party No Campaign. Jonathan Evans, until 1997 MP for Brecon and Radnor and a

Welsh Office Minister, told me that he had "a number of conversations with leading Labour Party figures not in Parliament about
their participation in a Joint All Party Campaign."

The Yes for Wales Campaign was particularly concerned about
the position of some of those in local government, particularly in
Cardiff. Kevin Brennan, a leading councillor in Cardiff, decided
to try and get the bulk of Cardiff's Labour councillors to sign up
for Yes for Wales. "A number of them did so with alacrity, and
were very happy to do so. A number of them were quite happy to
do so but sort of said, well, we won the election, it was in the
manifesto, yes I suppose that's our policy, I'll sign up and support
it." Brennan signed up 40 out of the 56 councillors "as a kind of
insurance policy which I never used.... If there was ever an attempt
to portray Cardiff Council and Cardiff Labour Group as being
against devolution or sceptical on it in public, then it was my
intention to say that the vast majority have already signed up in
support of Yes for Wales."

After the election, the Conservatives were even more in need of
allies to form a joint campaign. They had lost all their seats in
Wales. What few activists they had left were shell-shocked. "In my
wildest dreams I didn't think it could be as bad as it was," remembered Nick Bourne, the Conservative's leading No campaigner.
The party had no elected leadership in Wales, and no effective
organisation left. They also had no money to finance a No
Campaign. And at a UK level, their party faced a leadership election. Until the result of that was known, they could not determine
the nature of the Campaign, or who their leading figures in Wales
would be.

Outside the Commons, it had taken some time for a No
Campaign to establish itself. The first sign came from two women
from the Rhondda who had campaigned to keep the name
Rhondda in the title of their new local council. News of their plan
surfaced at the end of the week that the Referendum Bill was
published in mid-May. Carys Pugh subsequently told the Neill
Committee on Standards in Public Life in 1998 that she and Betty
Bowen planned to collect signatures against the Assembly plans.
They planned to hand them to Tony Blair sometime in August.
They began collecting signatures in Tonypandy. Viscount
Tonypandy himself declared his opposition to an Assembly and
forecast a No-vote in late May. There were rumours that a leading
businessman would front the No Campaign, but Yes for Wales was
getting reports that most wanted nothing to do with publicly

opposing one of the new Government's flagship policies. The Conservatives met in conference in Rhayader to discuss their own plans in early June. They had their own dissidents: some Conservatives were thinking hard about their party's position. The Conservative meeting confirmed that a non-party Chairman would be needed to lead their No Campaign, and hinted at Tonypandy as a possibility. The Conservative Chairman Audrey Hull revealed that the Conservatives had held a meeting in Westminster to discuss their views, with former Prime Minister John Major and other members of the Shadow Cabinet. There would be no Conservative money for the campaign, but they promised that a campaign would be up and running in two weeks.

In the absence of an organised public No Campaign, the activities of Llew Smith, MP for Blaenau Gwent, were a godsend to the Conservatives. Smith's opposition to devolution became an issue almost as soon as the Referendum Bill was published. Ron Davies' comments about expecting Labour dissidents to toe the line were turned into a major story by the *Daily Post*, and picked up subsequently by some of the nationals. Davies had made it clear that campaigning against, or being associated with a No Campaign, was inappropriate behaviour for Labour MPs.

Davies' calculation was clear: "I decided that we would have to take them on at a very early stage. It was worth having a public punch up with Llew in the hope that we could get them into submission but in the knowledge that if we couldn't get them into submission it would certainly encourage a lot of other people not to put their heads above the parapet. It wasn't a very pleasant time for us, you know, it just wasn't a very pleasant time but as a tactic it worked." Davies' view of the situation was not shared by all his Ministerial colleagues, several of whom thought it was a tactical error, enabling Smith to exploit the freedom of speech issue, though some now acknowledge that it did pay off in that few others were as vocal in campaigning. Smith complained to the Whips that he was being picked on. Some MPs spoke up for Smith's right to speak out. Smith had already alleged that Ron Davies had threatened him with expulsion before the election. Davies says he merely pointed out to Smith that if he did not stop rebelling against party policy then he had to understand that the party was likely to take action against him.

The debates on the Referendum (Scotland and Wales) Bill provided a focus for the Labour dissidents to raise some questions about the Government's proposals in advance of the referendum campaign itself. This was deeply frustrating for Yes supporters. Nick Ainger remembers "You had people like Denzil [Davies], masters of the place, being able to do a very good job of probing and teasing and so on, and our own members had still not found their feet, being very very frustrated." Speaking on the Second Reading on 21 May, Ted Rowlands, a long-time devolution supporter, explained how he had himself been rather contemptuous of what he had seen as the Welsh Labour's Old Guard in the 1960s. But he had come to feel that they had been more in touch with public opinion than he. He was concerned about the fact that the Bill enabled a pre-legislative referendum, rather than a post-legislative referendum. He said "we may create difficulties for some of our colleagues" who might find that their local area had voted differently from they themselves. He ended: "I shall exercise the same right to say yes or no as, I am glad to say, the clause will give my constituents." The next day, Peter Hain said "we say to each and every Labour supporter, this is a loyalty vote in your new Labour Government. Do not side with the Tories in undermining such a crucial part of our programme by voting No or by not bothering to vote at all." The Labour MP for Swansea West, Alan Williams, raised the issue of freedom of speech for backbenchers. He said "I was somewhat concerned by suggestions that the Secretary of State for Wales had said that it would be a disciplinary matter if Labour members dared to speak against devolution." He also asked why the Wales referendum would come after the Scottish one. Two days later Llew Smith spoke out, saying that he and other party members were entitled to freedom of speech.

This issue of the right of backbenchers to express their views trundled on largely behind the scenes until a month later, on 23 June, Llew Smith became the darling of the Tory benches when he revealed that he had complained to Labour's Chief Whip that he had been threatened with expulsion by Ron Davies. He also alleged that Davies' Special Adviser, Huw Roberts, had threatened Smith's local Council that they would be penalised if they sought to see Ron Davies with Smith present. Roberts is very clear that he had a very one-sided conversation in which he largely listened to Smith. Smith kept saying he wouldn't be threatened and Roberts kept reminding him that he had not made any threats, he was ringing on behalf of the Secretary of State to find out what Smith was planning to do next. Roberts reminded Smith that the Assembly had been in Labour's manifesto but Smith replied that no-one in Blaenau Gwent backed the government's policy. "I reported this back to Ron who said 'Well, I think he's wrong' and asked me to ring Bernard Assinder." Assinder was the Leader of Blaenau Gwent Council. Assinder confirmed that the constituency had passed a resolution supporting party policy. "I said to Bernard 'well, probably best if you don't come in with Llew because I think Llew and Ron are not going to exactly get on very well'." Assinder reported this to his group, and then the story was leaked to Smith who claimed that Blaenau Gwent had been threatened, and so had he. The issue began as a purely Welsh story, linked to the *Western Mail*. Smith's claims that he had been threatened were investigated by Labour's Chief Whip Nick Brown.

A letter written by Assinder to Brown surfaced in Prime Minister's Questions. Somehow, the new Leader of the Conservative Party, William Hague, had a copy of the letter and raised it in his first question time with Blair:

> Mr Hague: When the hon. Member for Blaenau Gwent [Mr Smith] says that he was threatened with expulsion from the Labour party if he campaigned against a Welsh Assembly in the forthcoming referendum and the Secretary of State of Wales denies that, which one is telling the truth?
> The Prime Minister: I can assure the right hon. Gentleman, and I again welcome him to the Dispatch Box, that no one has been threatened with expulsion. People are perfectly entitled to state their position, provided, of course, that they do so in accordance with the rules of the parliamentary party.
> Mr Hague: So let the whole House get it clear: when the hon. Member for Blaenau Gwent says that he was told twice that he would be kicked out of the Labour party if he stood for his beliefs, we have the Prime Minister's personal assurance that he was not telling the truth.
> The Prime Minister: I can give my personal assurance that no such threat was made.
> Mr Hague: In that case, who authorised Mr. Huw Roberts – a special adviser at the Welsh Office – to tell local council officials that their relationship with the Welsh Office would be jeopardised if their local Member of Parliament did not support the policy of the Labour party? Do not local council officials have a higher responsibility to the wider electorate, and not to the unity of the Labour party?
> The Prime Minister: That is absolutely right. I can tell the right hon. Gentleman that I have asked for an investigation into this matter, and I am told – [Interruption.] If hon. Members would just wait a minute. I am told that that allegation is untrue as well, so perhaps the right hon. Gentleman will now withdraw it.
> Mr Hague: The whole House will hope that it is untrue and the whole House will look forward to seeing the result of the investigation in due

course. Just so we have this absolutely clear, when the Secretary of State for Wales tells *The Daily Telegraph* that individuals in the Labour party must not flout the party election manifesto, but the Secretary of State for Scotland tells the House, as he did a few weeks ago, that any Member of Parliament has a right to speak his or her mind as he sees fit, which one is speaking for the Government?

The Prime Minister: I have just made it clear – [Hon. Members: "No."] Perhaps I will make it clear again. One: Members of Parliament are perfectly entitled to speak their mind. Two: there is no truth in the allegation that pressure was put on councils or that they had been told that they could not have the resources or any of the rest of it. If that were the case, it would be quite wrong. It is not the case, and perhaps now the right hon. Gentleman will withdraw the allegation.

Mr Hague: Will the Prime Minister therefore –

Hon. Members: Withdraw.

Madam Speaker: Order. The House will come to order.

Mr Hague: Will the Prime Minister therefore give us a cast-iron guarantee that he will come to the House with the result of that investigation? Does he not regard it as an extraordinary state of affairs that different Cabinet Ministers give conflicting views on this matter and that investigations into it have to be mounted? What will he do to stop the arrogant behaviour of his Government on these matters and to ensure that there is an honest and open debate?

The Prime Minister: Unfortunately, and I understand these problems, I think that the right hon. Gentleman prepared his last question before he heard the answer. I have just made it clear that I investigated the matter this morning. There is no truth in these allegations. People are perfectly entitled to speak their mind. They are entitled to do that and that has been made clear by everyone concerned. It is important that we now get on and debate the principles that underline the devolution debate. I can only say to the right hon. Gentleman that, if he carries on with points like this, no wonder he has no Members of Parliament left in Wales or Scotland.

Assinder amplified his meaning in a second letter to the Chief Whip exonerating Roberts. Smith appeared on Newsnight that night, saying that he wanted a meeting with the Prime Minister and the chance to put his case to the Commons Standards and Privileges Committee. Hague followed up the question with a letter to Blair the next day, enclosing the *Newsnight* transcript and demanding that Blair investigate whether someone had lied to him and calling for the matter to be referred to the Committee on Standards and Privileges. Hague repeated his question in a speech to the Scottish Conservative Party Conference in Perth the next day. Meanwhile, Alan Williams MP tabled a series of questions to Ron Davies concerning the Roberts-Assinder-Smith issues.

The issue was beginning to get out of hand for the Government. It also caused Yes for Wales great concern. Members felt that the Government was not getting enough support from pro-devolution MPs. They feared that if Labour could not orchestrate its MPs to come out and make the positive case for devolution now, how did they expect to do so in the heat of the referendum campaign proper? The night of Hague's speech in Perth, several Yes for Wales Steering Committee Members met at the Cardiff home of Eluned Morgan to mobilise support. She recalls: "A lot of people felt frustrated and felt that Llew represented everything that they didn't want to be associated with in the Wales Labour Party." She spoke to a number of Labour MPs, including Jackie Lawrence and Betty Williams who were as concerned as she was. That day, Llew Smith had published an article in the *Guardian* making his case. Kevin Morgan, as Chair of Yes for Wales, had sought space for a reply but the *Guardian* would only agree to a letter. His response to Smith argued the politics clearly. Smith's position, he said, reflected "the familiar refrain of the centralist tradition within British Labourism. Its message is simple: real power lies at Westminster, so let's focus on capturing the 'state machine' in London and we will legislate for your needs from the centre."

Driving home after the meeting, where they had agreed to urge pro-devolution Labour MPs to support the Government against Smith, some of the Yes for Wales officers heard Peter Mandelson, on the BBC's *Any Questions* programme, say that of course Llew Smith was entitled to have his say. This was clearly a signal from the Prime Minister, to say enough was enough. The 'free speech' issue was over, but the dissidents had also been told that they could not campaign against Labour policy in an organised way. In fact, Blair had made this point clear at a meeting of the Parliamentary Labour Party two days after Hague had first questioned him about it. He had told Labour MPs that they could express their views without fear of expulsion, but also said that colleagues were entitled to express their differences of view about such matters, though they were under an obligation to do so in a reasonable and comradely way. The PLP's code of conduct required colleagues to refrain from personal attacks on other colleagues and to act in harmony with the policies of the Parliamentary Labour Party. This was widely interpreted as meaning that they should not be involved in a sustained campaign against Labour Party policy. Smith said he was happy with the PM's assurances and dropped his plans to complain to the Standards and Privileges Committee.

Davies' objective had been to take on the first avowed dissident MP and get it clearly established that Labour MPs, while free to express their views, would not be allowed to join up with others from across the party spectrum to campaign against party policy. By standing up to Smith, Davies felt he had made the position clear to other potential rebels. That may be so. But the issue distracted from the positive case for devolution for some time. Nick Ainger confesses "it did undoubtedly colour the early stages, so we weren't setting off on a positive message." Rhodri Morgan felt "it was quite a frustrating period because we couldn't effectively kill the Llew story." On the other hand, it was certainly the view of some prominent No campaigners that potential dissidents in and outside Parliament decided to sit on their hands after this.

By 9 July the No Campaign of Carys Pugh and Betty Bowen had an apparent backer in Sir Julian Hodge, Wales' ninth richest man. The 92-year-old told the *South Wales Echo* from his home in Jersey that his intervention had come after talks with Viscount Tonypandy. He said, "I have no political reason to oppose it, but as a businessman I don't think it's good for Wales." The immediate reaction of Yes for Wales was to ridicule the No Campaign as consisting of "Tories, tax-exiles and Tonypandy". The following day, Viscount Tonypandy told the *Times* he was looking for a strategist to run the No Campaign. Tonypandy's last political involvement had been not with the Labour Party, whom he had served as Secretary of State for Wales, but with the Referendum Party. He told the *Times* "The anti-Europe campaign saved Britain in the nick of time. I think the idea of a federal Europe has been killed stone-dead and we can do the same here in Wales." Tonypandy alighted on Matthew Gunther-Bushell, a former junior aide to disgraced Conservative Minister Jonathan Aitken, who had got involved with the Referendum Party. Ministers and Yes campaigners, unkindly and probably unwisely in retrospect, contrasted the youthful focus of the Yes Campaign and the elderly nature of the No Campaign.

Hodge's involvement appears to have been triggered by Carys Pugh. She told the Neill Committee, "I rang Viscount Tonypandy. He was president of our Campaign – I call him George. I said 'George, I can't afford to do any more.' He said 'Don't worry about this. Leave it with me. I'll have a word with Julian'." Pugh said Tonypandy himself donated £100, and two Labour MPs anonymously gave £50.

Tonypandy was the link between the embryonic No Campaign and the Conservative Party. Nick Bourne had been contacted by Matthew Gunther-Bushell who was keen to get involved. They both went to see Tonypandy at his Cardiff home. He was very helpful and gave them contact numbers for Betty Bowen and Carys Pugh. They went straight round to see Carys Pugh and went through the letters she had received. Meanwhile, Martin Perry, the Conservative Party's Wales Director, and Lyndon Jones, the Party's agent in Brecon and Radnor, were making contact with a number of business people. Perry was well-connected with the business community through the Cardiff and County Club. Through these connections they met up with Robert Hodge.

The first business meeting of the embryonic Just Say No campaign was held at the St Mellon's Hotel. The business meetings included Nick Bourne, Betty Bowen, Carys Pugh, Robert Hodge, Lyndon Jones, Martin Perry, Matthew Gunther-Bushell and Jonathan Evans. They were desperate to find someone who could be an articulate public spokesperson who would be identifiably from a Labour background. Their candidate in Cardiff Central, David Melding, had suggested the name of Tim Williams to Martin Perry. Williams, a Welsh-speaking historian who had once worked for Plaid Cymru MPs, had been a nationalist in his school-days but later turned against nationalism and was critical of the Welsh language and devolution movements in Wales, contributing articles which went against the grain of the consensus of the Welsh chattering classes. He leaped at the chance to take part in the Campaign.

The No Campaign tried to create two spoilers for Yes for Wales. First, the announcement about Julian Hodge happened ahead of the Yes for Wales conference. The actual launch of what was to be called the Just Say No Campaign (a negative title which Gunther-Bushell allegedly hated) took place the day before the White Paper. Yes for Wales' main response to the launch of the No Campaign on 21 July was largely to ignore it, though a small demonstration with a Yes banner and children in Yes sweatshirts greeted those attending the No campaign offices. The Yes Campaign was far more concerned about the publication of the White Paper. Viscount Tonypandy was named as President of the No Campaign. Robert Hodge was the Chairman. Others named included Professor Nick Bourne, Tim Williams, and the Rhondda two, Carys Pugh and Betty Bowen. One celebrity – the former Wales soccer captain Gary Speed – was found for the No

Campaign by *Wales on Sunday*. They had approached other sporting celebrities themselves but none was prepared to come out in support.

More damaging to the Yes Campaign that week was the way in which information about Assembly members' salaries was put into the public domain. The figures were given in a response to a question to the Secretary of State by Swansea MP Alan Williams, rather than through a planned and managed announcement. It was a clumsy and damaging mistake which failed to give any real context for the decision, nor did it properly state that the independent Senior Salaries Review Board would be looking at the levels of pay. The figures were quickly grasped by the Conservative spokesman Michael Ancram in the Commons and became a key piece of No Campaign propaganda.

Anti-Assembly MPs had made their views plain in their reaction to the statement on the White Paper by the Secretary of State, published 22 July. At the end of the week several of them also criticised the Yes Campaign in an adjournment debate on the White Paper. Alan Williams attacked Peter Hain for having asked for blind loyalty in the Referendum Bill debate some weeks before. He and Denzil Davies claimed that Yes for Wales had been conducting their campaign on the basis of verbal abuse. Ted Rowlands said that "we should stop peddling the notion that individual Labour members who dare to criticise the White Paper or who are opposed to devolution are Tories." Davies and Rowlands both argued that a big opportunity had been missed to reform the quangos. The debate was also marked by a speech from one of the 1979 dissidents, Donald Anderson, who explained why he had changed his mind and was now voting Yes.

At the end of the week the Yes Campaign was drawn into its first spat with the No Campaign, when the bizarre claim was made that the No Campaign headquarters had been threatened by a petrol-bomb attack. Just Say No issued a statement headed 'Petrol bomb attempt at No Campaign office', claiming that "the very worst kind of nationalism is once again rearing its head in Wales." The press release – inflammatory in all senses – was largely ridiculed by the Welsh media, with the BBC refusing to even cover the story. Yes for Wales spoke to the police about the incident and it seemed that they could find no evidence whatever to support the claim in the release. But it suggested Yes for Wales should be prepared for more juvenile and irresponsible outbursts. In fact we had expected the No side to indulge in such 'dirty tricks', and had prepared accordingly. That weekend's *Wales on Sunday* carried details of a memo to be issued to all Yes Campaign groups warning that more dirty tricks could be expected from the No camp.

Over the summer, the Yes Campaign revised its strategy towards Just Say No (JSN). It decided to deal with the No Campaign in a number of ways. The main emphasis would be to depict the No Campaign as largely a Conservative front. Yes for Wales groups collected evidence that the No Campaign was largely staffed by local Conservative activists. Yes for Wales was able to point out that Just Say No leaflets were modelled on the core 'tax-bombshell' message of the Conservatives 1992 election campaign. (The leaflets claimed that the Assembly would cost everyone in Wales £1200 in tax each year, just as Conservative advertising had done in 1992). We also found evidence that the Just Say No Campaign was trying to silence its Conservative supporters by pulling them out of debates.

Yes for Wales sought to assure people that William Hague was the No Campaign's real leader. He had launched their Campaign petition at the Royal Welsh Show on 22 July, on the day the White Paper was published. He returned to Wales to lead their last ten days of campaigning. Robin Gibson-Watt in Brecon and Radnor was Constituency chairman of the local Tories; Bridgend Tories supplied all the leafleters and canvassers for the local No Campaign; the No stand at the Vale of Glamorgan Show was manned by Tory councillors; Just Say No materials at the Anglesey show were distributed from the Conservative stall; Just Say No Campaign leaders in Newport were former Conservative candidates Alan Cairns and David Davies; the Denbigh Just Say No Campaign was led by Conservative Cllr Stuart Andrew.

Even then, the Yes for Wales Campaign did not know the full extent of Conservative involvement in the No Campaign. While Carys Pugh, Betty Bowen and Tim Williams were frequently used as spokespeople for the No Campaign, behind the scenes the No campaign headquarters was being directed by Lyndon Jones, the Conservative Party agent in Jonathan Evans' former seat in Brecon and Radnor. Other Brecon and Radnor Conservatives were highly active.

The attempt to depict No campaigners as Tories was deliberate, and it was determined that Labour MPs coming out in support of the No Campaign would be depicted as friends of the Conservatives. This tactic was completely misunderstood by the MPs themselves, not least later in the campaign when the Yes

Campaign tagged them 'Thatcher's Friends'. The phrase was coined when Margaret Thatcher headed north to Scotland to campaign against devolution. At an individual level no-one could take that allegation seriously, but the point was to get Thatcher's name associated with the No Campaign, as she and John Redwood were valuable bogeys. A leading *Western Mail* journalist saw it as one of the Yes for Wales Campaign's most effective interventions. The No Campaign was relying on emotional, fear-based arguments (fear of the Welsh language, North versus South) and there seemed little time to argue the detail of devolution. When towards the end of the campaign Labour MPs' calls for a No-vote were announced one by one by JSN, Yes for Wales did not at that stage know of the level of collaboration between some of the No-voting MPs and the Just Say No Campaign.

Our second line of attack was to point out the dangers of a No-vote for Wales, to illustrate more precisely how Wales would get left behind. The Yes Campaign developed a position, spelt out by Professors Kevin Morgan and Phil Cooke, on what would be the costs to Wales of voting No. They pointed to monies lost by Wales under the Conservatives – the £105 million returned by John Redwood to the Treasury, the loss of £46 million of EU monies by Clwyd, the cuts in development area status, and the imbalance in spending between Scotland and Wales – as the costs of voting No.

The third line would be to point up contradictions within the No Campaign, exploiting what Nigel Jenkins, the writer, described as Just Say No's "treasurable battiness". The first signs of disagreement in the No Campaign surfaced at the Eisteddfod, with one former Conservative agent attacking them. Elwyn Jones said "I now want nothing to do with a campaign which is autocratic and has little understanding of the Welsh way of life." He described the No Campaign as shambolic. His comments were pounced on by YFW and were despatched to journalists in all media, as well as to local groups. To an extent, Yes for Wales was keen for certain of the No campaigners to have a considerable amount of air-time as we believed that they presented an off-putting image to ordinary people. When Carys Pugh, particularly, attacked Tony Blair as a "Tory in Red" and said she wanted to see Peter Hain sent back to South Africa, we felt it was the kind of own-goal the No Campaign could have done without.

The Yes for Wales Campaign planned to monitor claims made by the No Campaign, and respond sharply to them. The first campaign mailing to local Yes for Wales groups included 'No can't be right', a response to the No arguments. Just Say No leaflets had claimed the support of the CBI in Wales, and in the latter stages of the campaign Yes for Wales tipped off *Wales on Sunday* that these claims were continuing to be made, despite the CBI's refusal to get involved. The newspaper managed to get an on-the-record quote from the Director of the Wales CBI Elizabeth Haywood denouncing this as "a lie". Yes for Wales then tipped off the *Financial Times*, which repeated the story, enabling the campaign in Wales, unlike that in Scotland, to avoid the charge that business was opposed to devolution. The CBI Chairman, Ian Spratling, attacked Just Say No for "dirty campaigning" in suggesting job losses and closures were likely if Wales voted Yes. Spratling, who had had regular discussions with Ron Davies on behalf of the CBI, said that these comments were to the detriment of Wales and were sending the wrong signals to inward investors.

What did surprise us was the operation of the balance rules by the broadcasters. Both the Yes for Wales Campaign and the Labour campaign had planned a range of announcements and events to ensure consistent media attention, and particularly TV and radio coverage. To some extent, the media war depended on the approach taken by the main broadcasters to the issue of impartiality. Complaints were made by Yes campaigners to both BBC Wales and the BBC in London over their coverage of the launch of the No Campaign. The problem for the Yes Campaign was that the No Campaign was entitled to balance and had to do very little to get it. The No campaign ran a series of launches around Wales, at which their spokespeople would let off 2,000 balloons. They also had a campaign bus which trundled round the Valleys. The broadcasters had to cover them, no matter that the events were the same throughout, and there was little organisational effort compared to that undertaken by Yes for Wales and the Labour Yes campaign. Despite having less money than they had originally hoped for, the No Campaign had significant coverage. Carys Pugh was effusive in her praise for the broadcasters when she appeared before the Neill Committee, saying they had saved her thousands in advertising costs: "I had excellent support from the media, both TV and radio."

The most telling critic of the Government's proposals, in practice, was Denzil Davies, who focused precisely and effectively on a limited number of issues largely linked to Europe. His claim that Wales would lose out in Europe because no-one from the

Assembly would be able to sit in on the Council of Ministers had a definite resonance with farmers. Yes for Wales was receiving feedback from July onwards that this was causing problems and took action to redress it. No campaigners used it at public meetings like the one held by the *South Wales Echo* in Bridgend. Davies made the claim on a number of occasions and achieved widespread coverage in parts of rural Wales where this mattered. The Labour Party was also concerned about his closeness to Dr Alan Williams MP. There was a belief that Williams, MP for Carmarthen East and Dinefwr, had been persuaded that he could only hope to hold his seat against the nationalists if there were no Assembly. There was a widespread fear among Labour officials that Williams would come out against the Assembly in the last week. Williams was known to have become more and more critical of the Government's proposals, particularly in relation to the quangos, which he did not believe went far enough. There was considerable behind-the-scenes activity by the Labour Party to ensure that this did not happen. Another critic, Ted Rowlands, also wrote an effective article in *The Times* that was critical of the arguments being used by the Yes-side, but eventually declared himself to be voting Yes.

Though Yes campaigners would generally begrudge saying it, Just Say No ran a relatively effective campaign, though their most obvious weakness was the lack of a grassroots base. "In some areas we were very thin on the ground," confesses Nick Bourne. They produced well-targeted literature, though it was unclear how much of it got distributed. "It was not circulated as widely as we would have liked", Robert Hodge told the Neill Committee. Their arguments were the arguments which Yes campaigners had anticipated, focusing largely on cost, bureaucracy and 'jobs for the boys'. In particular they argued that the Assembly would cost £117 million over four years and this could pay for 1400 teachers, 1500 nurses or six new schools. They said services would have to be cut to pay for the Assembly, while taxes would rise. The Assembly would set North against South and Welsh against English. There was some confusion, not least in the last stages after the Scottish vote, as to whether they believed that the Assembly would be a talking shop or a slippery slope to nationalism. But for the No Campaign, inconsistency did not matter. What mattered was whether their message was making an emotional appeal to their supporters or was worrying potential Yes voters. They did not have to explain complicated proposals, just to argue against what others were proposing. But their existence made it more respectable to vote No.

Eight: Summer Days

The National Eisteddfod in Bala was the setting for the first meeting of the expanded Yes for Wales Steering Committee on 2 August, where the plans for the final stages of the campaign were outlined to activists. The Bala meeting was attended by several local Yes for Wales groups, including Wrexham, Caernarfon, Swansea, Cardiff, Ceredigion, Pontypridd and Neath. In late July I had crafted an approach to the last four weeks. This set out themes for daily and weekly media coverage for what the Yes campaigns had collectively termed the Campaign Proper – the period when the focus of the London media would be back on Wales, and when people had returned from holiday and were now needed to make up their own minds. Yes for Wales had its own grid of activities for the final stages. The Campaign Proper would be launched after the August Bank Holiday, with clear themes for each of the weeks. The first week's theme would be *All Wales Supports an Assembly* (August 25-29), to be promoted through local and regional campaign re-launches; *Wales Needs a Voice* would follow (August 30-September 5), to be promoted through publications and press conferences on particular topics: Wales needs a voice for economics, for housing etc; then *The No Campaign is a Tory Front* (September 6-12), to challenge the No Campaign, pointing out that business is unhappy with the No Campaign, most of the No Campaign's activists are Conservatives; and finally *Scotland Voted Yes: Don't Let Wales Get Left Behind* (September 13-18).

We also outlined our media strategy at Bala, which was later distributed to local groups. The media strategy made clear that our key aim was to run a positive campaign for a Yes-vote, identifying the idea of a Yes-vote with popular figures in Welsh life and culture. At the same time, however, the Campaign must have solid answers about the questions and fears people had about the Assembly. The strategy document acknowledged that the political parties also had their own campaigns in place, and would be working in some cases alongside the Yes Campaign and in others through it. The paper said that the No Campaign was expected to campaign on divisive themes, setting Welsh-speakers against non-Welsh speakers, running possibly "the crudest, most negative campaign Wales has ever seen", focusing on cost and bureaucracy. Yes for Wales would not waste much time in answering the No Campaign: its main focus would have to be on selling devolution as a good thing for Wales. Although it would need to rebut lies and distortions, it should move back onto its own ground as soon as possible. The document argued that the Yes Campaign should certainly refrain from attacking individuals and should certainly not attack people just because they were old. The positive messages to be projected included:

– Wales needs a voice
– An Assembly will be good for jobs, for the international profile of Wales, for inward investment
– Wales needs to decide its own priorities on key issues
– An All-Wales Assembly will give Welsh issues more time than the House of Commons

The paper recognised that the Campaign had no money for advertising. The Welsh broadcast media was to be the priority, along with the *Daily Mirror*. We were concerned about those areas of Wales where people could tune into English TV programmes, and would take up the issue of campaign coverage with the broadcasters in the neighbouring areas. There were plans for specific themed articles for the *Western Mail*. Tabloid papers in Wales (*Daily Post, Wales on Sunday, South Wales Echo, South Wales Evening Post* etc) were to be fed a diet of local and celebrity linked stories. The London-based media, the paper noted, had largely decided that Wales was where Labour's agenda was vulnerable, and that would govern the tenor of their coverage. The *Mirror* remained the Campaign's most important outlet, because of the breadth of its reach.

The Bala meeting also heard that the stock of promotional materials had been expanded since the Yes for Wales conference. There were now balloons, T-shirts, car-stickers, posters, campaign ribbons, recruitment leaflets, plastic carrier bags and letterheads for local campaign use. Mari James had produced a draft campaign leaflet to be tested at the Eisteddfod, which would be produced centrally so that it could be used across Wales. It would also be used as a template for local groups. Val Feld had produced pledge cards for local groups to use to sign up pledges of commitment to vote Yes. These would be collated centrally and signatories would be mailed further information to encourage them to turn out and vote.

The Campaign was also able to introduce the team working on our behalf. There were three people in Cardiff, led by Daran Hill, with Kate Stokes, Press Officer, and Beryl Wichard who acted as Secretary (later Blodwen Jones took over). North West Wales was covered by Jill Torkington, experienced in voluntary sector campaigning; North-East Wales by Claire Bryant, a former student activist; in West Wales, working from Eluned Morgan's office was Anna McMorrin, focusing on organising sectoral groups and helping to liaise with the rock bands; covering the Valleys was city high-flier Darren Evans. The Liberal Democrats' organiser Mel ab Owain was responsible for mid-Wales. The Steering Committee also heard that Mari James, one of the two Vice-Chairs, was to be based largely full-time in the Yes for Wales office from now on. As an experienced campaigner herself, she could offer more hands-on guidance to the office and to local groups. As well as taking on specific roles, the Campaign officers had taken responsibility for certain tasks. Kevin Morgan (Chair) and Mari James (Vice-Chair) were to be the main public faces of the Campaign, undertaking most of the media interviews and debates. James would also co-ordinate the mailings to groups and liaise with the political parties. They, along with Hywel Francis (National Convenor), who would also undertake a lot of the Welsh language media interviews, were to be the Campaign's main speakers at public meetings. Val Feld (Treasurer) would speak frequently at meetings and organise Women Say Yes. She would be the main liaison with ethnic minority organisations, many of whom were very active. Eleri Carrog, the other Vice-Chair, was to be active across North Wales and in the Welsh-language media. I was to have specific responsibility for planning the media campaign, dealing with the media response to the No Campaign, and for liaison with the Government.

The National Eisteddfod was very important. It was a great opportunity to identify additional supporters and to raise money. Five thousand names were collected in support of the Yes campaign, and about £2,000 was raised for the Campaign. It was an excellent distribution point for literature and more T-shirts were sold there than at any other time. A rally was held at the Eisteddfod, with speakers including Labour MP Gareth Thomas, Plaid's Elfyn Llwyd, Lord Geraint, and the academic and Welsh-language activist Elan Closs Stephens. Artists like Mary Lloyd Jones and other cultural figures took part in photocalls during the week. At the end of the week, a number of activists from Cymdeithas yr Iaith set off from Bala to walk to Cardiff, which they intended to reach two weeks later having collected signatures on a petition on route.

After Bala, a detailed media briefing pack was drawn up. This was sent out to the Welsh and London media, in advance of the Campaign Proper, and made available to those foreign journalists who requested it. The pack contained an introduction to the Yes for Wales Campaign; a list of activities since Yes for Wales was founded; information on the breadth of its support, including business, celebrity and Conservative support; local and sectoral groups; funding; the Yes Campaign's view of the Just Say No Campaign and the dissident Labour MPs; polling results; and a list of future activities.

With Mari James now located in the Campaign Office, its ability to serve local groups had grown. Regular mailings were sent to local groups and other supporters. The first, in early August, included a ten-point summary of the White Paper; tips on campaign techniques; draft press releases; arguments against the No line; and the Yes Campaign's media strategy. We now had more volunteers in the office, stuffing envelopes, making calls and taking orders for materials. James found that calls coming into the office were now taking a lot of time. Another telephone line was rented and another room. During August she organised regular weekly meetings with the political parties. This 'Wednesday Group' included Andrew Davies for the Labour Party, Mike German or Judy Lewis for the Liberal Democrats, and Karl Davies or Dafydd Williams (on occasion, Ieuan Wyn Jones or Cynog Dafis) for Plaid Cymru.

Rowntree's release of extra money for the Yes Campaign, coupled with a steady flow of income from donations, allowed the Yes Campaign to embark on at least the elements of an advertising campaign. A van was hired with an advertisement for the Yes Campaign and a phone number to ring to support the Campaign. The Advan drove all over Wales and was available to the Campaign for local meetings and celebrity photocalls.

At a local level, the campaigning was becoming more intense. But it was a hard slog through the summer, for Yes for Wales and all the political parties. Other organisations were beginning to focus more readily on the Campaign. The work done by Newport Council leader Harry Jones was beginning to pay off. Torfaen council came out in favour. So did Carmarthenshire County Council, Gwynedd and Ynys Môn Councils. Celebrities continued to give their support, with Glamorgan cricketers Tony Cottey and Steve Watkin breaking off from their home game at Colwyn Bay to support the Conwy group. The Cooperative Party came out in favour. Friends of the Earth declared their support.

On 7 August, the Government opened its information hotline, a dedicated telephone number which members of the public could ring to find out information. Those answering the phones were only able to give out factual information; if people wanted detail on the Yes or No arguments they were referred to the Yes for Wales and Just Say No campaigns. This became a serious – and unanticipated – problem for the Yes Campaign. The phones rang constantly with callers who wanted to know more. "It wasn't unusual for you to put the telephone down after a telephone conversation to find that 10 or 14 telephone messages had come in," remembers Daran Hill.

There was significant collaboration on the ground between the Yes Campaign and members of the different parties. Yes for Wales groups launched with all-party platforms of MPs and others in Abergavenny, Pontypridd, Pembrokeshire, Llanelli, Porthmadog, Pwllheli and many other places. A Campaign shop was opened in Ystradgynlais by Labour's Julie Morgan MP and Rhodri Morgan MP, Liberal Democrat Richard Livsey MP, Plaid's Marc Phillips and the Yes Campaign convenor Hywel Francis. Ethnic minority supporters were beginning to be identified. Cymdeithas yr Iaith came out in favour of a vote for "Yes – and more". Meanwhile a survey of Labour councillors found 70% of them saying they would vote Yes. The Federation of Small Businesses came out against. The letters pages of the newspapers, particularly the *Western Mail*, were filling up. The *South Wales Echo* began a phone poll.

In August the campaign relied largely on events and photo-opportunities. On 14 August the Labour Party campaign for the Valleys was launched by Peter Hain and Ron Davies. They met in the Rhondda and Porth then travelled separately across the Valleys that day. Hain took the campaign to Llew Smith's Blaenau Gwent seat, where the local Yes group was already very active on an all-party basis. The Campaign carried on all through the month. Minibuses carried campaigners into town centres for leafleting and canvassing. Labour had four minibuses working in several different locations. The idea was that the local organiser would take the minibus out and it wouldn't return to Transport House in Cardiff until it was dark. Each would have about twelve people on board and there would be music playing, to create a splash in the communities in which the bus travelled. The campaigners on the bus would leaflet a few streets, knock on a few doors, and introduce whoever their campaign celebrity was (it was frequently Peter Hain). There were balloons and street stalls in some of the places. Labour was using phone banks to mobilise volunteers to come and join the bus wherever it stopped. Yes for Wales also had a bus which toured the Valleys, which was paid for by the Democratic Left.

But the campaign wasn't all glitz. Yes for Wales was looking to find opportunities to make the case that the Assembly would bring the quangos under control. One was the rumour that the Welsh Office was about to extend the term of office of the Chairman of S4C, Prys Edwards. The campaign called for the post to be advertised under Nolan rules. The press statement from Yes for Wales was taken up by the *Western Mail*, which managed to get an admission from Edwards that he was going to leave the post in six months time.

Labour's pledge to bring Cabinet and other Ministers into Wales was carried out. The rock group the Stereophonics declared their support in a photocall outside the HMV shop in Cardiff's Queen Street with Peter Mandelson. The Stereophonics' drummer Stuart Cable said "I think devolution is important to give young people in Wales better job opportunities." Stunts and photocalls predominated, with Cabinet Member Clare Short MP eating a pizza with the Yes for Wales logo (made from leeks and laverbread) in the Topo Gigio restaurant in Cardiff. Agriculture Minister Jeff Rooker visited farmers in Llangollen. Home Office Minister and Cardiff South and Penarth MP Alun Michael visited and spoke at the Denbighshire and Flintshire show, warning that without an Assembly, "Wales will lose out to the English regions".

Artists Say Yes was launched by the sculptor Angharad Jones and the painter Mary Lloyd Jones. The latter had designed two banners in her characteristic bold style which had already been displayed at the Eisteddfod. Angharad Jones's sculpture of the Mabinogion character, Blodeuwedd, was erected by the Norwegian Church in Cardiff Bay. Health-workers Say Yes was launched. The Welsh Rail-users Campaign came out for an Assembly. Catholics Say Yes was launched. The *South Wales Echo* decided to run a series of meetings where both the Yes and No cases could be put forward, in Merthyr, Pontypridd, Caerphilly and Cardiff.

The Pontypridd meeting was fairly bitter. Hywel Francis from the Yes Campaign with Mike German from the Liberal Democrats debated with Llew Smith and Tim Williams. The room was packed, primarily with local Yes supporters from Pontypridd and the surrounding area. Llew Smith was greeted with cries of "Stop moaning Llew", as he complained he had been called a Tory for coming out against the Assembly. Smith and Williams attacked the proponents of an assembly as encouraging nationalism. But there were many, many Labour supporters amongst the Yes Campaign in Pontypridd, and their arguments were laughed out of court. Hywel's line was "This is not about dividing Wales or nationalism whatever that may be. It's about giving Wales a fresh democratic mandate." Hywel spoke at many meetings during the summer on behalf of Yes for Wales in Abergavenny, the Rhondda, Tonpentre, Treherbert, Merthyr and Pontypool.

Yes for Wales spoke regularly to the different parties to get their feedback. Peter Hain was worried about the Campaign on the ground. It was one of the most difficult campaigns in which he had been involved. Not enough people were out there campaigning. He was worried that the arguments were not getting to people on the doorstep. Hain had been back and forth across Wales leading small groups of Labour activists into town centres and knocking on doors. He was both elated by the response when voters were actually contacted face to face but frustrated at how little of this was going on. The No Campaign had been claiming strong support from Valleys councillors and tried to claim the support of Rhondda Cynon Taff leader Billy Murphy, who came out and declared he was voting Yes. Kevin Morgan was also worried about the Valleys. "I would go up to the Cynon Valley regularly to see my parents and in the rugby club there was simply very little support even among our natural supporters and that always worried me." Morgan believed "there was a deep rational cynicism there among our real heartlands." He was tired of the argument put forward by one or two London journalists. "The implication was that Labour voters, particularly working-class Labour voters in the Valleys were feckless and quite frankly stupid, and this wasn't what was coming through to me in places like Rhigos rugby club." Morgan believed that Valleys people had a rational basis for their cynicism about their locally-elected councillors, and they were concerned about the prospect of more elected politicians. Kim Howells found the same in his campaigning.

At this point the Yes Campaign decided it would need to increase its level of spending for the duration of the Campaign and made an appeal for an additional £20,000. The Campaign said that it needed to counter what our press release called the "crazy statements" of the Just Say No Campaign. We thought Just Say No was funded by large sums from Sir Julian Hodge. The announcement was partly made to counter claims that the Yes-side luxuriated in government sponsorship. But actually, Yes for Wales needed even more. Meanwhile Ron Davies announced that the abolition and merger of quangos would pay for the Assembly.

The Yes for Wales Campaign was never as strong on the ground as the impression it tried to give out through the media. Activity across Wales was uneven, and there were areas where there were no Yes groups at all. There were also problems with the production of leaflets. Initially, Yes for Wales had relied on templates of leaflets, adapting local group leaflets and passing out materials that could be incorporated into leaflets locally. The shortage of funds meant that the Campaign was not in a position to produce a bulk order of leaflets before July, and there was a feeling that the leaflets needed to incorporate the White Paper and the arguments expressed within it. Yes for Wales had understood that the Government summary of the White Paper, and a number of fact-sheets, would be released at the time of the White Paper itself or shortly after. Instead, the distribution of the document was delayed until after the Bank Holiday. This meant that there was no centrally produced literature to be distributed across Wales.

Literature was produced for different sectoral groups. An excellent leaflet was produced for Women Say Yes, for instance, and there were leaflets produced for ethnic minority groups. Val Feld remembers "we produced all these leaflets in the different languages and they just went, I mean thousands of them." Val was delighted – and stunned – by the response from ethnic minority groups. She attended a big festival in Swansea for Indian and Pakistani independence and set up a Yes for Wales stall. She found that there was a real desire to support the Campaign, "They understood exactly what this was about because they knew about colonialism." She found activists from the ethnic minority communities were highly active in the campaign, such as Councillors Cherry Short and Jaswant Singh in Cardiff and Naz Malik in Swansea. Over the August Bank Holiday there was an important meeting of ethnic minority organisations addressed by Ron Davies, Cherry Short, CRE Commissioner Ray Singh, and activist Jazz Iheamache.

During August, demands from local groups grew. There was a feeling expressed by several that the Pledge Card assumed that people were committed to the campaign. By contrast, the No Campaign had sharp, well-focused literature. Members of the Steering Committee themselves were privately concerned that a central leaflet was not available. It was also starting to cause some difficulties with local groups and with Plaid Cymru, who felt that they had been promised leaflets which had not materialised. By late August it was clear that not enough literature was getting out. Labour MEP Eluned Morgan believed, "The whole of the leafleting strategy, the communication on the ground, was a disaster. People weren't getting any copies." Some Steering Committee members believed that there was insufficient centralised control over the leaflets at that crucial stage – that too many individuals were developing communication materials for local circulation and use, each with strong ideas of their own. This resulted in materials that were not as effective as they might have been, and fear of criticism prevented others producing material at all. Daran Hill, however, believed that the local literature was effective. "Lots of local groups were producing their own, and I think they were amongst some of the best literature that was coming out because they were locally guided." The campaign did produce a template for local groups to produce their own leaflets in mid-August, along with a campaign pack.

Within the Labour Party campaign, there were different problems. Despite the regular weekly strategy meetings there were internal tensions amongst the Welsh Office Ministers and between them and Transport House in Cardiff, between Wales Labour Party Executive members and Alan Barnard of Millbank, and between Transport House officials and their own national referendum co-ordinator Andrew Davies. One particular dispute arose over the funding of one of the Labour leaflets. It was originally to have been funded by Trades Unions for the Labour Party (TULP). Terry Thomas felt that the leaflet should therefore carry an acknowledgement of this, and thought Barnard had agreed to this. In fact, the acknowledgement was ultimately carried in a small strap line. To see it, "you had to use a magnifying glass" said one Labour insider. It was widely believed that Thomas and Barnard did not see eye to eye. Barnard, nicknamed the Governor-General, controlled the budget on behalf of Millbank, and therefore ultimately controlled the campaign.

Labour's campaign on the ground was also patchy. Two constituency MPs who campaigned hard were Rhodri and Julie Morgan. "Cardiff West and Cardiff North decided to campaign jointly. Because of the summer we thought we might have shorter numbers and with people away on holidays it was easier to organise rotas," said Rhodri Morgan. The Morgans found opinion in North

Cardiff particularly running heavily against devolution: "It was horrific, we estimated opinion running 7:1 against devolution." Morgan warned Transport House of the issues being raised. 'It's a gravy train': the Ron-Llew row; the slide to nationalism; quangos will stay; the Scots will get more; a general sense of what good will it do?

But when they went on holiday to West Wales, later in the month, they found things quite different. "We had a couple of sessions in Cardigan and Aberporth. Aberporth was very good, and was the reverse of Whitchurch, a very strong impression of pro-devolution sentiment. The same in Cardigan, although not quite so good." Nick Ainger, campaigning in his own constituency, found things were very good in the Carmarthen area. His constituency party undertook some canvassing, leafleting, regular street stalls, attending shows and events. "We did events, balloons, outside the Somerfield store in Tenby, which is a main sort of area to meet the people, in Tudor Square in Tenby, outside the Co-op in Pembroke Dock." Alun Michael, Labour MP for Cardiff South and Penarth and a Home Office Minister, found

> I was struck then at the fact that whenever you talked to people, if you talked about the institution and the Assembly, they regarded that as nothing to do with them. Those things, the processes of account-ability and the creativity that can come from the Assembly are very much matters that are of interest to politicians and academics and journalists, but not to ordinary people. On the hand if you started to talk to people about their health service and were they satisfied that they had enough say in, for instance, the future of Llandough Hospital or the way in which GP services are driven, or the way schools are organised, they would engage with it and the idea of having an assembly representative who could be held accountable for decisions in Wales was much more attractive and people started to realise what it was all about.

Hain and Davies meanwhile were still criss-crossing Wales. Hain was becoming particularly concerned that the Campaign had to take people so carefully through the arguments. He felt that if there were enough people out, able to canvass one to one, the message could get across. But there weren't enough people. He knew that the media campaign and the events, while important, would not be enough. There was too little understanding of the current system of government, let alone Labour's proposed changes. He was also staggered by the level of hostility he encountered to the Welsh language in parts of the Valleys, and he found deep concern about separatism.

Where they were able to reach people, they were getting posters up. Hain had an excellent experience in the Garw valley, where there was an estate covered with posters. He also recalled talking to four or five pensioners in Pontypridd market, accompanied by several camera crews and journalists, and finding them initially hostile, but by the time he had worked through the arguments about a "Voice for Wales" and the impact on jobs they were asking for stickers. Old-fashioned grass-roots campaigning was what was needed. And Hain knew that Labour's safest seats were rarely accustomed to needing to do that. Jon Owen Jones, then a Government Whip and a year later a Minister, said it almost needed an alternative party structure to create a national campaign. It was difficult for others to campaign in areas not their own. Safe seats did not have the level of preparation and organisation that Labour's target seats had had.

Yes for Wales was succeeding in bringing people together across the parties. Mari James' weekly party meetings were now sharing information, coordinating events and passing on intelligence about developments on the ground and requests from the media. There was considerable collaboration on the ground. Eluned Morgan was campaigning more with Yes for Wales. She found herself sharing platforms with Plaid, the Liberal Democrats and even one Conservative, Viscount St David. "Sharing a platform with a hereditary peer was just something that I wouldn't have dreamed of doing before this campaign, and that was a very strange experience." She was very positive about the way in which people shed their differences. "The same thing in Montgomeryshire, I shared a platform with Lembit Öpik and Helen Mary Jones [of Plaid], so there was a lot of that going on and people were just trying to raise consciousness there."

Even a seat like Brecon and Radnor, where Labour members had worked hard but lost to the Liberal Democrats, saw the two parties splitting up the seat to target the areas in which they were strongest. Livsey was active for the Liberal Democrats all over Wales. "I went to Swansea, I went to Cardiff, Llanelli, Carmarthen, right across the Southern half of Wales. I didn't get to North Wales as much as I would have liked. I went over once into Ceredigion where I'd lived for fourteen years anyway." He recalls campaigning in Newport, Gwent, with Tyrone O'Sullivan and Paul Flynn. "The thing that struck me was that a lot of the English-born people living and working in Newport who were in favour of devolution were sending their children to Welsh schools, they were very angry about the low level of wages in Wales, the low wage economy and the fact that they felt just as exploited as the native Welsh population." In the Valleys, the bus funded by the Democratic Left, the party built after the closure of the Communist Party, was widely welcomed by local Yes groups in the areas it visited. Peter Polish, the Democratic Left secretary, also ensured that the Party's journal *Red Kite* carried several articles and features on the Campaign, and helped with the production of cheap leaflets and posters.

It wasn't possible to create all-party cooperation all over Wales, however. Gareth Thomas MP recalled, "we didn't have the same sort of degree of on the ground co-operation between the parties in North Wales. That appears to have been the case. Probably that's a reflection of the extent to which we'd fought fairly hard-hitting campaigns against each other in the General Election." Thomas acknowledged that for Labour in some places in North Wales, the Yes Campaign was more likely to be viewed as a Plaid front. The overall Labour strategy of focusing on its heartland areas was also more problematic in North Wales, where areas were not so monolithically Labour. In parts of North Wales, Plaid themselves accepted that they were the Yes Campaign. "In some areas, like my own constituency, to all intents and purposes Plaid was the Yes Campaign," said Dafydd Wigley. "There were some Labour people, there were half a dozen Labour activists, Tom Jones, Transport and General and one or two of his colleagues who did work hard." The Wrexham group led by Labour councillor Stella Matthews was very active.

In the Valleys, Darren Evans was working hard to get local groups off the ground. Some clearly ran themselves, like Neath and Port Talbot. Pontypridd was another model group, led by lecturer Dave Egan. Evans set up groups in the Cynon Valley, with Tyrone O'Sullivan and Plaid member Phil Richards and the Liberal Democrats. Merthyr he found to be a nightmare. But there were strong groups in the Rhondda led by local activist Cliff True. There was also a group in Torfaen, and the very active group in Blaenau Gwent. Each had about 10-15 activists. Evans was based at the NUM building in Pontypridd, where the photocopying facilities were particularly useful.

Plaid's campaign was, according to Dafydd Wigley, largely an invisible one. "Most of the campaign was going on out of sight by means of telephone campaigning. It grew as the campaigning went on, people realised that you were able to talk." In some areas this worked particularly well. "In my own constituency we phoned some 13,000 out of the 16,500 telephone numbers that are in my constituency. I think we had about 10,000 or so responses which we could action, and we did in fact send out targeted letters for those who had voted Plaid in the General Election in my name, and for those who had voted for one of the other parties in the name of the Yes Campaign."

The telephoning was done under the name of Yes for Wales in three shifts, 2-4 pm, 4.30-6.30 pm and 7-9.30 pm. Wigley said there was no difficulty in getting a large crowd to do the telephoning. The same technique was undertaken in Meirionydd and Anglesey. Cardiff Plaid members led by their local Chairman Owen John Thomas operated a successful telephone canvassing operation in the Valleys as well, covering 50,000 homes. The results were fed back to Plaid's headquarters in Cardiff on a nightly basis. An important role was played by Ieuan Wyn Jones. "Ieuan Wyn particularly took this on because he's a pragmatic Baptist and there's no better person than a pragmatic Baptist," said Dafydd Elis-Thomas. Jones explained that the party had to train up its activists in the technology and methodology. "It was a mammoth task," he said.

Labour, in contrast, did less telephone canvassing. Barnard found himself being pushed to set up an extensive telephone canvassing operation. But having worked out how many voters there were in Wales, how many volunteers Labour had, how many telephone lines and how many calls they could make, he decided that it would make hardly a dint in the number of voters. Instead, Labour used phones to mobilise volunteers for events or to get the message out through a telephone tree, and occasionally to test reaction from voters. Andrew Davies reckoned that Labour had very few workers and it was inevitable that their key activities were focused around events and the media, no matter how difficult that was. Coordination between the Government, the Labour Party, and the Yes Campaign was held together by informal meetings every two to three weeks, and near daily telephone contact. Weekly meetings were also held between Yes for Wales and the three pro-devolution political parties.

In Ceredigion, Plaid Cymru was providing much of the funding for the Yes Campaign. Cynog Dafis was disappointed that there wasn't any national Yes for Wales literature early on. The Plaid member of the local Steering Committee pressed for the distribution of a locally-produced leaflet. Dafis said "In Ceredigion the local Yes for Wales Campaign produced its own pamphlet, and

Plaid Cymru I think paid for most of it, and we put in £500."
There was some joint activity with Labour in Cardigan and
Aberystwyth on the streets through Yes for Wales, but he felt that
the local campaign was not well run because Plaid did not put its
own machine in to run it.

But where local campaigns were well-run, local literature did the
job. Neath's local question and answer leaflet was widely circulated
around South Wales and drawn on by many groups. Kevin
Brennan of the Cardiff Yes for Wales group remembers: "We had
produced our own materials and so on, so we were actually quite
reasonably geared up, possibly to be able to do as much as
anybody would have been. We had a very good core support team
and Committee meetings weekly." His colleague, media academic
and former Councillor Geoff Mungham remembers good local
support from businesses with £10,000 raised in cash and kind, and
huge activity and presence in Splott Market. But Brennan felt that
the Campaign didn't have enough people going out on the
doorstep. "There wasn't enough door to door doorstep campaigning going on, we were alright at the stunts and events but the actual
meat and drink of door to door campaigning wasn't happening."
The group did leaflet football and rugby matches and also Cardiff
railway station, which also helped to get the message through to the
Valleys via local commuters. Val Feld remembers that "the
Swansea group was great once it got going." She found that people
had little trouble working together. "Plaid and the Lib Dems were
the two sort of most powerful groups" in the local Yes Campaign.
Labour ran its own campaign in Swansea but there was collaboration between the two.

All of these issues were reviewed when the Yes for Wales
Steering Committee met in Neath Civic Centre on Saturday 23
August. The campaigners were at a high point of expectation. Just
two days before, Neil Jenkins, the Wales and British Lions back
had undertaken a photocall at Pontypridd's Sardis Road ground:
he was precisely the kind of Valleys-based popular celebrity the
campaign was looking for. His kicking had helped deliver the
British Lions' victories in South Africa earlier in the summer.
There was also a certain poignancy in the fact that he was a particular hero of Just Say No's Tim Williams.

Yes for Wales Convenor Hywel Francis told activists not to be
complacent about the chances of a Yes-vote. "If we lose in
September, the case for an Assembly is lost for a generation. The
summer silly season is over and the campaign begins in earnest

next week. From now until 18 September we must strain every sinew to deliver the biggest possible vote for an Assembly."

He also urged Yes campaigners to remind the public that the Yes Campaign had no public money and no millionaire backers. "We have to raise every penny that we spend. We need to raise another twenty thousand pounds to get our message across. We know that the No Campaign plans a major advertising push in the last few weeks."

At the Neath meeting, there were representatives from Bridgend and Ogmore, Blaenau Gwent, Llanelli, Neath, Aberavon, Ceredigion, Ystradgynlais/Brecon and Radnor, Swansea and Cardiff, as well as the Wales Labour Party, Plaid Cymru, the Welsh Liberal Democrats, Democratic Left and Unison. The officers outlined the Campaign timetable for the final month, explaining how the Campaign would be re-launched on the Tuesday following the Bank Holiday. More materials would be available from the Cardiff office. Leaflets and campaign newspapers were particularly stressed as a priority by local groups.

Themes for the final weeks were outlined. Officers had already briefed local groups that they wanted local launches in the week after the Bank Holiday to illustrate the campaign theme 'All Wales Supports an Assembly'. There were a number of press conferences, public meetings and debates scheduled for the week. The following day, Cymdeithas yr Iaith completed its walk from Bala to Cardiff. Catatonia played a gig in Swansea with the Yes for Wales banner behind. (Cerys Matthews from Catatonia had already featured on the front cover of August's issue of *Barn*, wearing a Yes for Wales T-shirt). The Super Furry Animals wore Yes for Wales T-shirts at one of their gigs. Yes for Wales itself had hoped to organise a concert with a number of the top Welsh bands, but it proved impossible to get agreement on a date and to find a sponsor.

Campaigners were in good heart. The parties themselves had a lot to report. The Labour Party had distributed its first leaflet and a second would be unveiled the following week along with bus advertising. Unison had mailed out to all their members. The Liberal Democrats were active through local Yes Campaigns but were producing their own Yes posters. Plaid were mobilising their own voters and working through Yes groups. They explained how they were undertaking telephone polling. The Llanelli and Ceredigion and Cardiff groups had been leafleting using their own locally-produced leaflets. Cardiff had produced credit-card sized pledge cards. Several groups were holding local meetings and manning street stalls. Ystradgynlais were working through local rugby clubs. Brecon and Radnor had had a specific focus on farmers. Most groups said they were not expecting to canvass as they anticipated local political parties taking responsibility for that. A mailing had just gone out to all Yes supporters across Wales.

The National Campaign had a range of matters to announce at its press conference on 26 August. Again, there had been careful planning in the lead-up to the post-Bank Holiday launch. Journalists had been told in advance that the press conference would launch the Yes Campaign's final drive for victory, outline its strategy for the final stages, reveal more celebrity names and an advertising poster. Behind the scenes the former Brookside actor Stifyn Parri – a founder of SWS, Sociable, Welsh and Sexy – had been working hard at getting celebrity support. Yes for Wales had stories targeted at different newspapers. The office was open on the Bank Holiday Monday lining up stories in the *Financial Times* for the business community (encouraging the paper to run the story that the Welsh CBI had denounced a No Campaign leaflet). The name of Jason Hughes (the actor who had played Warren in the cult TV series *This Life*) was let out as a Yes supporter. (In the Welsh version of the press release, it was suggested that he had been a star of *That's Life* rather than *This Life*!) For the tabloids, there was the news that celebrities supporting Yes for Wales now included Ruth Madoc, which was picked up by the *Daily Mirror* on the Wednesday. The campaign was also able to announce that it had received a message of support from Bryn Terfel who led a long list of celebrities including actresses Rakie Ayola and Lisa Palfrey, actors Matthew Rhys, Brian Hibberd, Andrew Howard, Keith Allen, Ioan Gruffydd, and Mark Lewis Jones; the producer of the cult film *Twin Town* set in Swansea, Kevin Allen, and opera singers Dennis O'Neill and Gwyn Hughes Jones.

The press conference, attended by Mari James, Val Feld, Kevin Morgan, Eluned Morgan and myself, saw the announcement of events across Wales that week. There were to be further press conferences in Swansea, Cardiff, Meirionydd. There were leafleting blitzes in Porthcawl, Bridgend, Llanelli, Swansea, Pontypool, Montgomeryshire, Ceredigion, Brynmawr, Neath, Cardiff and Aberavon. Public meetings were planned in Wrexham and Ebbw Vale, Cynon Valley and Flintshire, and a concert and meeting in Haverfordwest. Women Say Yes were to hold a rally at Whitland's Hywel Dda Memorial Park.

The Campaign also unveiled its new poster, 'Time to Take Over the Remote Control,' which was to tour Wales on the Advan. The poster was designed by Harry Barlow, of the advertising agency Issue Communications, who had worked for many campaigning organisations, including trades unions and local authorities as well as charities. A photocall was held outside the National Museum with Kevin Morgan, Val Feld and Eluned Morgan.

The same morning Ron Davies began the delivery of the government's shorter version of the White Paper with a photocall in Cardiff. Peter Hain launched it the next day in North Wales. The leaflet was to be delivered door to door during the week. Yes for Wales campaigners were relieved that it was finally going out.

The next day, the Liberal Democrats re-launched their campaign. Richard Livsey and Lembit Öpik called the next 24 days the most important in Wales' history. The Assembly was critical for Wales' economy and for jobs. The same day, Ron Davies outlined the importance of the Nolan principles for members of the Assembly, who must be people of high calibre. He welcomed a statement from the CBI which asked him to answer six questions about the Assembly, including the right of business to be consulted on legislation affecting it, the need for an Annual Report measuring performance and a statutory limit on the costs of the Assembly. In Wrexham that evening, Steering Committee member Stella Matthews had organised the Wrexham Says Yes launch with Labour MPs Martyn Jones and Dr John Marek, Liberal Democrat Peer Lord Thomas of Gresford and Plaid Cymru peer Dafydd Elis-Thomas. The following day Flintshire Says Yes was launched by Labour MP Barry Jones, Lord Thomas, former Clwyd County Council Chief Executive Mervyn Phillips, Flintshire County Council Leader Tom Middlehurst and Denbighshire County Council Chairman Eryl Williams.

There was now real momentum behind the Campaign and a string of events every day. More actors including Judith Humphries and most of the cast of *Pobol y Cwm*, Boyd Clack (who jokingly suggested opponents should have their throats cut), and many others came out in favour at the Actors Say Yes launches in Cardiff and Bangor later in the week. Mari Gwilym, who organised fifty actors to turn out at Theatr Gwynedd, said "if we don't act now we will lose this opportunity". The broadcasters were fixing regular slots in news programmes and the media in general were now beginning to give the Campaign the flavour of a by-election. The Liberal Democrats, Plaid and the Welsh Greens signed a joint declaration in favour of the Assembly at a press conference where they were represented by Richard Livsey (Liberal Democrats), Cynog Dafis (Plaid) and Kevin Jakeway (Greens). The declaration included several points arguing for the democratisation of Welsh life, an effective voice in Europe, a commitment to sustainability, and to proportional representation as a basis for inclusivity. Daran Hill was staggered by the level of press interest for this. "We didn't expect it to be big, and I remember Mari and I being amazed how big it was in terms of the amount of attention it received."

There was a further statement that day issued by Yes for Wales. Concerned by a claim made earlier in the week by Denzil Davies in the *Western Mail's* agriculture section, that Welsh farmers would lose out in Europe under an Assembly, Yes for Wales issued a joint statement from Labour MEP Eluned Morgan, LibDem MP Richard Livsey and Plaid MP Cynog Dafis on the benefits to agriculture of the Assembly. They knew that Denzil Davies had been peddling this line for some weeks to useful effect and it needed countering. Their statement pointed out that agriculture was already devolved. It referred to the damage done to Welsh agriculture under the Conservatives. It explained that the Secretary of State for Wales had always had the right to attend Ministerial meetings in Europe but had never taken it up. Now the Secretary of State would have the full backing of the Assembly. Next day the *Western Mail* said "The Yes for Wales rebuttal machine was cranked up yesterday to head off fears that a Welsh Assembly might be bad for rural Wales."

That day, Labour's business manifesto for the Assembly, *A Positive Partnership,* was launched at the offices of Epitaxial Products International Ltd outside Cardiff by Ron Davies, former WDA Chief Executive David Waterstone, and Nick Williams, Managing Director of the company Euroclad. It said that the Assembly would mean a better skilled workforce, modern infrastructure, more investment and strong small businesses. Davies was also able to respond to the CBI statement earlier in the week, promising that business would be consulted by the Assembly on key decisions.

There were other events too. Yes for Wales launched its campaign for the Valleys in Nantgarw, with Hywel Francis, Unison official Linda Lumb, local engineering employer Gwyn Williams, Councillor Jeff Jones, Leader of Bridgend Council and Kim Howells, MP for Pontypridd and Minister for Lifelong Learning. The theme of the press conference was "The Valleys Say Yes to

Jobs, Education and Training." Howells, who had been attacked as a devo-sceptic by nationalists amongst others, called for the people of the South Wales Valleys to support the Government's proposals for a Welsh Assembly.

Michael Foot joined young Labour campaigners for devolution in Cardiff and Merthyr. The actress Julie Christie joined Eluned Morgan and the self-styled King of Hay Richard Booth to launch Hay on Wye Says Yes, taking the campaign to the border. Unison helped to coordinate the launch of Health-workers Say Yes.

Later that afternoon, the *Western Mail* called to ask for Yes for Wales' comments on the opinion poll it would be running the next day. It was the first since the beginning of July. *Western Mail* reporter Nick Horton teased the Campaign that it had not yet got to 50%, but it was clearly ahead and apparently gaining ground. When the Yes for Wales officers met that evening for their weekly meeting, they believed the Campaign was on a roll.

Nine: Death of a Princess

The North American Gymanfu Ganu was coming to an end on Saturday 30 August when Dafydd Wigley was asked to do an interview for an American television station. There in Milwaukee, his wife Elinor had just finished playing her harp in front of four thousand people. Wigley had been on a brief trip, giving three lectures on the referendum on four days. Dafydd Iwan had also flown out for the concert. Wigley recalls "As I was being interviewed, they had a fax message brought forward to the interviewer which said that there'd been this accident in Paris." Wigley was interviewed on his reaction to the news that Diana, Princess of Wales had been injured in a car crash. By the time he got back to his hotel late that night, the news had come through that Diana had been killed. "Next morning of course, when I got up to go for breakfast, the whole television crew's waiting for me down there to comment." Wigley was aware, at one level, of the absurdity of the interviews, thousands of miles from home, "She was Princess of Wales, I was an MP for Wales, I mean they assumed we were at least first cousins." The Plaid Cymru President was conscious not only of the immediate tragedy of the bereavement, but of the potential impact on the referendum campaign, though like most people he was not aware of the kind of momentum that the tragedy would gather in Britain.

About the same time as Dafydd Wigley had retired for the night, several thousand miles away, in his London flat, Alun Michael was being woken by a 5.30 am call from the Labour Press Office at Millbank. He had travelled to London to appear on *Breakfast with Frost* to explain the Government's plans for dealing with sex offenders. Now he was briefed on the situation and told he would be making the first official government response. He spoke to David Hill, the Labour Party's Chief Press Officer, and discussed the approach to be taken. From the early hours, right through until lunchtime, the Cardiff South MP did one broadcast after another, giving the Government reaction to the tragedy.

John Osmond, the Director of the Institute for Welsh Affairs, was also in the United States, about to leave Newark airport to fly back to Britain. "I went to get a cup of coffee from this black woman who was serving and she heard my accent, she asked me if I was English and I said 'no I'm Welsh actually' and she said 'ah gee, you must be so sad'." Osmond saw the television and realised what had happened. What strikes him now most forcefully was the statement by the Prime Minister. "I remember thinking how bloody amazing Blair was, seizing that, you know the talent of that man, the way he kind of took hold of that whole event and turned it round."

For the Yes Campaign, there were hard choices. I woke up that morning and put on the radio to listen to the Radio Wales farming programme. I was worried about the impact of statements over the previous few weeks by Denzil Davies suggesting Wales' farmers might lose out in Europe because the Assembly Ministers would not have the power to attend European Council meetings. Activists in the rural areas of Wales had been warning about the impact of these statements on the ground, and Yes for Wales had lined up a story to address the issue. Instead of the farming programme, I found James Naughtie of Radio Four's *Today* programme. It took a few minutes before it dawned that there had been some serious tragedy. I heard one of the commentators talking about the young Royal Princes and the "violence" of their mother's death. It sounded like there had been an assassination. It was several minutes before the radio bulletin explained what had happened.

That day, the Yes Campaign tried to make sense of what the impact would be on the Campaign itself. There were phone calls back and forth between members of the Steering Committee, Government insiders and Ministers. For a while, it seemed that the Government might be pressured into abandoning the referendum; some figures in Scotland Forward, the Yes Campaign in Scotland, themselves wondered if that might have to happen. I spoke to Nigel Smith, the businessman who had founded and now led Scotland Forward, and made it clear that the Welsh Campaign wanted to carry on. The Steering Committee had to make a decision about its press conference the next day. The Campaign had lined up two Conservative supporters of devolution to come to Cardiff and declare their support. It was obvious that this press conference would have to be cancelled, but I didn't want the Campaign to make any statements until it was clear what the Government was going to say. I was conscious that it was important that all of the pro-devolution organisations reacted as one. Mari James was in the Yes for Wales office on the day; it was Daran's first Sunday off in weeks. She was also clear that the Campaign would have to post-pone and cancel events, but it was still not clear for how long. She had the job of co-ordinating the response, and letting the media and the local Yes groups know what the plan was. Mari and I spoke to members of the Steering Committee, staff, and key activists such as the Rev. Aled Edwards, one of the founders of the Christian Ministers Say Yes group and active in the Cardiff campaign. Edwards was emphatic that activity would have to be suspended. We didn't need telling. But it took quite some time during the day for the Government's position to be finalised. Eventually, at 3 o'clock, we agreed a press statement saying that the Yes for Wales Campaign was suspending national campaigning on devolution and asking local groups to do likewise. "The people of Wales will grieve for Diana. Our thoughts are with the Prince of Wales and his sons and members of the Royal Family and the other families who have lost their loved ones in the Paris tragedy," said the statement.

The suspension of campaigning meant that there would be no press conferences on Monday 1 September or Tuesday 2 September. On the Monday, Buckingham Palace announced the funeral arrangements. Mari issued a further press release, announcing that Yes for Wales had suspended its national and public campaigning up to and including the day of the funeral. She organised a mailing to all Yes for Wales groups telling them that the Campaign would re-launch on the morning of Monday 8 September. Groups were asked to cancel public meetings and leafleting. She also clarified that it was acceptable to carry on with routine private organisational meetings, working out what materials would be needed for the rest of the campaign and ordering them, and planning last-minute distribution of the Campaign newspaper. She pointed out that the postponement of activity made the final weekend of 13 and 14 September even more crucial, and plans should be in hand for town centre leafleting and other activities.

The political parties had to make similar decisions. Alan Barnard had gone back to London that weekend to see his team, Chelsea, win their first home game of the season 4-2 against Southampton. He had been planning to travel back to Cardiff on the Sunday morning. Instead, after hearing the news, he made some phone calls and it was agreed he should go into Millbank on Monday to determine what the campaign could and couldn't do. The Wales Labour Party's organiser, Andrew Davies, had heard the news on radio in bed. He discussed it later in the day with the Wales Labour

Party Chairman, Terry Thomas, and they both concluded that it could have a significant effect on the Campaign.

For Yes campaigners, the tragedy broke the momentum that the Campaign believed had been achieved. The day before Diana's death, the *Western Mail* had run the first opinion poll for almost two months. The figures showed the Yes Campaign well ahead. 'Wales heads for a Yes vote' was the headline. The research had taken place during the middle of August, before the Government had begun to distribute its summary of the White Paper. The poll put the Yes Campaign on 42%, the No Campaign on 22%. After the don't-knows had been squeezed, the Yes total rose to 48% and the No total to 26%. The Campaign appeared to be strengthening in the Valleys, the result of much of the effort by both the Labour Party and Yes for Wales. Yes for Wales welcomed the poll, but in its statement focused on the need to avoid complacency: "These findings are very encouraging. But the only poll that matters is the one on September 18. This is not a time for complacency. We are urging all our local groups and our activists to redouble their efforts. We must ensure a good turn-out and a clear victory."

For activists the poll confirmed what was happening on the ground. Nick Ainger had told the Secretary of State that in the Carmarthen area the Yes Campaign was walking it, at least two to one. "I think when the opinion poll gave us that really positive message then it sort of confirmed the core message that we'd received. I mean, I think it's fair to say that things were running our way." Reports the day before Diana's death had been universally good across Wales. Ron Davies himself felt that on the Saturday, 30 August, the day before Diana's death, "things were really good. I remember going home that night, and thinking great, we've got it, it's coming our way." Peter Hain had been campaigning on that Saturday in Merthyr Tydfil, where the reception had been fantastic. To Hain, the Campaign felt like it was moving ahead for the first time. In North Wales, Home Secretary Jack Straw had been campaigning and again the mood was positive. Jon Owen Jones MP felt the tide was turning. In Wrexham that day there was a stunning success which was noted by campaigners across Wales. The rugby international between Wales and Romania, held at Wrexham's Racecourse ground, was leafleted by Stella Matthews' Wrexham Yes for Wales troops, and those watching at home on television could see a mass of Yes for Wales stickers adorning the spectators in the ground.

Kevin Morgan felt that the Campaign had gained momentum

153

steadily during August. "I felt we were building up a momentum in the last two weeks of August and suddenly we were completely derailed. At that time my sense was that this will be a profoundly important event for the No Campaign, that suddenly Britishness would take precedence over Welshness. At worst, Welshness, a vote for the Yes-vote, could even be construed by some people as almost a form of disloyalty, that was what I was worried about." Rhodri Morgan believed it did have an impact on Britishness. "If you were in a uniform you were against devolution, that seemed to be the rule, and maybe it was the same thing basically, it was like cloaking you in a uniform, we were all in the British army under Diana as it were." Dafydd Elis-Thomas also noted its impact: "I think it just froze the whole thing. I think it froze the whole debate, the opportunity of taking the debate on. And I know that there were certain initiatives the Yes Campaign had which we couldn't use because of all that." Ieuan Wyn Jones felt it broke the momentum, but that there was little evidence when Plaid resumed telephone canvassing that any real difference had been made. The Liberal Democrat Leader in Wales, Richard Livsey, was "extremely uneasy" about the potential impact on the Campaign.

Daran Hill remembers that it had a major practical effect on the campaign. "Suddenly this happened, [it] knocked a few days out of our Campaign period, and we had to compress all our Campaign activity down into a few weeks, and a lot of press conferences and themes that we were hoping to run with." Among the events which the Yes Campaign had to cancel were a planned seminar for business to be organised by the Business Forum on Devolution just two days before Diana's funeral was scheduled. But the biggest impact of all was on the Campaign's media strategy. A good relationship had been built with the *Daily Mirror*, who had run a series of stories in the week before Diana's death on the celebrities joining the Yes Campaign. But with Diana's death filling several pages – indeed, most of the issue – for all of the following week and much of the week after, there was little space to focus on the Campaign, and the possibility of dedicated Welsh issues was lost until the last few days.

By the time of Diana's death, the Campaign had been underway on the ground in earnest throughout Wales for five weeks. The White Paper launch had been the catalyst. At last, the Campaign had a clear policy on which to focus. The Yes Campaign knew what it was defending against the No Campaign. It had a No Campaign to aim at. Events were being organised all over Wales by the Yes Campaign and its local groups.

Diana's death had knocked all this activity off course. Peter Hain admitted to the *Western Mail* that the Campaign had lost momentum. He was worried about the impact on turnout in particular. Labour had been due to launch a full General Election-style campaign, he revealed. The academic political scientist, Denis Balsom, felt that people had forgotten about devolution. Months after the event, Philip Gould surmised that only an 'earthquake' could have come between his prediction of a clear Yes win and the final result. Diana was it. Nothing else in his long experience of polling and focus groups could explain the difference. One right-wing commentator, Simon Heffer, claimed that the event was damaging to devolution as it would ensure a rekindling of national unity. This was rebutted by the Yes Campaign, reminding the press that devolution was not about the break-up of Britain. During the course of the week leading up to the funeral, there were rows about whether or not the campaigning moratorium had been broken. Low-level leafleting had been allowed for, but the No Campaign attacked Labour for allowing it.

Yes for Wales' officers had to grip the campaign and determine how best to re-launch. The plan for the last fortnight was considerably revised. Events were reshuffled. We relaunched on 8 September, the day that William Hague returned to Wales to lead the Conservative No Campaign. Yes for Wales greeted Hague as the "real leader of the No Campaign" in a press release revealing the extent of Conservative organisational support for the No Campaign at the local level. Yes for Wales accused Hague of treating Wales like an English county, pointing out that Hague had used the same form of words to appoint Jonathan Evans spokesman for Wales as he had in appointing David Harris spokesman for Cornwall. According to the Yes Campaign, "Mr Hague's policy for Wales is the word NO. No Welsh MPs, No Shadow Secretary for Wales, No to an Assembly". Labour also pursued the real leader line, with Peter Hain saying that the No Campaign was purely a Tory front. They also attacked his performance on the spending costs of quangos.

But Yes for Wales' re-launch press conference had a more positive focus. The Campaign knew it had to promote the benefits of an Assembly, as well as counter the attacks from the No camp. Yes for Wales launched *The Economic Case for An Assembly* with Professor Philip Cooke, Professor of Regional Development and Director of the Centre of Advanced Studies (CASS) at University College Cardiff, and Professor Kevin Morgan, this time in his academic capacity as Professor of European Regional Development.

Yes for Wales was again able to announce further local activities for the Campaign as local groups got into gear again. Amongst the announcements was the news that local Yes Campaign shops were to be opened in Llangefni and Caernarfon. There were to be public meetings in Cwmbran, Pyle, Pembrokeshire, Brynmawr, Aberdare, Aberystwyth, Maesteg, Llanidloes, Colwyn Bay, Machynlleth, Welshpool, Coity, Bridgend, Monmouth, Barry, Cardiff and Newtown. Leafleting blitzes went on in Clwyd, Alyn and Deeside, Wrexham, Carmarthen, Holyhead, Pwllheli, Arfon, Llangefni, Newtown, Conwy, Bala and Meirionydd.

The Labour campaign also got back on track. The day before, Culture Secretary Chris Smith had undertaken a series of engagements in Wales and had joined the Cardiff Yes Campaign at Splott market. On Monday, Ron Davies announced ten pledges for the Assembly. He said a Labour Assembly would make education the priority; find work for young people; divert NHS money from bureaucracy to treatment; cut the cost of the quangos; modernise British democracy; give a voice to every region of Wales; represent all communities in Wales, both Welsh- and English-speaking; support farmers and improve rural services; clean up politics and change the selection system for candidates; create an economic powerhouse. He also announced that there would be a cabinet style of government in the Assembly, one of the issues which the CBI had felt strongly about. A poll of CBI members seemed to show them marginally in favour.

MPs and Ministers returned to the fray and the Government announced a range of Ministers would be visiting Wales in the last ten days. That evening Lawyers Say Yes was launched in Cardiff by Attorney General John Morris QC MP, the former Secretary of State for Wales. He said that the Tories had a history of opposing transfers of power to Wales, beginning with their opposition to the creation of the post of Secretary of State for Wales.

There was now real intensity in the campaign, and Labour and the Yes Campaign were in danger of falling over each other. Even though Scotland was into the last few days of its campaign, the London media was actively covering Wales. They had decided Scotland was a foregone conclusion and Wales was where the action was. Some newspapers had begun speculating about the fate of the Secretary of State if he lost, and there had been one or two highly partisan profiles of him and whispering about the possible successor. At the same time, the No Campaign was coordinating a series of announcements from the dissident Labour MPs who had begun to declare their opposition. The Yes Campaign response was sharp and brutal. "Tony Blair says Yes. Ray Powell says No. We're glad it's not the other way around". On the Tuesday, with the news that Mrs Thatcher was campaigning in Scotland for a No-vote, the Yes Campaign rushed out a release labelling the dissident Labour MPs as 'Thatcher's Friends'.

Yes for Wales, true to its promise of several months before, had also found two Conservative supporters of devolution, former MEP Peter Price and former Young Conservative Chairman Phil Pedley and held a press conference with them. Pedley said "The more I have heard and seen of the Just Say No Campaign posturing, the more appalled I have become that some Conservatives are pandering to such infantile histrionics."

Press conferences were now a daily event. Anxious to hit the European theme once more and counter 'No' propaganda, Yes for Wales held a press conference with Welsh members of the Committee on the Regions, who said: "Wales will be the Cinderella of Europe without an Assembly". The press conference once again brought together members of different parties, with Councillors Dr John Evans from Caerphilly, Eurig Wyn from Gwynedd, and Brian Smith of Torfaen. They said "Wales needs an Assembly working with local government and our partners in Europe to improve our economy which is currently the poorest in mainland Britain. Not only do we need devolution but we need devolved government within Wales. The proposed national economic development agency will be a means to that end with regional offices established for North Wales, Mid Wales, South Wales and South-East Wales working closely with local authorities and local businesses."

That press conference took place on the morning that the *Guardian* published a poll suggesting the vote was on a knife-edge. The *Western Mail* the next day was headlined "Poll says Yes support is wobbling". The poll had the vote at 37% Yes and 36% No, with 27% undecided. It was a real shock for the Yes for Wales Campaign, and for Labour. HTV had been in the middle of fieldwork for a poll over the weekend of Diana's death, but had cancelled it when the tragedy occurred. The poll heightened the tension in the Yes Campaign, though publicly the view was expressed that it was a rogue. For Yes for Wales, Daran Hill expressed surprise that a poll should have been held over a period of national mourning. The poll had relied on a UK-wide survey plus a booster sample for Wales. Labour's North Wales coordinator Gareth Thomas said that Labour had some doubts about it, but that it showed there was no room for complacency. Comparing the poll to those in 1979 did calm people's nerves though. A week before the vote in Wales in 1979, the No camp had been leading by 58% to 27%.

In Swansea that day, the local Yes group put on a press conference to draw attention to the importance of the Assembly for young people. A further important intervention came on the benefits front, with the Institute of Welsh Affairs issuing its report on the likely impact of an Assembly on the Welsh economy. Written by Professor Ross MacKay of University College of North Wales, Bangor and Rick Audas of Newcastle University, it argued that Welsh prosperity had declined relative to the rest of Britain over the previous twenty years. Brian Morgan of University College Cardiff, in a commentary on the report, said that his experience as Chief Economist of the WDA had been that the Welsh Office had failed to defend Wales. Gerry Holtham, the Welsh-born Director of the Institute of Public Policy Research, wrote the foreword to the document again calling for an Assembly.

Labour launched its campaign scratch-card, in a photocall in Whitchurch High Street with Ron Davies and English Regions Minister Dick Caborn, who used the opportunity to warn Wales that Regional Development Agencies were coming to England. The scratch-cards were a stunt dreamed up by Alan Barnard to get the participation of ordinary Labour voters. This involved people scratching off numbers to find the real benefits of the Assembly. Thousands were distributed. Meanwhile, Housing and Local Government minister Hilary Armstrong visited tenants in Cardiff.

That night, one of the main Conservative No campaigners, Jonathan Evans, told a *Guardian* public meeting in Cardiff that he expected some "surprising people" would still come out and declare they would be voting No. Labour and Yes campaigners were concerned that Evans might know of another possible Labour dissident. The *Guardian* meeting was the setting for the only photocall of the campaign involving the three Leaders of the pro-devolution political parties, Ron Davies, Richard Livsey and Dafydd Wigley.

By Thursday, the morning of the Scottish vote, there were almost too many press conferences addressing a range of issues. Yes for Wales organised a photocall for Rugby player Nigel Walker with Ron Davies. In Treforest, Kim Howells joined Pontypridd

Yes for Wales campaigner Dave Egan, Dr John Pugh of the University of Wales Institute, Dr Sonia Reynolds of the Amman Valley Initiative and Matthew Kent, president of the Students Union at the University of Glamorgan for a press conference on education. Ron Davies issued a statement on Europe, designed to counter claims by Denzil Davies that Wales would be less powerful under an Assembly. Ron Davies said that he had cleared through Cabinet that Wales would have the same powers in Europe as Scotland. Wales, like Scotland, would have nine areas of similar powers, including the right to scrutinise European legislative proposals, the right to open a representative office, and the right to be involved in negotiations on the structural funds. A statement was issued by Alan Kreppel, the Managing Director of Cardiff Bus, one of Wales' largest bus companies, saying an Assembly was essential to improve Wales' transport system. Liberal Democrat Leader Paddy Ashdown was in Carmarthen campaigning with farmers, before moving on to Port Talbot, the Rhondda and Pontypridd. That day, the *South Wales Echo* issued a supplement which listed the views of all Wales' MPs, demonstrating that only a few were opposed. Ted Rowlands, MP for Merthyr, while attacking the Yes for Wales claim that those voting No were 'Thatcher's Friends', nevertheless said he would be voting Yes. Welsh Office Minister Win Griffiths spoke to the Federation of Master Builders. Plaid Cymru's Ieuan Wyn Jones said that the Assembly would be good for agriculture. A Spanish MEP, Juan Colon, joined the campaign alongside South Wales' Wayne David MEP. The new Tory Peer, Lord (Wyn) Roberts, appeared to concede Wales was heading for a Yes-vote when he said that he would seek to strengthen the Devolution Bill when it reached the Lords.

That night, Labour held a rally in Llantrisant with Kim Howells, Deputy Prime Minister John Prescott and Siân Lloyd. Cardiff Yes for Wales supporters gathered in the Yes for Wales office to watch the Scottish votes come in, with a posse of broadcasters and journalists there to record the reaction. Mari James, Vice-Chair of the campaign, had left for Scotland two days before, where she took part in a *Panorama* devolution debate on the eve of the Scottish poll. Links between the Welsh and Scottish campaigns were very good, and they provided photo-opportunities for the Yes Campaign to cash in on the Scottish victory. The size of the Scottish result delighted Yes for Wales supporters – but what would it mean for Wales?

The next day, Friday 12 September, Yes for Wales joined Ron

Davies to welcome Chancellor Gordon Brown at Cardiff station with a congratulations card, and a banner with the final week's message, 'Scotland Voted Yes – Don't Let Wales Get Left Behind'. A congratulations card was handed to victorious Yes campaigners in Scotland as well. Brown travelled to meet miners at Tower Colliery, where he declared "a new Wales is emerging as we modernise our economy and modernise our institutions." He also visited Merthyr with Alun Michael. Later that day at a press conference Ron Davies announced that Assembly candidates would be properly vetted to ensure high calibre candidates came forward, addressing one of the concerns of the CBI.

Yes for Wales had planned for the Scottish victory and press releases were tailored for Wrexham, Swansea, Newport and Cardiff to welcome it. During the morning the Prime Minister flew to Scotland to congratulate campaigners there and it soon became clear that he was on his way to Cardiff as well, to speak to the crowds and to lay a stone at the new Millennium Stadium. The Labour Party was desperate for the right atmosphere to be generated when Blair arrived at the bandstand at Queen Street, but lacked the contacts. Blodwen Jones, the Campaign administrator, arranged for the WNO's Brass Ensemble to appear to play in the bandstand. Yes banners and Labour banners were present in the crowd as Blair urged a Yes-vote in Wales as well, and Yes and Labour leaflets were distributed in the crowd as the Just Say No Campaign began an argument in front of the cameras. The Prime Minister said that devolution meant a straight choice between government by quangos and government by the people. But Yes for Wales campaigners were disappointed by the attitude of the Labour campaign, which had ensured no Yes for Wales banners appeared in front of Blair.

During the week Yes for Wales had organised national leaflets for distribution across Wales and taken orders for a four-page campaign newspaper to be distributed across Wales by local activists over the final weekend. The newspapers were delivered at the Cardiff office while Blair was speaking in Queen Street. I wrote the paper overnight in tabloid style. It featured Neil Jenkins wearing a Yes for Wales T-shirt on the front page. The newspaper put once more the standard message that Wales must not get left behind, and urged voters to back an Assembly for jobs, schools, housing, roads and hospitals. It repeated the line that only the Conservatives opposed an Assembly, and listed the supporters and opponents of the idea. It also answered people's questions about the costs of the Assembly and how it would be paid for. Nearly 200,000 copies were distributed across Wales that afternoon from the Yes for Wales office. Howard Matthews, husband of Councillor Stella Matthews, the driving force behind Yes for Wales in the North-East, drove a large batch to North Wales. Darren Evans took 60,000 to 70,000 up to the Valleys. They went very fast. Others went to local groups around Wales and via Plaid Cymru and the Liberal Democrats. They were distributed over the weekend through door-to-door deliveries and at street-stalls and stunts.

Yes for Wales was mindful of the polls and aware that another opinion poll was being carried out for HTV that weekend. The Campaign was also made aware that in some parts of Cardiff at least, insufficient work had been undertaken to get the message out, though the Cardiff group itself was undertaking a wide variety of activity. Around Wales that weekend, there was a mass of leaflet delivering and canvassing. Rallies were held in several places, particularly throughout West and North-West Wales. As Peter Hain put it "If we generate the activity on the ground we will get a decisive victory".

The Campaign on the ground was in full swing. There was a literary night in Cardiff, featuring readings by Rhodri Morgan, Raymond Garlick, Menna Elfyn, Mario Basini, Nigel Jenkins, Mike Jenkins, Robert Minhinnick, Alun Rees, Kate Baillie, Herbert Williams, Catherine Fisher, and Wayne David MEP. In Swansea, the local group had organised a whole day of local rock bands in the Castle gardens. *Pobol y Cwm* actors, organised by Judith Humphries and Catrin Fychan, joined Peter Hain in Neath for his final Saturday's campaigning. They had been turning out all round Wales for Yes for Wales. Darren Evans found them very valuable in the Valleys. They had also turned out in Carmarthen when we had news that No campaigners were holding a launch there.

The Labour campaign was also increasing the tempo. David Hill, the Labour Party's Chief Press Spokesman was despatched to Wales from Scotland to help coordinate the media campaign. On Sunday, Donald Dewar also arrived from Scotland to join the Labour Party campaign and Yes campaigners, though again Labour was determined this was their event. Dewar said at a photocall, "Like Scotland, Wales is a nation which believes in itself. Like Scotland, Wales believes in a strong UK." A photocall was held at City Hall, with the slogan 'Scotland Voted Yes – Don't Let

Wales get Left Behind' as the main focus. This was reported widely on television and became the front page of the *Western Mail* the next day. (Yes campaigners had to intervene with the Liberal Democrats after their leader went completely off-message on the BBC's *Breakfast with Frost* programme, saying it was arrogant to think the people of Wales would necessarily follow the people of Scotland. Privately briefed by the Yes for Wales Campaign Ashdown corrected the interpretation of his comments the following day.) Dewar joined the Cardiff Yes Campaign and Welsh Office Ministers in Cardiff's Splott Market.

The Cardiff group, led by Geoff Mungham and Aled Edwards organised eighty people to come to the Yes for Wales headquarters that evening to deliver both Yes for Wales and Labour leaflets in those areas of Cardiff which had not received them. Edwards had taken the names of all those from Cardiff who had signed up for Yes for Wales at the Eisteddfod. He spent 6-7 days ringing them from the Labour Party offices to get them to turn up. There were Plaid Cymru supporters leaving the headquarters with hundreds of Labour Party leaflets under their arms. They recognised the urgency of ensuring that the message got out and accepted that it didn't matter whether it was Labour or Yes Campaign leaflets they were distributing. That was a common view in the last week.

Local campaigning reached its peak, with yet more meetings, rallies and leaflet drops. It was becoming difficult to keep up, and only a sketch of the final events can be made. Further photocalls were held, including one with Sports Minister Tony Banks, Peter Hain and Cardiff and Wales rugby captain Jonathan Humphries, and then in Swansea with Welsh women's squash champion Tegwen Malik. The Prime Minister came back to Wales to visit Wrexham, where he was mobbed in a greeting more like that for a football team or a film star, and also the Toyota plant on Deeside. Several Welsh rock bands were announced as supporters by Musicians Say Yes. David Blunkett visited Powys to talk of Labour's plans for better schools. Asian MP Keith Vaz met ethnic minority organisations. Dafydd Wigley told housing campaigners at the Cymdeithas Tai Eryri annual meeting that an Assembly would be good for housing. Meanwhile Employment Minister Stephen Byers was campaigning in Flintshire. The *South Wales Echo* telephone poll, which up till now had shown a No majority, finally swung towards Yes.

Yes for Wales published an analysis of the arguments about the funding of Wales and the Assembly. Written by Rhodri Morgan

and Kevin Brennan, *The Money Myth* pointed out that Wales
received no real subsidy from the UK Treasury, as non-domestic
spending such as the Defence budget, which benefited other parts
of the UK, was not counted. The publication on housing and the
Assembly, written by Welsh Federation of Housing Associations
Director Gareth Hughes and myself was published. This argued
that significant savings would be achieved from the merger of Tai
Cymru and the Welsh Office. Labour's Finance and Industry
Group launched its Welsh branch with a statement urging industry to back the Assembly. Paediatricians Vote Yes was launched –
the grandest sounding Yes group yet. Paddy Ashdown campaigned
again in South and Mid Wales. Ted Rowlands, one of the MPs
with doubts, warned that he was afraid that the role of the
Secretary of State would be that of a eunuch after the Assembly,
but re-confirmed he would vote Yes.

Everyone was waiting for the HTV poll. Finally, on Monday
evening, it was published. Conducted by NOP, it put to rest the
fears of Yes campaigners who had been rocked by the *Guardian*
poll the previous week. The position was still tight. The poll found
that the Yes-vote was just ahead. 50% were certain to vote. 37%
said they would vote Yes, 29% No, but 34% remained undecided.
Of those certain to vote, 42% said they would vote Yes, 34% No,
but a further 23% remained undecided. 74% said that the Scotland
result made no difference to them. 35% wanted tax-raising powers,
47% did not. 57% would have preferred law-making powers,
against 31% who did not. On the positive side, 56% believed that
the Assembly would make the Welsh Office and quangos more
accountable, and 55% believed it would give Wales a stronger voice
in Europe and London. On the anti-side, 61% believed it would
cost money that should be better spent on health and education.
43% believed it would be a talking shop.

Now the Yes Campaign found itself the victim of vandalism.
The A-frame van carrying the slogan "Time to take over the
remote control" was attacked near Swansea where it had been
parked overnight. The section saying 'Vote Yes' had been cut out
with a Stanley-knife. The section was being repaired when the Yes
Campaign managed to get HTV along to film it for that evening's
news. The Just Say No Campaign was asked to comment and was
clearly taken aback. In Swansea itself, Yes banners were removed
from bridges on the entrances to the town.

The Campaign kept up its momentum over the last few days.
Peter Hain toured the LG plant at Newport and warned of threats

to jobs if the Assembly did not go ahead. Kim Howells gave a similar message: "A No-vote on Thursday will mean Wales gets left behind economically. Left behind Scotland, left behind London, and left behind the regions of England." Hain was worried about the response he had found in Islwyn. Darren Evans was still not convinced that the Valleys would come through. Five Sundays standing outside either Pontypridd or Aberdare Tesco's had shown him how hard it was to interest people, let alone persuade them.

The *Daily Mirror*, which had dropped Yes coverage in the aftermath of Diana's funeral, came back into the campaign in the last few days to urge a Yes-vote. On the day before polling it carried an article by Manchester United Manager Alex Ferguson, who said "The Tories treated Wales like a lower division team, not a proud country with a distinctive contribution to make to the UK. A Welsh Assembly is a vital part of Tony Blair's vision for a new Britain." Ferguson's intervention had been requested by the Rev. Aled Edwards, who suggested it to Andrew Davies. He was concerned that the message of support from Ryan Giggs had not been received in North Wales. He knew that many North Walians were fanatical United supporters, and that Ferguson was a Labour supporter, so he had urged Labour to arrange the intervention.

That day John Prescott visited Newport, as did William Hague. The Deputy Prime Minister's message to Wales was "Go for it". Prescott's visit, like Blair's the previous Monday, was picked up throughout the media. Hague's presence offered another opportunity to take a swipe at Conservative involvement in the No Campaign. The *Western Mail* revealed that Mrs Thatcher had been urged to keep out of Wales after her disastrous visit to Scotland the week before. MPs from over the border were joining the Yes Campaign by now. Twenty Labour MPs from England and Scotland visited Clwyd, met by a Scottish piper and local MP Chris Ruane. Others came to Newport. Transport Secretary Gavin Strang visited Wales, as did Social Security Secretary Harriet Harman, who urged a Yes-vote for the sake of children. The Cardiff-born novelist Ken Follett, and his wife Barbara, a Hertfordshire Labour MP (known as Barbie and Ken in the Valleys), visited Swansea. A Cardiff estate agent forecast in the *Western Mail* that there would be over 3,000 new jobs for Cardiff created by the Assembly.

Local groups were gearing up for the final day. 120,000 'final day' leaflets had been sent out to local groups by Yes for Wales. These were very simple and aimed at getting the vote out. The

Labour campaign had also produced its own leaflets for the last day. Mailings were going out to several thousand supporters on the Yes for Wales database. Eluned Morgan dropped into the Yes for Wales office in Cardiff and found "a real fun atmosphere". We had also arranged for a local businessman to donate the cost of a private plane to fly over the Valleys with the message "Vote Yes – support Blair" on polling day. The night before the poll, campaigners in Machynlleth held a candle-lit vigil.

Ten: Waiting for Carmarthen

At last, it was the eighteenth of September. The day dawned with the *Daily Mirror* again producing a front page dedicated to Wales, urging people to vote Yes. Inside was the message: "Go For It Wales". The *Western Mail* carried pictures of a wide range of people from all backgrounds of Welsh life, for whom the Assembly could be said to matter, urging a vote for all our futures. Internally, there had been a battle over the front page. One camp in the editorial team wanted the front-page to be a collage of Welsh symbols, featuring a young woman in a "traditional" Welsh costume looking out over the Brecon Beacons. There was a more modernist camp however which felt this was backward-looking, and wanted to stress that the Assembly was for everyone.

It was a glorious day across most of Wales, with temperatures reaching 24°C in some places. Throughout the country, Yes campaigners summoned up their energies for one last push. Hywel Francis began the day in Ystradgynlais, where there had been an effective local campaign throughout. He was to spend the day in and around the southern areas of Powys, before returning to the Neath Valley in the evening. Dafydd Wigley spent the morning in his Caernarfon constituency. On election day his habit was to visit every one of the 92 polling stations. He did the rounds of as many as he could, before setting off for Cardiff. Richard Livsey campaigned in Powys during the day. He worked particularly in the areas which he knew would be weak for the Yes Campaign, trying to raise morale. He found that the Tories were not working as hard as they have normally. They were clearly still demoralised by the General Election. "The vibes were good," he recalled. "There were more people persuaded to vote Yes than I would have expected." Kim Howells was out in a speaker car in Pontypridd. Val Feld spent the day in the Swansea campaign shop, frequently having to ring the electoral registration office on her mobile phone to check people's eligibility to vote, and where they should go to vote. "We were still persuading people right up until the close," she said, "we had this sort of shop on the corner right in the very centre of town which was decorated with lots of posters and banners and things like that." Troops of people left the Swansea shop to go leafleting around the supermarkets, the bus station, the railway station, with loudspeakers carrying the message. Andrew Davies was also in Swansea. He was concerned about the level of activity. The Labour Party effort in the city was split between the referendum and a local council by-election. In Clwyd, Gareth Thomas worked across the council boundaries of his constituency. Cynog Dafis undertook a whistle-stop tour of Ceredigion, working till late that night.

Eluned Morgan started the day in St David's, where she found people at the polling station, raring to go. "There was quite a buzz there," she recalled "but there wasn't the buzz of a general election by a long shot." She spent most of the day – from 11.00 to 5.00 – in Llanelli. This was very comforting. Lots of people were out, most were positive and had been to vote. She went on to Ystradgynlais where she spent 2-3 hours in a loudspeaker car. It was very quiet compared to Llanelli, but the work had clearly already been done.

The Welsh Office team also campaigned in their localities. Nick Ainger went out with a loud-speaker van, first of all in Pembroke and Pembroke Dock, moving slowly further and further east to Carmarthen. Peter Hain was campaigning in Neath. "There was a fantastic reception," he recalled. All day he worked in the constituency, getting a good response from local people. "One guy worried the life out of me," he recalled later. "He told me that he got into the polling booth, his pencil in his hand, and kept wavering between yes and no. In the end, he told me, he thought what does Labour want, and what does my MP want? They're both Yes, so that's what I'll vote." Ron Davies was also getting a good response in Caerphilly town centre: "There was a really good atmosphere. All the signs were that it was good."

Not all of the team found things so positive. Huw Roberts spent part of the day in the Vale of Glamorgan with Labour MP John Smith. He found no momentum at all. Huw saw the Yes for Wales plane up above, urging people to vote for Blair today and started saying the same message through the loud-speaker. Then John Smith told him the leafleters they were working with were Plaid Cymru members! In Cardiff, Kevin Brennan was downcast. "I was convinced we were going to lose, prior to the night of the event, not least through campaigning in places like Ely, where core Labour Party areas were. Having been on the streets with Eluned Morgan the day before the event, when we spoke to a group of pensioners and spoke to people out on the street it was clear to me that we would have problems, although things would be better than '79." Daran Hill was surprised to find a total absence of election-style activity, with nobody at the polling stations. Rhodri Morgan recalled working in Pentrebane trying to persuade some single mothers to vote at the polling station opposite the school where they were picking up their children. "They would not go over to vote, they couldn't see the relevance at all." Elsewhere in the Valleys, Darren Evans spent some of the morning checking his groups had sufficient leaflets, then went out with loudspeakers around Abercynon, before heading off to Merthyr for the count in the evening. He was still nervous. He wasn't sure enough had been done. He knew that experienced Labour campaigners from Millbank who had been staffing Labour's campaign minibuses had been shocked by how little the local parties had done in some areas.

In Cardiff, the Yes for Wales office was pushing its volunteers out to leaflet the City Centre. Leafleters were posted in Queen Street and some were sent down to the bus station. Volunteers were despatched up to Merthyr and the Valleys. The Cardiff West Labour Party was working particularly hard. Alan Barnard went out with some of the volunteers from Transport House to knock on doors.

During the day, the Yes Campaign phoned around the local groups, to try to get some sense of what was going on. The response was patchy. Little seemed to be happening in North-East Wales in particular, and the same seemed true of Merthyr. In other areas, things were better. But it was hard to get a real picture. When I phoned Alan Barnard in the early evening to compare notes, we discussed the border areas in particular. Barnard thought it would be fifty-fifty in Newport. The absence of the kind of polling day activity that the political parties would normally have mounted in elections meant that we were deficient in our intelligence gathering.

I was thinking through the potential responses for the Campaign, depending on the different outcomes. Having checked these through with Mari James, they were faxed out to the leading Yes campaigners and to the Yes Campaign workers around Wales, so that the Campaign would at least be on message immediately the polls closed. All of the Campaign's officers had tasks assigned to them. Kevin Morgan, Val Feld, Mari James and Hywel Francis were to be in the count at the College of Music and Drama, to take part in interviews where needed. Eleri Carrog would be at Cardiff Castle, for Channel Four. I was to compere the Yes for Wales party at the Park Hotel, accompanied by Daran Hill.

At 9 o'clock, Kevin, Mari and I met in Mari James' room in the Park to discuss our final views of what the Campaign should say in the early interviews. Mari reminded us that the first results were likely to come from areas where the campaign was least strong, and we should make that clear in our early pronouncements. I had been trying to get a feel for the BBC exit poll. By that stage the rumours were that the Yes camp were eight points ahead. Morgan didn't want to hear it. "I don't want to know," he said. It was the right response. We would later find that the poll had been undermined by a computer sampling error. We agreed that the early stance would be quietly optimistic – optimistic, but not complacent.

Elsewhere, the Welsh Office team were also meeting. During the day, Ron Davies had been getting a steer from all at Transport House, including those from London, that it was going to be a 60-40 result in favour of the Yes Campaign. However, Davies, who had spent the day in his constituency, was concerned by what he found when he dropped in at the count there, "I went to the count and thought, oh shit, not too clever". When the Ministerial team met in the Welsh Office at 10.30, with colleagues from the Labour Party like Anita Gale and Gareth Hughes, there was an edge of nervousness. They agreed that there would be no comments from the Ministerial team of Davies, Peter Hain, or Win Griffiths until the early results were in. There would be just a simple statement from the Secretary of State as he arrived at the central count. Peter Hain remembers being grabbed by the media as soon as he arrived in the College of Music and Drama. "I felt it was important to be cautiously optimistic, but I wanted to stress how much we had had to do since 1979. I said that we had a mountain to climb." Hain arrived at about the time HTV had a leak that Wrexham had voted No. His comments were seen as down-beat by several of those observing his interviews, journalists and Yes campaigners included. For Kevin Morgan, ever the pessimist throughout the summer, "that was my first image, and that was a profoundly de-motivating sight, to see Peter Hain in what I took him to be saying was reducing our expectations, stacking up reasons why we might not win." The *Western Mail's* Nick Horton took a similar view.

Inside the inner sanctum of the College, the Principal's office where the Ministerial team was based, several TVs were lined up to allow the team to watch coverage on the different channels. Hain's Ministerial colleagues watched in amazement as Hain appeared to move from one TV set to the next as the media passed him along the line.

In the Pen and Wig, a pub just off Cathays Park mainly used by lawyers, civil servants and academics, the Cardiff group was gathering. "I met up with the Cardiff campaigners and told them 'don't get all worked up'. They were all happy. 'No, no, no, I don't think we've made it,'" said Kevin Brennan. In Seven Sisters, Hywel Francis finished his day with a pint in the rugby club. His son Dafydd had worked the club and had identified only four people against. "It was an interesting contrast with 1979," he said.

Francis went to the Neath count, then drove on to Cardiff. He heard his MP, Peter Hain, on the radio. He thought Hain sounded despondent. Then he heard Jon Owen Jones and Kevin Morgan. He thought Jones was talking in terms of defeat.

The Cardiff result – or at least, the expectation of it – had a profoundly dispiriting effect on the Yes campaigners as Cardiff activists arrived at both the Park Hotel and the College of Music and Drama. In the Cardiff count, "it looked not too bad in some areas, but in others it looked an absolute dead loss," remembered Kevin Brennan.

At the Park Hotel, where the party was just getting underway, I was trying to get the television feed to the big screen to work, so that people could watch the results. I went into the bar to get a diet coke. Ian Courtney from the Cardiff campaign told me that Cardiff was bad. He looked very depressed. I tried to cheer him up. I wanted the atmosphere of a party, not a wake. In the College of Music and Drama, Andrew Davies felt that a mood of defeatism set in early, "the Cardiff result was key. Cardiff people infected the mood of all of us". Mari James found that the pattern established itself soon after they arrived at the college. Everyone from the Valleys was on a high, confident that things would go well. Those from Cardiff and the Vale were discouraged and depressed. She took an early call on her mobile from Darren Evans, the Yes for Wales Valleys organiser, who gave very upbeat news from Merthyr and Rhondda Cynon Taff.

In the College of Music and Drama, Eluned Morgan found people excited but apprehensive, which took her aback: she hadn't considered losing. Dafydd Wigley, on the other hand, was convinced the campaign had lost. "It didn't feel right, there wasn't enough momentum," he recalled. Hywel Francis felt an air of tension and anxiety in the College when he arrived. The first person he saw was one of his oldest friends, Merfyn Jones, History Professor in Bangor, who had been active in the campaign there. They were comparing notes when Hywel saw Richard Livsey, with whom he had worked in Ystradgynlais. Livsey told him "I think we'll sneak it". He found Mari James upbeat and armed with statistics, but Kevin Morgan, who had just been undertaking interviews, was very downhearted, and already concerned about splits in the Labour Party. "I just kept repeating the mantra, it's basically a numbers game, it's not over till it's over, we have to wait till the late results."

In Colwyn Bay, Gareth Thomas stayed at the count for no more than quarter of an hour. He could tell from the boxes coming in that the results were "extraordinarily bad". He had still been thinking in general election terms of a uniform swing across the country. He saw a lot of Tory activists who had not been seen before. Clearly they were on a high. Thomas didn't have the heart to stay at the count. Instead, he went home and stayed glued to the television all night.

The first result was Wrexham. Yes for Wales knew we would lose here, but we were interested in the size of the vote. The No Campaign won by 4,000. In the Park Hotel, Ieuan Wyn Jones turned to me and said "that's all right". In the College of Music and Drama, Alan Barnard was delighted. He had thought the Campaign would get pasted in Wrexham, where he felt there had been a lack of enthusiasm. It was almost an hour before another result came through. But unofficially rumours were already coming through of defeats for the Yes Campaign in Denbighshire and Flintshire. HTV, eager to be first with the results, was flashing the latest unverified results on screen, while the BBC waited for the official announcements. Shortly before the Denbighshire result, just after 1 am, HTV's Keith Raffan said that Dafydd Wigley had told him that Conwy had also gone No.

Daran Hill and I in the Park Hotel were in touch by mobile phone with Mari James in the College. Mari had heard from Carwyn Jones, a Labour Councillor in Bridgend who was the leader of the local Yes for Wales group, that they had won there. Carwyn was one of our most reliable activists. It was getting a bit gloomy in the Park, so I decided to announce the Bridgend result early. A big cheer went up at the news. It was the first positive sign the assembled Yes campaigners had heard. I had even had to call off the Jazz duo the Campaign had booked as people felt the music was too gloomy.

By now the cliches were flowing furiously. "It's too close to call," said Denis Balsom on HTV, a refrain that was repeated by virtually every broadcaster during the course of the night, including

Patrick Hannan on Radio Wales and Peter Snow on the BBC. "It's going down to the wire," they all said later.

Shortly after 1 am HTV ran a story saying they had a hint of a Yes-vote in Ceredigion, but that Powys had gone No. News that the campaign had won Merthyr, broadcast on the BBC direct from the count at 1.18, provided a great fillip and really buoyed the campaign workers in the Park. There had been little Yes campaigning done in Merthyr, with some volunteers sent up in the days before to aid Darren Evans.

The news of the likely defeat in Cardiff, which was all round the Yes camp by this stage, finally surfaced on HTV at 1.25, just after news came in that Anglesey had gone Yes, but by a surprisingly small margin. Mari James and I were trying to get actual details to allow us to calculate the likely totals for the Yes and No camps. Neither of us had any information from Carmarthen.

Then came a result which put a smile on the faces of all the Yes Campaign teams, no matter where they were watching the results. Blaenau Gwent had voted Yes, against the urging of its MP Llew Smith, who had caused such a distraction earlier in the summer. In the Park the cheering went on for some time. Shortly after, I introduced the local council leader, Bernard Assinder, to speak from the lectern, to cheers and applause. Meanwhile, in Carmarthen, Nick Ainger had been taking samples as the boxes came in. In the first few boxes in Carmarthen, the overall result seemed to be 2:1. Some boxes were better than 2:1. By 1.30, he reckoned he knew the rough outcome.

By half past one unconfirmed reports were coming in that the campaign had won Rhondda Cynon Taff and Swansea, with big majorities in each case. Unfortunately the majorities were significantly over-estimated. Torfaen's result came in, the narrowest of all defeats for the Yes camp.

Just after 2 am, the Cardiff result officially came in. Recriminations were already starting against Labour MPs, and some councillors, who were alleged to have done nothing in the Campaign. Plaid and Liberal Democrat representatives attacked Labour on TV for the timidity of its proposals. Labour Yes-supporters attacked those who had allegedly sat on their hands.

Yes activists in the College overheard veteran Wales Labour fixers discussing what should be done if Wales voted No. For some of the older Labour hands, it was a question of ensuring the right people got the quango jobs – for others, using the Welsh Local Government Association. Some wanted a new Secretary of State.

Kevin Brennan, Kevin Morgan and Geoff Mungham went into the inner sanctum to see Ron Davies at about 2 am, to commiserate with him. He was in the Principal's room with Hain, Griffiths, Huw Roberts, and Des Clifford, the Welsh Office Press Officer. Brennan remembered: "Outside in the bar area, David Hill [Labour's Chief Press Spokesperson] was, I believe, at that point preparing a statement which conceded defeat." Brennan said they found Ron in quite "an ebullient mood". They'd gone in to tell him not to do "anything daft", like resign. Morgan remembers saying to Davies "We are going down tonight and there's going to be some terrible recriminations in the Party." Davies told him he didn't want any recriminations in the Party. That could wait till the morning! He said there were still some big votes left to come in. "What I thought was an absolutely heroically optimistic thing to say," said Morgan. "They'd come to comfort me: I felt more like comforting them!" Davies recalled. "I was deeply touched by these people." Brennan conceded on air shortly after, saying "It looks like it's not going to go for a Yes-vote." He wasn't the only one to do so. Jenny Randerson and Kirsty Williams for the Liberal Democrats both did, and so did several Labour figures. Newport West MP Paul Flynn told Radio Wales "we're bracing ourselves for disappointing news".

Hywel Francis walked over to the Park Hotel in the pouring rain, abjectly depressed. Leaving the College of Music and Drama, he saw Richard Livsey. "How are we going to sneak it?" he asked. "The Tories couldn't get their vote out," said Livsey. "If it's below 10,000 in Powys, we've done it." At the Park Hotel, he saw Tyrone O'Sullivan. "We've had it," Hywel said to him. "No, we haven't," replied Tyrone, "we haven't had any of the Valleys' results yet."

Peter Hain came over to the Park Hotel about 2.30 just after the stunning result from Neath and Port Talbot was declared. Hain got a hero's welcome, entering to chants of "Neath, Neath, Neath", traditionally heard at his local rugby ground. Peter delivered a fighting speech, thanking the Yes for Wales campaigners, and saying that theirs had been the cause of hope against fear. But he seemed strangely downbeat, unwilling to suggest a victory was likely. His speech enthused the crowd however, and the chants of Neath, Neath, Neath were repeated as he left.

For the Yes Campaign officers, depressed as most were by 2.30 in the morning, it was a question of what to do about the debts. In the College, Hywel Francis got a commitment from Terry Thomas that the GMB would pick up £5,000. Val Feld and Mari James were considering fundraising schemes. In the Park Hotel, I was wondering if anyone would donate money to a defeated campaign. I also wondered, if the Campaign went down, whether we should call for a different kind of devolution to the regions of Wales.

In the College, the mood was getting worse. Val Feld remembers a small group of Tories cheering the results as everyone else got more and more despondent. She recalls telling Huw Roberts that Ron Davies must not resign. "Derek Gregory kept saying 'hang on, hang on, it will be all right'." Eluned Morgan remembers "I had conceded very early on in the evening, in my own mind. I was very upset, and very angry." She conceded on screen. Mari James however was keeping an eye on the running total based on the unofficial figures being phoned in. "This put the Yes figure higher than the official total." She was blocking out her concerns: "I went into denial."

The atmosphere was getting very downbeat. On the big screen, Peter Snow's BBC computer had finally coughed up a prediction, and it was that the No Campaign would make it. By now, I couldn't make the figures add up any longer, especially when Ceredigion came in lower than I had expected. The Vale of Glamorgan also went against us, though by less than we'd feared earlier that night.

I'd been on and off my mobile all night to Mari James, Huw Roberts, and others in the counts around Wales, and had a pretty clear view of the results that were likely to come in. I'd been keeping score since the first result, but it seemed that a Yes-vote was now beyond them. For nearly two hours I'd been telling the media in interviews, among them Steve Evans of BBC Radio, Michael Crick of BBC TV, and Peter Cullimore of HTV, that it was too close to call. Now I couldn't see a way to a majority. I went to find my wife, Ann, who was drinking with Eluned Morgan and Channel Four's Jon Snow in the bar area, and told them I thought the Yes Campaign was out by 1,500 votes. I said the same to Siân Lloyd, one of many TV personalities who had worked so hard for the Campaign, and to my brother, Geoff, who had come down from London to help. But I was determined not to say anything on air about this, despite the promptings of the journalists present. I decided that in my next interview I wouldn't concede, but I would say it was looking disappointing. Then I would attack the No Campaign for its xenophobia and also criticise those who had sat on their hands and done nothing for the Campaign. Some members of Plaid and the Liberal Democrats had begun to rebuke Labour: Labour devolution supporters had begun to attack Labour dissidents. After the Conwy result, just before 3 am, I phoned Kevin Morgan and asked him to come over to the Park. Val Feld remembers Kevin Morgan saying to her "we've got to be with the rest when the last result comes through."

In the College of Music and Drama, Andrew Davies was also trying to get the results from Labour's people in the counts on his mobile phone. He was aware of how depressing the night was growing: "I'd given up a pensionable job for a leap in the dark," he thought. The result he wanted was Carmarthen. He spoke to Nick Ainger in the Carmarthen count. "We've just had a tip-off, I don't know how reliable it is, I'll have to check it out, but it's 23," said Ainger. "23 what?" said Davies. "23,000" said Ainger. "The vote?" said Davies. "No, the majority," Ainger replied. Davies sent Ainger off to check, and went to tell Anita Gale, Alan Barnard and Andrew Bold who were collating the results for the Wales Labour Party. "Everyone was lifted. The mood was so awful," recalls Davies, who says everyone thought it was lost at this point. Davies tried phoning Ainger several times, but the mobile connection wasn't very good. Ainger confirmed it was 23,000. Mari James was also having difficulty getting the result. She had a call through on her mobile answerphone but the voice was indistinct, though it seemed to say "20,000". Later, Chris Roberts, Eluned Morgan's agent, explained why it was so difficult to get a clear view of the Carmarthen result. Rather than the bundles of votes being put in a place where they could be seen, they were bundled on the stage, and only those with access to the stage could see them, so only they could make any accurate judgement on how the vote was going. The point was that officials wanted to keep the result secret until they had told Cardiff. It was clear that the Yes Campaign knew that they were ahead, but they didn't get a real sign of the figures until about ten minutes or so before it was faxed through to the Welsh Office just before 3 am. Even then they didn't know if the Yes camp had won, as they didn't know the Powys or Gwynedd scores.

Andrew Davies passed the word on to other Labour Party officials. Huw Roberts wouldn't let the result go up to Ron Davies until it had been verified by the Welsh Office officials. "We were getting information from our people in the counts, but it was surprisingly patchy. We'd already had the disappointment of the Rhondda result. A great result in retrospect, but we'd been told it was 12,000 votes higher," Roberts was later to recall, "That threw our calculations." He admitted that it made the team a lot more cautious. He held back the Carmarthen result from Davies until he could get it from the Welsh Office officials, rather than unofficially from Labour party managers. He reckons that Labour officials had it about ten minutes before Ron Davies.

Roberts was in the inner sanctum of the College with Ron Davies, Peter Hain and Win Griffiths, Des Clifford, Welsh Office Press Officer, and David Hill, Labour Party spin-doctor from London. They had been keeping a close eye on the overall numbers, trying not to get too fixated on individual results. "I knew that we could win," said Ron Davies, "but I knew that it looked grim." He was coming to the view that if the result went wrong, he would probably have to resign. He asked Des Clifford to prepare an alternative statement in case the result went against him.

Dafydd Wigley went in to see Ron Davies just before 3.00 in the morning. He was there with Huw Roberts, Peter Hain, Win Griffiths, Richard Livsey and some Welsh Office officials. Wigley felt the atmosphere was quiet, very down. There were seven results to go and he was totally convinced it would be lost. He was distraught, barely concealing his tears.

"The Powys one was the one we were trying to get hold of," remembers Ron Davies. "I met Wigley in the course of the evening and he told us the figures from Gwynedd. We had provisional figures from Carmarthen, and we couldn't get hold of Powys figures. We didn't even know the turnout in Powys, and I had assumed that it was going to be more heavily against than it actually was."

Contrary to rumour, Davies did know the Carmarthen result before he went for his famous walkabout around the College of Music and Drama: "We decided to have a little joke on the media." Other senior figures in the Labour and other parties were still not convinced a year later. Certainly film of the evening records a very tense Davies. Kevin Morgan remembers "I thought he cut a very sad figure at this point, a very poignant figure at this point." BBC Wales Political Editor Glyn Mathias confirms that the press reaction was "He's just putting a brave face on it". Nick Horton called him "Ron de Niro – he should get an Oscar, he was so convincing." Horton phoned the newsdesk of the *Western Mail*, where the front page was being prepared as Wales Says No, to confirm it was a No-vote. Then shortly after he was taken aside by a press officer from the Welsh Office and shown the figures. "I ran to the phones. For the first time in my life I probably said the words 'Hold the Front Page'," he remembers.

Ron Davies had not gone for his walkabout until he had been given the official figures by John Adams, his other Special Adviser. Adams was waiting by the fax machine, with civil servants. Powys and Carmarthen came in nearly together. John Shortridge, a senior civil servant, calculated the totals, then Adams went through to the small office that Davies was using. The Secretary of State was on his own, trying to make a phone call to get the Powys figures. Davies took the figures from him, looked at them, then said to Huw Roberts, "Right Huw, come on, we're going for a walk around". Adams thinks Roberts didn't know for sure until he and Davies were half way along the corridor.

In Aberystwyth, Cynog Dafis was with a group of older Plaid activists in the Marine Hotel. A younger group of supporters were in the Coops. "I was surprisingly unemotional. There were people there, and I didn't expect it of them, who were distraught when it looked like we were going to lose." Meanwhile, in Colwyn Bay, Gareth Thomas' younger daughter couldn't sleep. She asked her father, "are the No-people going to win?" She went to bed thinking they had.

The Powys result came through. The majority for No was rather less than we'd feared, and Hywel Francis knew it was less than the 10,000 Richard Livsey had said would mean defeat. Shortly after this, Kevin Morgan and Val Feld arrived in the Park Hotel. They'd travelled back with Derek Gregory and Terry Thomas. Val remembers "Derek was the one person that all the way through kept saying hang on, hang on, it'll be all right." I introduced Kevin, who began the speech of his life. Without actually conceding, he told the assembled troops that the Campaign had to start again, that it would go on. There had to be a constitutional convention. "Throughout this campaign, there has only been one issue. Do we have the self-confidence in Wales to take more control of our own affairs? Not enough people in Wales have enough self-confidence." From the audience, Hywel Francis shouted "we haven't lost yet, Kev". Then on the large screen the news came of the Gwynedd result. It was huge, far bigger than anyone in the Park had expected. I was standing by Kevin on the rostrum. Daran Hill came up to me. He had been keeping score. "We can still do it," he said, "it depends on Carmarthen." At that moment, a journalist from Radio Five Live told me, "You know there's a rumour going around the College that you've done it?"

In the Park, Yes Campaign organisers were dashing to and fro, trying to get the actual figures from Carmarthen on their mobiles.

"It's still too close to call," we told reporters. Viewers at home watching S4C had by now got an inkling of the likely result from Carmarthen. In the College, Mari James had warned Yes supporters earlier not to sit in the front seats in case the result turned out to be a No. Now she had to get some to return to the front rows. She had been on the phone back and forth to Carmarthen, as had Simon Brooks, editor of *Barn*. At about the same time they both got calls confirming the figures.

The tension by now was palpable. A few were in the know, but most were not. By now many people had left the Park to drown their sorrows elsewhere. The result seemed to take an age. It wasn't helped by the abysmal Welsh of the local returning officer. Recently arrived from England, he had been urged by his colleagues not to attempt the Welsh. As the result came through in Welsh on the big screen in the Park, the BBC presenter Huw Edwards cut in before the English to confirm the verdict. In the College, there was greater expectancy as the rumour had got out to a wider audience.

Eluned Morgan recalls the moment of the announcement in the Park: "The whole atmosphere changed within seconds. It was the most emotional time of my whole life. It was a moment of going from absolute loss to absolute joy."

There was pandemonium. Everyone seemed to be hugging everyone else. Hywel Francis swung Eluned Morgan around. Kevin Morgan was in tears. I sent Daran Hill off to find the champagne the Campaign had ordered, which he'd told the Park employees to put away only forty minutes before. Campaign workers Blodwen Jones and Kate Stokes went off to find the 150 Welsh flags that had been ordered and started handing them out. Then the chants started, "Wales, Wales, Wales" like the chorus at a rugby international.

I invited the former Brookside actor Stifyn Parri, the coordinator of SWS, who had helped organise celebrities for the Campaign, up to the lectern to open the champagne, and started filling glasses. Kevin Morgan was being interviewed for television. "It's true theatre," he said. "It's extraordinary what's happened. What fiction could ever replicate this true drama here. I left from the count thinking we'd lost. I made a speech thinking we'd lost and nearly conceding." "It's brilliant, I'm the happiest I've ever been in my life," said Siân Lloyd.

Then the singing started. Choruses of *Hen Wlad Fy Nhadau* echoed around the room. The party was in full swing again, though the bars were about to close, except for the residents' bar. Ian Courtney, more cheerful now, bought me a beer.

In the College, Ron Davies was welcoming the result. "Good Morning," he paused. "And it is a very good morning in Wales." He invited Richard Livsey and Dafydd Wigley to join him and his Ministers on the stage. Then they all walked over to the Park, accompanied by their advisers and officials, and other MPs, including Paul Flynn and Huw Edwards, and Peers such as Viscount St David, the Conservative Peer who had supported the Yes Campaign.

In the Park, the Ministers' arrival was announced. "One Ron Davies, there's only one Ron Davies," sang the crowd. Davies spoke to the assembled supporters and thanked them for all their work. The partying went on for another two hours. From the lectern, the staff, celebrities and local groups were thanked. There was a special cheer for the actors of *Pobol y Cwm*, christened Cwmderi'n Dweud Ie (Cwmderi Says Yes), after their fictional village.

Virtually the entire College of Music and Drama seemed to have decamped to the Park, with many leading figures from the Welsh media amongst them. It took a long time to clear the bar. When it was clear, the Campaign found that most of its banners had gone. Key campaigners had to autograph T-shirts, banners, leaflets. At some stage, a banner designed by the artist Mary Lloyd Jones disappeared. Mari James and I escaped to the residents' bar to plan the press conference. Outside, people were queueing in the rain, trying to get into the hotel. Shortly after, copies of the *Western Mail* arrived, with the headline 'Wales Votes Yes'. "People were desperate to have it confirmed in print," recalls Nick Horton.

At home in Colwyn Bay, Gareth Thomas was in tears. In Cardiff, Jon Owen Jones, who'd gone home after a night of interviews on S4C, saw the result and hitched a lift from his neighbour to the Park. Later his wife came downstairs to look for him and was alarmed to find him gone, fearing the worst. In the Marine Hotel in Aberystwyth, Cynog Dafis and the older campaign workers were joined by the younger crowd from the Coops. "It was an extremely moving thing," he remembers, "because you had this combination of old and young people, kissing each other and crying." In Carmarthen, Nick Ainger was waiting to do an interview. By the time the crew decided he wasn't needed, all the other Yes campaigners had gone home.

The Yes for Wales press conference took place a floor above the party at 6 am. Croissants, coffee and orange juice had been provided. At the back of the room sat the Secretary of State and his advisers, finally having persuaded someone to get them a drink. "I was desperate for a pint," recalled Ron Davies later, "but the bar was shut!"

Kevin Morgan opened the press conference. He said that the closeness of the result placed an enormous burden on those who would be elected to it to prove it can work. "I hope they can prove it to those people who didn't feel able to vote for us: those who abstained and those who voted No. For me personally, the biggest single message has been the enormous boost it will give to the self-confidence of our children and young people. It will begin the process of getting rid of those cultural stereotypes of the Welsh: that we are not enterprising, not innovative and that we can't create opportunities for ourselves. We've started today to signal to the world that we are about to create new opportunities. Right from the start, we said there was only one message: self-confidence. The question as to whether we in Wales had the self-confidence to assume more responsibility for our own decisions – and indeed, from our own mistakes. You don't learn, grow, develop, without learning from your own mistakes. There will be painful decisions ahead, but we want to make them ourselves. And is has to be said, trite as it might seem, that this has been a victory of hope over fear."

Mari James read out a message of congratulation from Scotland: "We waited for you through the night. You joined us. Congratulations". We pointed out our success in winning seats where there were MPs arguing for a No-vote or expressing doubts. We thanked everyone who had taken part, not least Ron Davies, sitting in the corner quietly sipping his drink. Then we went off to do a final round of interviews, and try to get some sleep before joining the official celebrations outside City Hall.

Dafydd Wigley arrived at the BBC in Llandaff to undertake interviews. The first person he saw was Rod Richards, defeated Tory MP for Clwyd West, a former Welsh Office Minister and virulent opponent of devolution. "Dafydd, now we've got to make the Assembly work for Wales," he told the startled Wigley. Truly, things had changed.

As she recalled the night six months later, Eluned Morgan was to speak for all involved in the Yes Campaign: "I don't think I'll ever experience anything like that ever again. The joy of knowing that you made a difference. You can be in politics forever, in terms of being in a campaign, but to make a difference to the result, is something extremely rare, to make a difference as an individual. What is nice is that everybody who got involved in that campaign can claim to have made a difference to the actual final result, and that is something that I don't think many people experience."

Eleven: Learning the Lessons

After the Campaign was over, the main objective of Yes for Wales was to pay its bills. We owed some £29,000. The Campaign's financial needs became the subject of a front page story in the *Western Mail* during October, and were fanned by anti-devolution campaigners who had never apparently heard of cash flow planning. Yes for Wales had spent beyond its known income deliberately, calculating that a victory would produce the necessary donors and the enthusiasm needed to hold a range of fundraising activities. The need to raise the funds also provided an important focus for holding the Campaign together in the aftermath of the Yes-vote. Many people turned out to support fundraising auctions in Ystradgynlais, Cardiff and Bala. There was a football match with stars from *Pobol y Cwm*. Sales of Campaign merchandise continued to roll in. The Yes for Wales banner painted by Mary Lloyd Jones which had disappeared from the Park Hotel on the night of the victory was returned to Blodwen Jones by a guilt-stricken supporter from the Valleys after its disappearance was mentioned in the *Western Mail*. Yes for Wales groups helped to raise half of the monies needed, and in December the Rowntree Trust came through with the rest.

What did the result finally mean? The swing in Wales from 1979, at 30%, was higher than that in Scotland (23%). The strongest support came in areas which shared some or all of the following characteristics: they were away from the English border; they were under Labour/Plaid political control; over 30% of the local population were Welsh-speakers; 70% were Welsh-born; over 40% were economically inactive.

Denis Balsom can relax: his Three-Wales model still largely holds good. And Gareth Hughes was right to say in a speech to the Welsh Federation of Housing Associations just a few weeks after the result that it was largely the disadvantaged areas which had voted Yes. Contrary to what the Conservatives claimed overnight, the result actually produced a less divided Wales than in 1979, with big swings to Yes in the Valleys (between 45-47%) and even in South-East Wales (34-38%). Turnout was better than in the 1995 council elections and the 1994 European elections. There were marginally higher turnouts in the Yes areas than in the No areas, suggesting that campaigning on the ground did have some impact. There is clear evidence, as Richard Wyn Jones, Dafydd Tristan and Geoffrey Evans of University College, Aberystwyth, have pointed out, of generational difference, with Under-45s voting Yes by 5:2, and over-45s No. Unfortunately for the Yes camp, the youngest age groups have a poor turn-out record, and the referendum proved to be no different. The Aberystwyth research suggests that the Yes Campaign succeeded in keeping a high proportion of would-be No voters at home. A high proportion of Yes voters made up their minds in the last week, so Scotland may have had some impact. Unlike in 1979 the No Campaign failed to get its vote out. There were clear differences by party. Plaid, with the greatest, and Labour, with the next highest, clearly delivered the votes.

Did the pollsters get it wrong? Bob Worcester, the veteran MORI pollster, argued shortly after the referendum that the media misinterpreted the polls and it was always a lot closer. By and large the Don't Knows don't vote, was his argument, and their views should not have been squeezed and taken into account by the news media. Welsh Office sources believe that there were problems in some of the questioning. Most media outlets asked straight Yes-No questions, and these were the least accurate. The *Guardian* did not do so and obtained the most accurate result ten days before.

Interesting calculations have been undertaken subsequently to assess what the expected vote would have been, given the known facts about party support in Wales and the divisions within political party voters on the issue. These calculations are compatible with a 54-46% victory, which was roughly in the area that more informed campaigners on both the Yes and No sides were expecting. It was also said to be roughly the figure coming through from the NOP poll being conducted by the BBC on the day before and the day of voting itself, and subsequent analysis of the data appears to show this to be true. Why didn't this happen? Differential turn-out amongst the generations may be part of the answer, though there was a clear sampling problem with the BBC poll.

Some have argued that it was the weakness of the proposals on offer that made the result so close. There is little overall evidence for this. The NOP poll conducted by the BBC found that 6% would have preferred independence; 32% would have liked tax-raising and law-making powers; 19% wanted what was on offer, and 43% wanted the status quo. Other polls found a clear difference in intention to vote were tax-raising and law-making powers on offer. Law-making powers tipped the balance to Yes; tax-raising powers tipped the balance to No.

Scotland appears to have had much less of an impact than expected. According to NOP, only 8% said it made them more likely to vote Yes, but 2% said it made it less likely. Most said it made no difference. The expected lift had been about 10%. Plaid Cymru's telephone canvassing did find a small but significant uplift in the likely Yes voters after the Scottish referendum.

Finally, it is the view of at least one of the polling experts that the death of Diana had a major effect on the result. There was little polling done around the time of Diana's death, largely out of respect. But ABC News did commission MORI to undertake a survey, with the interviews being carried out across the UK on 10-11 September. The question asked people whether they would say that the death of Diana and the events since her death had "made you more proud to be British, less proud to be British or has it made no difference to the way that you feel?" The answers were interesting:

More proud to be British	31
Less proud to be British	2
Made no difference	65
Don't Know	2

In terms of Britishness within Wales, the BBC's NOP poll found people describing themselves in the following proportions:

Welsh not British	17
More Welsh than British	24
Both Equally	38
More British than Welsh	7
British not Welsh	13

Since the victory in the small hours of 19 September 1997, many people have sought to explain the final result in Wales. On the night, and for months afterwards, commentators and No campaigners alike focused on the supposed 'East-West' split, in which western Council areas largely voted Yes and eastern Council areas largely voted No. This supposed East-West split in the votes has been one of the most misunderstood areas of debate, in and out of Wales. Immediately after the result, *The Times* political editor, Peter Riddell, repeated a widely-shared London consensus that Labour had been rescued by the nationalist (sic) areas of

Wales such as 'Carmarthen'. For the academic Laura McAllister, writing in *Parliamentary Affairs*, the closeness of the result was due to Labour's campaign failings. These allegedly included the decision to tie Welsh devolution to the issues of wider constitutional reform in the UK, and the decision to make support for Tony Blair a key element in the Labour Party campaign. McAllister sees Yes for Wales "as a qualified success, for it did construct a popular front for the rather diverse body of devolution supporters". But she claims that the Yes for Wales Campaign also was to blame for linking the referendum to Labour's General Election success. Kevin Williams has argued in *Planet* that Labour's Millbank machine failed to deliver its much-vaunted professional effect. "The dead hand of Millbank was at work. Despite claims to the latter, Labour's spin machine is a rusty edifice. The lionisation of Millbank and Mandelson is one of the great political myths of the twentieth century. In the referendum this rusty edifice, in the most corroded part of the body politic, found it difficult to crank into action."

The issue of the East-West split has been dealt with at length by a number of commentators. Shortly after the referendum, the Welsh-language magazine *Barn* demonstrated in an essay by Dafydd Tristan the extent of the disparity within geographical areas of Wales, rather than between them. Subsequently, in a subtle essay in *Planet*, Paul O'Leary has pointed out the absurdity of seeing Wales as split down the middle:

> Let's be clear about this: a full 39.3% of Yes votes were cast in the so-called No districts, revealing a much less polarised Wales than reports have suggested hitherto. There can be no question that support for devolution varied from one part of Wales to another. Nevertheless, nearly twice as many votes were cast in favour of devolution in Powys as were garnered in Merthyr Tydfil, yet Powys is shown on the map as a homogeneous No area. In fact, each one of the so-called No areas of Conwy, Wrexham, Pembrokeshire and Powys had larger Yes-votes than the so-called Yes areas of Merthyr, Blaenau Gwent, Anglesey and Ceredigion. And it was votes, not districts, that counted. In this context, it is as logical to say that it was Monmouthshire (with its 10,592 Yes votes) which tipped the balance, as it is to say that the honour belongs to Carmarthenshire.

Riddell's shaky grasp of the political geography of Wales, attributing an area represented by Labour to Plaid Cymru, has been rightly ridiculed by Patrick Hannan in *Planet* but is in any case demolished by O'Leary's analysis. The argument of McAllister, that the outcome failed to validate a Labour campaign which was

dependent on loyalty to Tony Blair, is based on a misunderstand-
ing of the task which Labour set itself, and the priorities Labour
identified given the specific nature of the referendum campaign.
That the Yes for Wales Campaign relied on playing the Blair card
is not borne out by an examination of any of the Yes for Wales
literature or that of its local groups distributed during the campaign,
with the sole exception of the aeroplane message, itself deliberately
targeted at Labour voters in South-East Wales. It would be more
accurate to say that Yes for Wales played the Neil Jenkins card.

It is clear that very few political science or media studies academics
ever get close enough to the heart of a campaign to understand the
objectives, strategy, and focus of campaign professionals. Neither
McAllister nor Williams have asked what the individual party
managers saw as their priorities or attempted to evaluate the
priorities they set themselves and whether in their own terms these
were achieved. Every campaign depends on taking decisions.
Sometimes these are decisions not to do things if resources mean
that they can only be half-heartedly attempted and will not result
in significant added value. Finely balanced judgements frequently
have to be made, and usually in the heat of action and under media
scrutiny, rather than in the calm academic study. With a few
exceptions, these shades of grey are rarely given space in academic
writing on campaigning.

Equally, it is perfectly clear that there were several different Yes
campaigns being run under the same umbrella, each with a different focus and priority. The campaigns run by the different political
parties had clearly different emphases, and the role of Yes for
Wales was something different again. The Plaid Cymru campaign
largely focused on getting out the vote in Plaid's heartland. Plaid
Cymru MPs focused their constituency work, canvassing on foot
or by telephone (particularly the latter), leafleting, and traditional
election activities (such as targeted letters) in the four Westminster
constituencies they held, plus the next best four. Their telephone
canvassing was usually carried out under the name of Yes for
Wales. Plaid also supplied telephone canvassing of the Valleys, and
provided foot-soldiers and local Yes for Wales committee members
in a range of local groups across Wales. But the geographic
compass which Plaid had to cover was narrower in range than that
of Labour. Delivering strong votes in Plaid areas – achieved in all
apart from Anglesey, despite a strong and active local group there
– was their priority. Like Labour, Plaid had significant internal
divisions of its own.

By contrast, Labour had to run a campaign that had a presence across Wales. Their focus was on making a noise in the key Labour heartland areas, blitzing council estates, appearing with street-stalls, leaflets, balloons and sometimes celebrities, bringing in Ministers and the Prime Minister. Their rationale for using the Prime Minister on their literature was very simple. Their focus-group research made it clear that Blair was popular and if devolution was presented as part of his plan to modernise Britain, then Labour voters would, by and large, turn out for it. Far from it being a mistake, as McAllister alleges, it was an essential part of their message. While there were clearly tensions within the Labour campaign in Wales (with Millbank holding the purse strings), contrary to Williams' allegations, Peter Mandelson helped to clarify what the boundaries were for government communication and the Millbank machine supplied a steady stream of Ministers, policy input, additional staff such as press officers, and volunteers to help staff the minibuses that took the message around the Valleys.

The trades unions also played an important role in funding the Campaign (Unison coming up trumps with a £10,000 donation) and providing officials to help with delivering the message and support on the ground. Labour's biggest problem was not Millbank, but the reality that in many constituencies it was unable to deliver the local grass-roots based campaign that was needed. As Peter Hain said in *Tribune* in June 1998: "The absence of a vigorous campaigning tradition in Labour's heartlands haunted it in the Welsh referendum: it was the difference between a narrow win and what should have been a comfortable victory." Hain believed what was needed was old-fashioned campaigning alongside the media glitz, but that there simply weren't enough activists to do this.

There is no question that the visible dissent among Labour MPs did harm the campaign, or that Labour Party members on the whole were simply not sufficiently engaged by the campaign.

The Liberal Democrats joined in local Yes campaigns and also focused on Powys and other areas where they had some strength, such as Conwy. Their full-time organiser Mel ab Owain was effectively seconded to the Yes for Wales Campaign in those areas. There were targeted mailings, despatched by the Yes for Wales Cardiff office who had ten volunteers stuffing envelopes over three days. While the research by Jones, Tristan and Evans suggests that Liberal Democrat voters were overall hostile to devolution, the impact in holding the No-vote down in Powys was critical.

For Yes for Wales itself, the principal achievement was providing the coherence of an overall umbrella to unite the parties. The Yes for Wales logo became the logo of the Campaign, adopted by the TV news bulletins which ultimately reached most people. Nationally, the Campaign helped to set the agenda with its press conferences. It was Yes for Wales which in late May came up with the critical slogan 'Don't Let Wales Get Left Behind', offering it to Peter Hain for testing at the Institute of Public Policy Research lunch in Cardiff in June. The phrase was later adopted by Labour as its 'final push' slogan as well. John Osmond believes that this notion that Wales would be out of step with the rest of Britain was a powerful argument for the Yes Campaign, in striking contrast with McAllister's claim that it was a weakness to link the issue of Welsh devolution with constitutional reform across Britain.

An independent observer, Glyn Mathias, the BBC Wales Political Editor, saw Yes for Wales as a success. Writing in *Planet*, he said, "The Yes for Wales Campaign were well prepared and well-organised. They rolled out lists of celebrities who backed a Yes-vote, and they staged a sequence of media events such as 'Teachers Say Yes' or 'Cardiff Says Yes'. The principal value of the Yes for Wales Campaign was to provide a platform on which the political parties in favour of devolution could come together. And in the absence of anything like the Constitutional Convention which gathered multi-backing for the Scottish Parliament, this was important. It allowed Plaid Cymru, in particular, a means to swallow their objections to the proposed Assembly and come in behind the government's plans." Mathias wondered how effective Yes for Wales was in getting outside the political classes, but then he didn't see the local Yes groups in action. Subsequently he has said his main criticism concerned Yes for Wales' sectoral group launches, which were more media events than events demonstrating really substantial support of individuals within sectors on the ground. Some disliked the celebrity element of the campaign. But Nigel Jenkins, the writer, was more realistic. Writing in *Red Kite* he said: "I suppose that in addition to the routine political footwork of leafleting and persuading we are going to have to rely on an inordinate amount of glitzification – rolling out the Terfels, Giggses and Tony Blair's gnashers – to give a shine to our rather dull-sounding d-word."

Mathias is right that the underlying lesson of the Yes for Wales Campaign is a political one: building a consensus for constitutional reform requires significant cultural change that takes years rather than months.

In a sense, Yes for Wales was not only seeking to achieve a Yes vote but also to fill the gap that in Scotland had been taken by the Scottish Constitutional Convention. The Convention had had nearly nine years to prepare the way for a Scottish Parliament. In 1992, Peter Hain and other Labour MPs, the Liberal Democrats and the Wales TUC, along with the Parliament for Wales Campaign at the peak of its impact, had all called for the Welsh equivalent of the Convention. It was only in February 1997 that Yes for Wales launched. It was only in March 1997 that the Wales Labour Party had agreed to adopt an element of PR. It was only in the summer of 1997 that the Welsh Liberal Democrats and Plaid Cymru finally agreed to come on board, officially, for the Yes Campaign. The existence of the Labour Government, ironically, made it more difficult to get the voters out again. Nor was there much time to sell the case. Unlike Scotland, the issue was essentially selling democratisation rather than identity.

The referendum also raised deeper questions concerning the role of governments in campaigning for their policies. The Government could not, officially, campaign in the referendum because Parliament had not passed its devolution proposals – merely its plans for the referendum. Ministers elected in a General Election campaign in which 'sleaze' had been a prominent theme were not about to sacrifice their reputation for straightforwardness and for appropriate standards of behaviour from Ministers and the Government machine. If anything, they erred towards caution in what could and could not be done by government in promoting the devolution case. The referendum came too soon after the election to allow them to consider whether they were being perhaps too 'institutionally correct' in their handling of the public promotion of the campaign. Ministers were concerned to ensure that they could not be accused of favouring one side through government. They were also seeking to establish new rules for a referendum process last used in 1979. Despite what Just Say No and the Conservative Opposition claimed, the government only spent £575,000 on its information campaign. £300,000 of this was associated with the White Paper and its publicity. About £13,000 was spent on research related to the presentation of the White Paper and about £23,000 evaluating the success of the White Paper campaign. Yes for Wales spent just over £150,000: the Labour Party perhaps more. Contrary to the absurd conclusion of the Neill Committee, which asserted that the result might have been different if public funding had been available for both sides, it is my belief that Yes for Wales would have been in a stronger position to make use of public funding than was Just Say No. Yes for Wales had a reasonably effective local network of activists. Supplemented by advertising, better polling and research, extensive telephone canvassing and more literature, this network could have been devastating. In fact, Yes for Wales itself was under-resourced. In an area lacking a homogeneous media, substantial sums of money are needed to mount a serious campaign: for advertising, leafleting and campaigning. Yes for Wales never had enough money. No commercial organisation seeking to make an impact in Wales would have spent so little.

The referendum also placed demands on broadcasters which resulted in the suspicion that the concept of impartiality was in effect exploited by the No Campaign. The overwhelming preponderance of activities by the Yes Campaign was not equalled by Just Say No, yet for the broadcasters there had to be a rough equivalence of air time between the two campaigns. (The BBC also made some complicated adjustments for party views.) This meant that a relatively inactive No Campaign, which existed in few places on the ground, was able to appear as active as the Yes Campaign. Just Say No gave extensive credit to the media for the boost television and radio coverage gave their campaign. The television organisations in the broadcast areas overlapping Wales never gave any real coverage to the Campaign. (78,000 Welsh homes watch Granada exclusively, for example. It is reckoned that perhaps 10% of the overlap area of about 40% of Wales actually choose to watch programmes from England). As far as the written media is concerned, London media penetration of Wales is actually stronger than in 1979. The Yes Campaign lost some important coverage in the *Daily Mirror* in the aftermath of Diana's death. The Welsh Office advertising campaign, designed to encourage people to vote whatever their views, was also pulled in this period, which may have affected turn-out. The Aberystwyth University research suggests that the Welsh Office's mini-booklet did have a positive effect in raising turn-out.

The speed of the campaign also dictated the priorities of the parties. It was the Yes for Wales view that the Government's explanation of its plans should have been distributed at the same time as the White Paper was published, so that the thirst for information could be immediately assuaged. In a country lacking the media homogeneity of Scotland, particularly in the printed press, the need for written material which voters could consider at length and in their own time was paramount. The Government's explanation of the White Paper, which was wholly objective, and not the kind of exhortatory publication Yes campaigners would have liked, would have received more attention if it had been distributed in the full glare of publicity as the White Paper was launched. Instead, it went out after the August Bank Holiday, a full five weeks later, arriving in people's homes in the days just before the death of Diana. This meant that in the five-week period after the White Paper Yes campaigners had to *explain* the government's proposals as well as *argue* for them. It had never been a priority of the Yes for Wales Campaign to explain the case in detail, just as it was not the focus of the Just Say No Campaign to really analyse the detail of the government's plans rather than relying on a few simple arguments. Yes for Wales saw its task as helping get out the vote.

Ron Davies himself believes that there were a number of factors affecting the performance of the Yes campaigns. Not enough was done before the General Election, nor was the Election itself used as the springboard for the Campaign. The sense of Welsh identity is not as strong as Scottish identity is, nor is there the sense of confidence that flows from that. Voters found the concept of the Assembly difficult to understand. At a practical level, the No Campaign argument that the project would be an expensive talking shop bore fruit. At a practical level, the TV overlap areas were clearly a problem – so was the Diana effect. Peter Hain believes that the Just Say No arguments were effectively targeted and difficult to refute, playing to people's fears. Eluned Morgan and Gareth Thomas both believe that the Campaign became too focused on the nature of Welshness. "It was a referendum on how Welsh you felt," said Gareth Thomas. "What came over in Ely," recalls Eluned Morgan "was this idea of 'I'm not as Welsh as you and therefore somehow or other I won't find myself represented or an expression of myself in this new Assembly'. The perception was definitely that this was about Welsh Wales, a different kind of Wales and that certainly didn't play well in Cardiff."

Yes for Wales itself achieved most in the areas where campaigning started earliest, with Neath the outstanding example. The speed of the Campaign made it hard for the Steering Committee, before July, to reach clear decisions on some issues, as people were coming from different backgrounds, different levels of campaign experience, and with different expectations of the Campaign and their roles within it. The kind of trust and ease of working that can be achieved in campaigns that have come together over time could not be achieved in a campaign which had little more than six months for people to get to know each other and which was never certain of its budget.

By the same token, coordination between the different parties and the Yes Campaign, while smoother than many feared, was not as streamlined as anyone would have wanted. A significant amount of time was lost in the run up to the publication of the White Paper arguing the toss over the freedom of the dissident Labour MPs to campaign for a No-vote. This was a serious distraction throughout the early part of the Campaign.

For Yes campaigners, the final Yes for Wales Steering Committee in Machynlleth, in late November 1997, was a time of reflection. There was real pride in the voices there, pride in feeling, in Eluned Morgan's words, "The joy of knowing that you made a difference." There was also considerable generosity between individuals from different political parties. Labour councillor Peter Law, who had spear-headed the Blaenau Gwent campaign, said that he felt very proud. As he put it, "Fifteen devo-warriors" had worked together to deliver their Yes: people from Plaid, Liberal Democrat, Labour and independent backgrounds. Carwyn Jones, from Bridgend, believed that the majority could have been larger if the overall Campaign had been stronger, but was delighted with the performance through most of the Bridgend and Ogmore constituencies (Ogmore had been won for devolution against its MP). A campaigner from Machynlleth itself (a group which had had little contact with the Yes for Wales office), spoke of "the joy of being here today" and insisted on handing everyone left-over candles from the eve-of-poll vigil held in the town. Another Labour councillor, Charles Henrywood from Neath, paid tribute to the other parties. "Plaid provided a hell of a lot of the foot-soldiers working on the ground." Elin Edwards from Ceredigion, a Plaid Cymru member, was delighted to be at the meeting and had found the experience of working with people from other parties, particularly on the women's Campaign, very powerful, and felt the whole Campaign experience had been very emotional for her. Liberal Democrat Leader in Wales, Richard Livsey MP, was delighted by a Campaign that he felt offered Wales something for the future, in terms of people working together across party political boundaries.

The Machynlleth meeting discussed a paper prepared by Mari James, Hywel Francis and myself suggesting that there might be a need for a continuing campaign to sustain the integrity of the result as the Government of Wales Bill went through its clauses. The paper stressed that Yes for Wales would be wound up. It had done its job. The idea of the new organisation was welcomed, but shortly afterwards the Secretary of State announced the National Assembly Advisory Group. With several Yes for Wales activists as members, the need for a new organisation disappeared. Yes for Wales was now part of the establishment.

The people of Wales signalled a decisive shift in their views on devolution over eighteen years. The very closeness of the result demonstrated that the work undertaken by the thousands of individuals across Wales involved in the Yes for Wales Campaign mattered. It had, after all, been too important to leave to the politicians.

Twelve:
The Birth of Post-devolution Politics

The resignation of Ron Davies, the architect of Welsh devolution, on 27 October 1998 thrust Wales back into the headlines. It meant that the birth of the National Assembly would continue in controversy. After his resignation, it became apparent how divided Wales remained. To a great extent, Ron Davies had held together a fractious coalition in support of devolution, within his own party and outside. With him gone, it seemed that the fissures were exposed for all to see. Personally, I think I was never prouder of Yes for Wales than in the days after Ron's resignation when it was colleagues from Yes for Wales who came forward, spontaneously, to defend him.

While opinion polls now seem to show endorsement of the National Assembly, the meaning of devolution for Wales will not be clear for some time to come. But perhaps it should not surprise us that in the making of the New Wales, old divisions should remain. The final session of the National Assembly Advisory Group, working to smooth the practical details of a new inclusive democracy, ended with a dinner at the Cardiff and County Club, an institution which only allows men as members. So the Old Wales is still here, striving to hold on to what it has. So much of what has passed as normal practice in Wales, for nearly twenty years under the Conservatives, and to an extent under Old Right-wing Labour, has been about preserving the privileges of unchallenged authority. Normal unthinking practice in public life in Wales has too often been about making sure the right chaps are in office. The tests of public value, efficiency and effectiveness have taken second place to keeping other chaps on-side. Radicals and risk-takers are seen as threats and dismissed as "not team-players". Cronyism was alive and well in Wales throughout the Conservative era. And they got away with it, because of the complacency of middle-class opinion in Wales. Instead of that complacency, or what we might on a good day call benign decency, a strong dose of 'rational cynicism' might be more useful.

The campaign for Welsh devolution is over, but the struggle to build a living and breathing Welsh democracy has barely started.

As two of our most important historians, Dai Smith and Hywel Francis, have written: "it will be up to the people of Wales to see if they can and will breathe as much citizenship and democratic life into the new institutions which they have now willed into being." Despite the vote, the old faces are still here, running many of the quangos. The cultural elite is still the cultural elite and remains unaccountable to the Assembly. The old guard still controls many town halls. Men outnumber women massively in senior posts in most Welsh institutions and four out of forty women MPs is still considered progress on what there was before.

We still live in a pre-devolution culture.

But there are far more optimistic signs in our modern Wales. Welsh popular culture is leaving most of this behind. It is a confident culture, not hung up on deference and the inferiority complex. It is creating waves across Britain and internationally. Who would have thought that Wales, in the space of a few years, could produce not one but four or five rock bands that are coming to dominate British rock culture (which of course, in the context of rock ultimately means dominating Europe!)? But Welsh institutions are lagging behind. That is why the attempts that have been made to re-brand Wales are important. It should not be about creating Cool Cymru – something that would be both exclusive and doomed to failure – but about modernising the image of Wales so that it actually reflects what Wales is becoming, not what it was.

Another optimistic sign is the higher profile of women in public life. The National Assembly will not so much consolidate this trend as dramatise it. For the first time in Wales, we will have a political institution that roughly makes up the gender balance of our society. The old establishment epitomised by the Cardiff and County Club is on the way out. Women with energy and intellect are transforming private, public and voluntary sector institutions in Wales with a new spirit of leadership. It's another sign of the new politics and the new Wales.

Our new inclusive democracy has to be fought for and won. It cannot be taken for granted. Can the National Assembly develop into a new creative institution that has the strength to change things? Can the cross-party spirit that brought about the victory now carry through radical changes in the ways we are governed? Ron Davies' famous phrase that devolution is not an event, but a process, is now under test. The National Assembly will in its first years face the real challenge of demonstrating it has a meaningful role to play in modernising Wales. The need for modernisation is obvious to all those who've been excluded from playing a meaningful role in Wales, not just in the last twenty years, but in the twenty before that. For those of us who have spent periods away and then come home, the urgency is just as strong. Kim Howells said to me a year after Labour's General Election victory: "when I look at the people who were active later in the second Devolution Campaign, there were a lot of people like me involved in it, like you, you think of Kevin Morgan, you think of a whole host of people who couldn't wait to get away in the mid '60s, and who all trooped back to Wales and then became involved in trying to make it a better place to live in. I've often thought about it and I think it's got something to do with modernising it, there was something very nice about trying to recapture a past that we all remembered, but it was a very cosy thing. Modernising it, I think, was something else again."

Modernising Wales is the most urgent task facing the Assembly: helping to bring into being an economy that is not about dependency, that is dynamic, but at the same time rebuilding our shattered communities which have been wrecked on the failed promises of previous 'modernisations'.

The importance of politics and political parties

When we set up Yes for Wales so many months ago, the Campaign coined a rather glib mantra that we repeated for some months to anyone who would listen. We said: "Devolution is too important to be left to the politicians." In our naïve arrogance, what we were saying was not only that Devolution had to be meaningful to ordinary people, but also that the arguments between the pro-devolution parties over what kind of Assembly we should have, what kind of powers, what kind of electoral system, were in danger of obscuring the overall case for devolution itself. A case that had to be sold to the people of Wales in the referendum and which could not be taken for granted.

Yes for Wales was right to do that, and it was important in the context of a campaign to persuade people to take a radical, bold and untested step. Yes for Wales created a movement that tried to focus on points of agreement not disagreement. A movement that brought together people with very different views.

That coalition was an important element in shaping the new politics of Wales. It created a dynamic in which people came to understand that monopolies on ideas did not exist. That there were some broad areas where people within parties could have more in common with each other than with some in their own parties: particularly when it came to political practice based on principles of openness, sharing, co-operating, working on solutions. That campaign itself opened up areas of agreement which will enable the National Assembly to develop its work co-operatively and in a spirit of solution.

The Yes for Wales Campaign was not, however, an anti-political campaign. Its enduring value, as a campaign which, unlike so many others, disbanded itself after achieving its goal, should be as a movement that restored some faith in politics. Too often, particularly in the last few months before an election, all we hear about politics is negative campaigning from each side. The truth of course is that negative campaigning can be highly effective. But negative campaigning entails a danger – the danger of undermining belief in the usefulness of political debate and the importance of political institutions.

We sometimes forget that we are all, at some time, politicians: in our work-places, in schools, in our homes, in our communities. The best political skills are everyday skills: the skills of dealing with power, sharing information, negotiating, managing and smoothing away conflict, determining priorities for action. Those skills happen at all levels of life. The worst political skills are those which involve the abuse of power: the exploitation of weakness, empire-building, denigration of others, hiding key information, using structure and process to delay and destroy.

Yes for Wales may have done something to remind people of the more positive political skills. In Wales, the new political landscape has every opportunity to function on the basis of key principles of selflessness, integrity, objectivity, accountability, openness, honesty, and leadership. Those are the principles of public life set out by Lord Nolan, and Ron Davies was right to set them out as the principles which should be at the forefront of the minds of those who stand for the National Assembly for Wales.

Yes for Wales has done its job. That campaign is over. Yes for Wales had, of necessity, to duck many more questions than it ever answered, in order to focus on its task. A different task faces the National Assembly. A government cannot be run like a campaign, as the New Labour Government itself has found. What this means is that the National Assembly will need the disciplines and structures of political parties if it is to challenge the enduring areas of mediocrity and inertia that afflict our civic society and our political machinery in Wales. We must be careful about what we mean by 'inclusivity'. It is right that the National Assembly should be open to all regardless of gender, race, physical ability, linguistic ability, or sexual orientation. It is right that within the National Assembly there should be structures to ensure that the different regions are properly represented and their needs are properly accommodated, and that this is a National Assembly not a Greater South Wales Assembly. It is right that the Assembly should be inclusive enough to recognise that there are many different 'Welshnesses' in Wales, to borrow a phrase of Dafydd Elis-Thomas. The referendum should not have been a referendum on Welshness, how Welsh you felt, as both Gareth Thomas and Eluned Morgan worried it might become. We have too many people in Wales already who think that theirs is the only real Welshness. The battle for the Assembly won, we can now start to think in terms of civic forms of Welshness which are not dependent on particular linguistic or cultural affiliations.

But 'inclusivity' has become the most over-worked word in English-speaking Wales. The National Assembly will be judged on outcomes, not on process. The Assembly was never an end in itself. Some of those who believed in an Assembly during the Tory years did so because in part they thought it would deliver certain outcomes that they wanted to see. There is no more guarantee that a National Assembly could produce some sort of green socialist paradise than any other political structure. As Ron Davies said in his pamphlet *Devolution, a process not an event* in early 1999: "The devolution process is enabling us to make our own decisions and set our own priorities, that is the important point. We test our constitution with experience and we do that in a pragmatic and not an ideologically-driven way."

Additionally, it would be entirely counter-productive to the standing of the National Assembly to confuse the need for greater inclusiveness in reaching decisions on broad issues of strategy with micro-management by a large executive body. If inclusiveness comes to mean slow decision-making, continual reference back to committee, repetitious calling for further information, it will damage the standing of the Assembly in the eyes of the people of Wales. There is also a danger in confusing inclusiveness in reaching decisions with inclusiveness on every aspect of implementation. Once decisions are taken, there should be clear lines of authority for implementing them: with appropriate mechanisms for accountability subsequently. Inclusivity and leadership are not always as compatible as some people seem to think. Inclusivity must not mean a false unity. More important is the ability to deliver real leadership – leadership based on a politics capable of recognising and reflecting difference and of negotiating division, rather than ignoring it, fudging it or trampling over it.

And that is why we need political parties. At the end of the day, the Assembly has to make decisions. Political parties which know their positions, which are clear about where they are coming from and where their points of difference lie, which are not the prisoners of single-issue campaigns, will ultimately be the best guarantor that inclusivity does not mean inertia. The National Assembly, and the post-devolution politics that should come in its wake, presents challenges for all the parties, whose rhetoric sometimes seems not to have caught up with the events of 18 September 1997. The Conservatives can no longer behave as though constitutional change is to be resisted for ever. The Liberal Democrats can no longer mark their difference from others by their commitment to constitutional change. Plaid Cymru has to show that its claim to be the Party of Wales is relevant to most of Wales. And Labour? Labour has to reconcile democracy in Wales with real democracy at every level of the Wales Labour Party, so that one member one vote means just that and not one activist, one vote – and Labour in London needs to relax about Labour in Wales. In other words, all the political parties have to show that they can offer leadership to post-devolution Wales. What worries me is the degree to which many within them are still carrying the baggage of pre-devolution Wales. Creating an Assembly does not will a new country into being. A new institution does not magically remove old conflicts, structural economic problems, poverty, poor housing or ill health. There has to be a political agenda for that Assembly to develop.

Cultural inertia

One of the biggest obstacles to dynamic change in Wales is the cultural inertia of our major institutions. And amongst the institutions that faces one of the biggest changes is the civil service. The Permanent Secretary of the Welsh Office, Rachel Lomax, had something to say on this when she spoke to the Institute of Welsh Affairs in November 1997. It is worth quoting her words in detail:

> We are going to have to get used to explaining ourselves in public. Our business will be conducted more openly than in the past, and we

199

will almost certainly find ourselves much more actively engaged with other bodies in Wales.... We will come under new – and entirely different – leadership. Instead of working to a Secretary of State who is a member of Cabinet, and at best represents one Welsh constituency, most of us will transfer to the Assembly, where our political masters will be directly answerable to people from all over Wales, who will work in an entirely new and almost certainly much more open way.... We will have to listen more actively and respond more fully. We may increasingly become organisers of advice and expertise, rather than monopoly suppliers... we will have to consciously shed the mindset – still rather ingrained in civil servants everywhere – which says that the only advice worth having comes from the civil service.

There are many officials in the Welsh Office and some of the quangos who are open to outside dialogue and discussion and prepared to take on points of difference and engage with outside views, who understand the importance of openness and of clear policies, guidance and principles governing particular decisions. Equally, there are still some public servants who need to do more to demonstrate that they have understood the importance of openness, participation and avoiding a monopoly on advice. They will have a shock if they try it on with the new Assembly members.

It was one of the main selling points of the Assembly proposals that Ministers in the Welsh Office have far too little time to spend on the detail of their remits and that the creation of an Assembly would enable a real focus on issues and decisions that required attention by elected representatives. One of the areas of greatest concern in Wales – and this is true of business as well as many other areas of civil society – is the widely-held view that decisions taken by officials behind closed doors need greater scrutiny. The diaries of the First Secretary and the Assembly Secretaries must not be so taken up with the operation of the Assembly, the need to prepare for committees and the Executive Committee that there is insufficient time for them to lead and drive their officials and scrutinise their efficiency and effectiveness. Particularly when it comes to dealing with the weight of secondary legislation that is likely to descend upon them and on which they will have to make decisions.

Above all the civil service in Whitehall will need to face up to the changes in Wales. Our new Secretary of State Alun Michael told me shortly after his appointment "A lot of government departments don't really understand what it's about. They think that because accountability for Welsh Office responsibility moves to

Wales that England and Wales departments – UK Departments – can forget about Wales. We actually need to be more strongly linked into their decision-making and have a stronger voice and make sure that Wales is understood."

Those Whitehall departments are still living in pre-devolution Britain.

An Entrepreneurial Wales

One of the reasons why public servants will have to change their approach is that the world in which Wales exists has changed radically. Our old nationalised industries have largely gone. Wales competes in a global market. Information travels around the world between decentralised companies faster and faster. They are often better informed than centralised public institutions. But small and medium enterprises are the keys to job-creation in Wales, and their needs are not always best met by centralised institutions, whether they are development agencies or banks. The kind of rigid mentalities that typify some public servants – those who just want to implement rules – often lack the flexibility to ensure fast decisions and the support needs of a diverse range of organisations.

Kim Howells has described his own experience in Wales in the mid-eighties. "We suddenly realised we weren't very good in Wales at entrepreneurship and at research and development and all of the kind of icons of post-industrial Britain. We were hopeless at it, and if we were going to do anything then we'd better tackle that right from the start. All those instincts I'd had about Wales being a horrible smug place, where people assumed we taught kids better, that we had a better education system, that somehow we had right-eousness on our side, it started to come through to me in a big way. I really started to resent what we had in Wales, it wasn't very much actually."

Thatcherism understandably gave some people in Wales a horror of the concept of entrepreneurialism, with its connotations of Arthur Daley or of all those unreadable books piled up in airports about the exploits of this or that big businessman. The entrepreneur as hero. As the French socialist leader Lionel Jospin said in London in 1998, "We say yes to market economy, but no to market society." But entrepreneurial skills are skills that are applicable in many different walks of life. Entrepreneurial skills are relevant in business, but they are the same or similar skills displayed by social entrepreneurs in charities, in community groups on council estates, in housing associations. They are creative and problem-solving skills. They are the skills developed by artists marketing their work, by independent television producers, by software pioneers, by pop groups taking control of their own labels. In a world where the old industrial manufacturing giants, with their standardised Fordist processes, are gone, thinking around problems, creating solutions are the order of the day, not following some blueprint. We need Welsh entrepreneurs, in business and in our communities. As Alun Michael says, "It's that creativeness, that dynamic devolution that I am keen to develop. I see it as a process which allows us to do things that people haven't thought of doing before, harnessing energies; which is why the Assembly can provide leadership to business in Wales, to local government in Wales, and to the voluntary sector in Wales, and make with them a strong partnership which is greater than the sum of its parts."

New Country

The devolution referendum put Wales on the map world-wide. There were camera crews from Turkey, France, the United States and many other places present in Cardiff on the night of our vote. Newspapers such as the *New York Times* and the *Chicago Tribune* faithfully recorded the result, as did CNN. Wales was out of the shadows.

We are making a new country within an old state. Making our new Wales will require deep resources of intellectual capital. A leading intellectual who actually played a major part in the making of a new democracy a few years ago said something very profound in calling for intellectuals in his country to focus on positive ways of building that new democracy, not carrying on a flat lament for what might have been:

> Our country is where it is. Its landscape is beautiful in some ways and devastated in others. Its natural resources and industries are structured in such a way. We speak the languages we speak, we have our own historical traditions and customs. The political right and left are the way they are here and not the way they are elsewhere, and no matter how much we might want to we cannot hope to change these things entirely. Why not try to understand the inner context of the fact, the potential, the problems and hopes connected with it and why not deal with it in the most appropriate and adequate way.

That was President Havel in the Czech Republic in 1991. That call for optimism, to action, is a necessary rally against cynicism and against what our most creative playwright, Ed Thomas, has called 'miserabilism'. We need to look outwards. We are building a new national institution, not building a wall around Wales. Wales needs to be looking to build new relationships outwards to Europe and across the world, but also within Britain, with Scotland, with England and its regions, in the UK with the new Northern Ireland Assembly and the Westminster Parliament and beyond that with the Council of the Isles.

Havel's call is a call for practical intellectuals. We need them in Wales. As those two Yes for Wales stalwarts Hywel Francis and Rob Humphries have written recently of their hopes for the Assembly in respect of adult education, "Much will depend, in terms of policy-making, on transforming the political culture of Wales. If this is so, then the people of Wales are already engaged in a process of learning and understanding. That is an essential prerequisite to influencing policies that impact on our daily lives. In order for such a process to be thoroughly democratic and inclusive, active citizenship must be at its heart." Too many of our existing intellectuals seem to have given up. They too are stuck in pre-devolution politics. When, in 1996, the Labour Party announced that there was to be a referendum on devolution in Wales, the level of deep cynicism and gloom amongst so many so-called intellectuals in Wales was striking. There seemed to be an astonishing failure of nerve: a fear of actually having to go out and persuade people to vote for devolution. There were too many who believed that devolution was unwinnable, and who instead of rallying immediately to the cause of a Yes-vote chose to waste time on the sidelines moaning that the pet system on which they'd laboured many hours wasn't going to be the one on offer. Some of our so-called intellectuals lost whatever influence they might have had at that point.

In the course of that period, the most important forums for intellectual life in Wales changed significantly. The Institute of Welsh Affairs became a key forum where practical ideas for reform in Wales could be debated. And the most important print forum for the intellectual debate in Wales was the *Western Mail*, which ran several series of articles that genuinely tested out all the areas of the National debate. Some of the smaller magazines that have seen themselves as a forum for intellectual debate seemed trapped in a kind of nostalgia for the '70s or even the early '80s: you know, the time when the Left was the Left and lost every battle. Sitting there waiting for the sell-out. Ned Thomas was right to close down *Planet* in 1980, recognising that had devolution been achieved, it would have required a new kind of cultural response. Can the existing publications engage with post-devolution Wales, in building a new civic society, as energetically as they attacked Wales under the Conservatives? Do they have the will? As Dafydd Elis-Thomas recently said in commenting on some of the pessimists within Plaid Cymru during the early stages of the 1997 campaign: "there are some people, fundamentalists in both religion and politics, people that I always find difficulty in talking to, they are about, if you like, deifying or raising up the ideology over and above the practical programme and they're the people who lead people into the wilderness and make them suffer for forty years and they're no bloody use to anybody."

New Wales – in a New Britain?

Devolution offers Wales another opportunity. We are contributing to building a new Britishness as part of this process. What did Gwyn Alf Williams say in that period of defeat in 1979? "We Welsh look like being the last of the British. There is some logic in this. We were, after all, the First." Wales now has voted for devolution and Gwyn Alf's comment is even more relevant today.

Wales is not England, but it is not Scotland either. The journalist Jonathan Freedland, author of a fine new book on what Britain – and the English in particular – could learn from the United States in terms of radical popular democracy, wrote a sensitive piece on Welsh devolution when he visited Wales during the referendum. Despite its heading, 'A gentler, kinder nationalism for Wales', Freedland's piece has meaning for all of us in Wales, not just those who want independence. "There is no Welsh equivalent of the Braveheartism on show north of the border, little of Scotland's defiant urge to shake off the yoke of English rule." Freedland noted that the Welsh campaign had more to do with democratisation than with nationalism. "Listening to the arguments, it becomes clear that what Labour is involved in here is something quite rare: politicians who can currently exercise power – and spend lots of money – with very little scrutiny, are pushing for a system that will oblige them to face much more. It is not clear if the significance of this action has quite sunk in, in Wales or beyond."

In the coming years, it is Wales' difference from Scotland, rather than its similarity, which may become more obvious. Scotland's flirtation with the SNP may or may not be a temporary one. It would be curious to see a Western European nation opting at the beginning of the twenty-first century for that most nineteenth-century of institutions, its own state. Scotland may be the last example of Benedict Anderson's thesis that nation-states are imagined communities dependent on the print-media for their shared sense of cohesion. Wales' sense of itself is far more mature. As the situation in Scotland becomes more uncertain, England needs Wales for Britishness to have meaning. The opportunity is there for a radical response – what John Lloyd, Associate Editor of the *New Statesman,* has called "civic unionism". Intellectual life in Wales in the '80s and early '90s has been too dominated by a nationalism of the mind. To a large extent, this has focused on the role of the Labour Party within political life in Wales. For years, significant numbers of intellectuals in Wales have seen Labour as the party of the centralist state. It was the failure of the centralist state against which Welsh and Scottish nationalism, the New Left and Radical Liberalism organised in the 1960s. During the 1970s the two most internationally-prominent Welsh intellectuals, Raymond Williams and Gwyn Alf Williams, joined Plaid Cymru, which at that time came to be almost an honorary part of the Green, Peace and Alternative Left outside Labour. They cast themselves as Welsh Europeans, a phrase which had some meaning in terms of an opposition to the *ancien régime,* but is scarcely a slogan for a multi-racial and multi-cultural society.

While Labour under Neil Kinnock, John Smith and Tony Blair slowly but surely came to terms with the constitutional and European agendas, many Labour MPs in Wales lagged behind. As Eluned Morgan pointed out during the referendum campaign, opposition to devolution in Wales often went hand in hand with Euroscepticism. While Old Labour persisted in opposition to political reform, the intellectual infatuation with nationalism was at its strongest. With the emergence of a more pro-European, pro-reform Labour Party, the scope for nationalist intellectual resurgence seems unlikely. The neutralising of the language issue between the political parties has also removed a further recruitment weapon. Intellectually, the devolution victory has given the Wales Labour Party the opportunity to ensure a radical politics in Wales that does not fall prey to nationalist illusion. If it chooses to do so, Labour has the opportunity to win the intellectual arguments for its programme in Wales on a popular basis, articulating specifically in a Welsh context proposals for political renewal that deepen the commitment to pluralism at every level of politics and civil society.

But it is too easy sometimes to cast the European Union as a marvellous modernising influence against a dormant old post-imperial Britain. In Wales a huge amount of breath is wasted on speeches about Wales in Europe as though our relationships on this island itself do not matter. Europe is too often treated uncritically. That is the old, pre-devolution politics.

There are radical Britishnesses as well as imperial Britishnesses. If Britishness is a historical construct, then we have a part in its construction. Britain is now and always has been now. Britain is an artefact that the British produce. The British make and remake Britain day by day and year by year. If they want to. If we want Britain, we will have to make Britain.

Post-devolution Britain exists. It is multi-cultural and multi-racial. The implications for England, for England-in-Britain, for the English who can no longer assume that British means English, may not yet be clear. But we should not assume that England's relationships with Wales or Scotland, and their institutions, or England's relationship with Westminster, will remain static. We may have to help the English come to terms with post-devolution Britain, but how nice to be able to patronise them for a change....

At a time when one of our most successful rock bands, Catatonia, has had a hit single named after the stars of an American Sci-Fi series which enjoys global success ('Mulder and Scully'), and another, the Manic Street Preachers, has produced an album named for Aneurin Bevan with songs about the Spanish Civil War, the Hillsborough Disaster and Tryweryn, it should perhaps be clear that the new generation in Wales lacks little in confidence or ambition. The old debates about Welsh identity, about the British Welsh, the Welsh Welsh, and Y Fro Gymraeg still have some meaning in terms of geographic mapping of election results. But Welsh identities are more fluid today. Wales' heroes today are not just white Welsh Europeans. They are often Welsh Afro-Caribbeans, or Welsh Asians. (European identity is also more complex.) There are fluent Welsh-speakers in all our ethnic minority communities. Occasionally, we even cheer Welsh heroes from England. The historian Kenneth O. Morgan has described devolution as post-modern politics. As Ed Thomas wrote during the devolution campaign, "old Wales is dead, and new Wales is already a possibility, an eclectic self-defined new Wales with attitude – upside down, inside out, postmodern – call it what you want, but it's real. It's a lie that tells truths. You may not like my style, but I no longer need anyone to dress me." We are living – most of us – in a Wales which has its own brand of postmodern irony. When Cardiff City scores the first goal in a game at Ninian Park, and it's happened a lot in the 1998-9 season, the chant goes up "One-Nil to the sheep-shaggers". That is a sign of the confidence to overturn those old insults.

That is not to say that some people in Wales are not still deeply confused about their own identity. The Last Night of the Welsh Proms at Cardiff's St David's Hall is an event that can only truly be described as bizarre. Welsh people waving Welsh flags and singing *Rule Britannia* and *Land of Hope and Glory* betray an extraordinary and contradictory imperial response. Those of us who have witnessed 2,000 Conservatives signing *Land of Hope and Glory* at the end of their party conference know precisely what this song is about. But this Last Night too is a 'Welshness'....

Though language increasingly ceases to be an issue which divides Wales, there were some undertones during the referendum campaign that suggest that the language issue still has the capacity to irritate some in the Valleys. On the other hand there are still some Welsh-speakers who use the term English to encompass those from Wales who do not speak Welsh. Some of them can only relate to Wales' modern rock scene insofar as the bands themselves relate to the Welsh language – they do not see that their Welshness is played out in many different ways. When the Manic Street Preachers put up a Welsh-language poster for their new album in St Mary's Street, Cardiff, they were immediately attacked by "some wombat who thought their grammar was a bit iffy", in the words of a memorable letter to the *Western Mail*. The Manics were equally memorably defended by Cymdeithas yr Iaith Gymraeg. But the transformation in attitudes on the language since 1979, in no small part due to S4C and more recently the Welsh Language Board, is significant. Language has to a large part disappeared as a place of political dispute (which is not to say that progress can be taken for granted).

It is a long time now since Gwyn Alf Williams asked and answered the question When was Wales? "If we want Wales, we will have to make Wales." We're making that new Wales here and now, with our own National Assembly. The polls suggest, however, we have a long way to go to demonstrate the day-to-day relevance of the National Assembly to people's lives. But at least polls now show most people in Wales believe they voted Yes on 18 September 1997.

No-one in Yes for Wales would begrudge them that belief.

Acknowledgements

There are many people who have helped to make this book what it is, and most of them know who they are. Special thanks must go to all those active in the Yes for Wales Campaign itself, in the local groups, amongst our supporters, celebrity or otherwise, and most particularly to my colleagues on the Steering Committee, notably Kevin Morgan, Mari James, Hywel Francis, and Val Feld, as well as our National Organiser, Daran Hill. All of them consented to long interviews and gave freely of their insights on the campaign and reminded me of moments and events, some of which I had forgotten, some of which I had not myself shared. Originally this book was to have been a joint effort with Mari, but her commitments on the Secretary of State's National Assembly Advisory Group overtook her. I am deeply grateful to her for her intensive input on several sections, and also to Hywel for his perspective as both an activist and a historian on Wales in the 1980s and early 1990s. What I know about contemporary Welsh history I owe to people like Hywel, Dai Smith and one of my lecturers at Bangor, Emlyn Sherrington, whom I was delighted to see surface as the Secretary of the Bangor Yes Campaign in 1997.

Like many people active in the 1997 Campaign, I remembered 1979. My own memories of that campaign are of the large meeting in Bangor, where I was a student union official, addressed by Michael Foot, and the day the results were announced, watching and waiting in the student union building in the vain hope that at least Gwynedd might go Yes. I left Wales that year, and though friends, relatives and ultimately work kept me in touch with Wales, returned to live here only in 1996. The process of writing about Wales between 1979 and 1995 has been one of filling in gaps in my own education. Others have the benefit of first-hand experience, and I am grateful to them for sharing their memories with me.

I am grateful to my publishers, Seren, and to Mick Felton particularly, for seeing the need for the book and following through on his instincts.

I am very grateful to all of the interviewees, many of whom contributed interviews which themselves frankly ought to be published in some other form in due course. Interviews conducted specially for this book included those with the leader of the Assembly campaign and the architect of the devolution project, Rt Hon Ron Davies MP; Peter Hain MP, who encouraged me in this venture throughout; Eluned Morgan MEP, who provided the best summing up of a Yes for Wales activist's experience; Rhodri Morgan MP; Dafydd Wigley MP; Dafydd Elis-Thomas; Richard Livsey MP; Cynog Dafis MP; Nick Ainger MP; Dr Kim Howells MP; Huw Roberts; Rt Hon Alun Michael MP; Jon Owen Jones MP; Gareth Thomas MP; Ieuan Wyn Jones MP; Geraint Talfan Davies; John Osmond; Gareth Hughes; Andrew Davies; Cllr Kevin Brennan; Alan Barnard; Pat McFadden; John Adams; Aled Eurig; Glyn Mathias; Rev. Aled Edwards; and Nick Horton. Geoff Mungham, Owen John Thomas, Lee Waters and Chris Roberts also helped me with some important points. Amongst our opponents, Jonathan Evans, Nick Bourne and David Melding were charming, tolerant of my needs and personally very helpful.

I am grateful to the following for permission to quote from the following works: to Verso for extracts from Kim Howells, 'Stopping Out: The Birth of a New Kind of Politics' from Hue Beynon (ed.), *Digging Deeper: Issues in the Miners' Strike* (London and New York: Verso, 1985), pp.139-148; to Dr Paul O'Leary for an extract from his article in *Planet*; to Faber and Faber for an extract from 'Epilgoce' by Vaclav Havel from *Summer Meditations* (Faber, 1982); to Penguin for extracts from Gwyn Alf Williams *When Was Wales?* (Penguin, 1985); Parliamentary copyright material from *Hansard* is reproduced with the permission of the Controller of Her Majesty's Stationery Office on behalf of Parliament.

I owe a special debt to my family for putting up with the writing of this book. To Gruffydd, who continues to indulge his step-father's sad and nostalgic support for Cardiff City, even to the extent of agreeing to a season-ticket, and to my step-daughter, Marged, who as a teenager is finally coming to enjoy the right kind of rock music, though it's about time she gave me back my Stereophonics CD.

My brother Geoff finally got me writing less ephemerally a few years ago, and sets a very challenging example of fluency and command. After the referendum result, my mother, Peggy, decided that Carmarthen was the only place to live, and who can blame her.

My final acknowledgement is to the woman who brought me back home and who to me embodies the New Wales – my wife Ann Beynon. She said 'Yes' before Wales did.

Notes on Sources

Throughout the book I refer to contemporary newspaper, magazine, TV and radio reports, as well as party publications, Yes for Wales and Campaign for a Welsh Assembly/Parliament for Wales documents. However, in some sections, notably the historical Chapters Two and Three and the analytical Chapter Eleven on the lessons of the campaign, a much wider range of sources is cited. The main sources are therefore recorded here.

Contemporary media: *Western Mail, Daily Post, South Wales Echo, Golwg, Barn, Planet, Y Cymro, New Welsh Review*; BBC Wales, HTV, BBC Wales for S4C, TV and radio transcripts and recordings. Also national newspapers, particularly the broadsheets (*Guardian, Times, Independent, Daily Telegraph* and *Financial Times*) and the *Daily Mirror*. Local newspapers monitored by Yes for Wales. (Yes for Wales press cuttings are deposited with the National Library of Wales.) Some of these sources are footnoted in detail in my chapter in Denis Balsom and J. Barry Jones ed., *The Road to the Assembly*, University of Wales Press, forthcoming in 1999.

For Chapters Two and Three the sources are various. The best account of the 1979 Referendum remains the book edited by David Foulkes, J. Barry Jones and R.A. Wilford, *The Welsh Veto* (University of Wales Press, 1993). Gwynfor Evans' biography is *For the Sake of Wales* (Welsh Academic Press, 1996). James Callaghan's autobiography is *Time and Chance* (Collins, 1987).

The Nuffield Election Studies and the Times Guides to the House of Commons 1979-87 are very valuable.

John Davies' comments are largely from his *A History of Wales* (Penguin, 1993) though for S4C see his *Broadcasting and the BBC in Wales* (University of Wales Press, 1994). John Osmond's books on Wales in this period are invaluable, notably *The National Question Again* (Gomer, 1985) see especially John's introduction, Denis Balsom's chapter on the Three Wales Model, John Davies' essay on Plaid and Donald Anderson's on Labour post-devolution. John Osmond's *Police Conspiracy* was published by Lolfa. See also *Divided Kingdom* (Constable, 1988) and *Welsh Europeans* (Seren, 1995).

Gwyn Alf Williams' lecture 'When was Wales?' was reprinted in his *The Welsh In Their History* (Croom Helm, 1995). His book *When Was Wales?* was published in 1985 by Penguin. Other quotations come from his essays in *Marxism Today* in the 1980s, and from his speech at the Campaign for a Welsh Assembly conference in 1988 (*Radical Wales*). David Marquand's book is *The New Reckoning* (Polity, 1997).

Robert Harris' book on Neil Kinnock is *The Making of Neil Kinnock* (Faber, 1984).

Dai Smith's quotes on Plaid come from his essay on Raymond Williams, originally written for *Planet*, subsequently reprinted in both *Aneurin Bevan and the World of South Wales* (University of Wales Press, 1993) and in Terry Eagleton ed, *Raymond Williams* (Polity, 1989). Also cited are *A People and a Proletariat* (Pluto, 1980) and *Wales! Wales?* (republished by Seren in 1999 as *Wales: A Question for History*) and his book written with Hywel Francis *The Fed* (Lawrence and Wishart, 1980, reprinted with new introduction, 1998).

Clive Betts' quotes are from his *The Political Conundrum* (Gomer, 1993).

Peter Hain's book *The Democratic Alternative* was published by Penguin in 1983.

Wales, the Imagined Nation, edited by Tony Curtis, was published by Poetry Wales Press in 1986.

Kim Howells' essay on the Miners' strike is from *Digging Deeper* (Verso, 1985).

For the battle for S4C, see Angharad Tomos and Jonathan Coe in *What's This Channel Four?*, S. Blanchard and D. Morley ed., (Comedia, 1982). Patrick Hannan's account is from his essay in the collection he edited, *Wales in Vision* (Gomer, 1990).

Hywel Francis is the historian of the Miners' strike. I have consulted a range of his essays from *Marxism Today, New Socialist, Llafur* and *Gulliver*. Accounts from the *New Statesman* are also quoted, notably Beatrix Campbell's interviews.

The 1994 Parliament for Wales Campaign Conference gave rise to the book *A Parliament for Wales* edited by John Osmond (Gomer, 1994).

I have written on Blairism in England in 'New Labour New England', in Mark Perryman ed., *The Blair Agenda* (Lawrence and Wishart, 1996), and in 'The England Debate', in *Renewal*, July 1995.

I am grateful to Kevin Morgan for showing me an early draft of his and Geoff Mungham's chapter 'Unfinished Business: Labour's devolution policy' to be published in the Denis Balsom and J. Barry Jones collection already cited.

Ron Davies' pamphlet *Devolution: a process not an event* was published by the Institute for Welsh Affairs in 1999.

For Chapter Eleven, key sources are the Welsh Referendum Survey which has been reported in a variety of articles by Richard Wyn Jones, Dafydd Tristram, Geoffrey Evans and Bethan Lewis of the Department of Political and International Relations at the University College of Wales, Aberystwyth. (See articles in *Barn*, *Agenda* (Institute of Welsh Affairs) in the autumn of 1997, and *Golwg*, and papers presented at the CREST conference in Cardiff, 18 September 1998).

Bob Worcester's comments are from MORI's publication, *British Public Opinion*. ABC News poll details carried out by MORI are from the same publication.

NOP details are from the detailed tables published to accompany their poll for the BBC.

Planet's post-referendum issues provide the essays by Kevin Williams, Patrick Hannan, Glyn Mathias and Paul O'Leary. Laura McAllister's essay is from *Parliamentary Affairs*.

I have also drawn on Yes for Wales' submission to the Neill Committee, and on the report of that Committee published in October 1998 for the funding of the No Campaign.

In chapter twelve, the Vaclav Havel quote comes from 'Epilogue' in *Summer Meditations* (Faber, 1992).

Hywel Francis and Rob Humphries' essay is *The Learning Country: Citizenship and the New Democracy in Wales*, Welsh Centre for Lifelong Learning, University of Wales, Swansea, January 1999.

Index

213

About the Author

Leighton Andrews is a political consultant and policy analyst who runs his own businesses in Cardiff and London, Political Context and Welsh Context. Born in Cardiff, he grew up in Barry and then in Dorset, returning to Wales to study English and History at the University College of North Wales, Bangor, where he was Deputy President of the Students' Union and a sabbatical officer. He has an MA in Labour History from the University of Sussex. He was a full-time Vice President of the National Union of Students from 1980-81. He has been Head of Public Affairs at the BBC in London, Campaign Director of the UN International Year of Shelter for the Homeless, and Parliamentary Officer of Age Concern. His previous public affairs consultancy experience was gained as Managing Director of Sallingbury Casey Ltd and Joint Managing Director of the Rowland Company. He was honorary political adviser to the Friends of John McCarthy. A specialist in media policy, he is Visiting Professor at the University of Westminster and Visiting Research Fellow at University College, Cardiff. Returning to Cardiff to live in 1996, he co-founded Yes for Wales with Peter Hain MP.